ON BEING HUMAN

ON BEING HUMAN

Fulton J. Sheen

ON BEING
HUMAN

Reflections on Life and Living

Doubleday & Company, Inc., Garden City, New York

Grateful acknowledgment is made to Alfred A. Knopf, Inc. for permission to reprint "On Children" from THE PROPHET by Kahlil Gibran, copyright 1923 by Alfred A. Knopf, Inc.

The articles in this book appeared in various newspapers across the country. Those published during the years 1949–53, 1955, 1957–60 were distributed by George Matthew Adams Service. Those published in 1966 and 1977 were distributed by Washington Star Syndicate (1966, 1977).

Library of Congress Cataloging in Publication Data

Sheen, Fulton J. (Fulton John), 1895–1979.
  On being human.

    Selections from Sheen's syndicated newspaper column "Bishop Sheen Writes" for the years 1949–1977.
    1. Meditations. I. Title.
BX2182.2.S43   242
AACR2
ISBN: 0-385-17783-6
Library of Congress Catalog Card Number 81–43373

Contents

III THE QUEST FOR HOLINESS

IV TRANQUILLITY OF SOUL

V LOVE

XX RENEWING THE WORLD

XXI PLAIN TALK

Introduction

DURING HIS LIFETIME, Fulton Sheen combined an amazing number of successful careers, any one of which would have been considered achieving the pinnacle of success by most men and women. A mesmerizing preacher who enthralled audiences wherever he preached. A renowned college professor. A leading radio and television personality who at the height of his TV career had the most popular show on the air. An avidly read columnist for almost four decades, published in newspapers all over the country. A prolific author with some sixty books to his credit. A convert-maker who numbered some of the most illustrious names in the United States among those he instructed in the Catholic faith. A tireless pleader for the poor and underprivileged in his role as National Director of the Society for the Propagation of the Faith.

But all of these faded into insignificance in his eyes when compared with the career and vocation that he most prized—that of priest. For in the priesthood, he felt, he was best able to follow in the footsteps of his Master, offering the Sacrifice He had commanded, forgiving sins and spreading the Good News of the Gospels. He considered a priest to be *alter Christus* and he dedicated his life to pursuing that ideal—a quest that was the common thread that bound all of his activities together as he preached and spread by every means at his command the teachings of Christ. The relation of man and God and man's quest for eternal life in God, to be found only by following the directives the Lord left, are the twin themes of his preaching and writings. He emphasized the necessity for complete abandonment to God's love and mercy if we are to find the peace of mind and soul all men and women seek. The articles included in this volume, which have never before been published in book form, cover an enormous range of topics, but underlying them all is the need to follow God's commandments if we are to achieve that peace in this world and the bliss and happiness of eternal life in His presence in the hereafter. Over and over he stresses the Divine teachings of the Ten Commandments and the two new commandments Christ gave us which summed up all the commandments: "You must love the Lord your God with all your heart, with all your soul, with all your mind and with all your strength," and "You must love your neighbor as yourself."

Writing with the characteristic Sheen style, humor and an incomparable ability to make the most abstruse topics understandable, he covers the whole range of human interests, discussing topics from nuclear bombs and world problems to the often petty problems and needs besetting the individual. The articles included in this volume were selected from hundreds of columns he published from the 1940s to a few months after his heart surgery in 1977. As you will see when you read them, they are as fresh and timely today as when they were written. Times change, as do our life styles, but human problems remain constant. So too are the teachings of the Master who taught for eternity. In the twentieth century no one was more eloquent and more effective in spreading those teachings than Fulton Sheen as he strove to be a worthy *alter Christus*. Even after death he continues that task in the writings he has left.

JOHN J. DELANEY

I

God and Man

Dialogue Between Human and Divine

WHAT IS faith? Some conceive it as believing that something will happen such as "I have faith that I will make a fortune before I am forty." Others think of it as self-confidence and self-assurance by which they make God a junior partner in some project of theirs: "I have faith that I will woo and win that rich girl." This is not faith but egotism; it is directed not to God, but to self.

Faith is related not to self-assurance but to God; not to an event, but to truth. In fact, there is often the greatest faith when there is the least prosperity. Such was the case with Job who, full of sores and sitting on a dunghill, said, "I will trust Him though He slay me." Faith is the acceptance of a truth on the authority of God revealing it. When a distinguished scientist tells me about the age of fossils, I accept it on natural faith. I never make a test of the bones to verify his estimate. But I have a sufficient motive in his credibility —namely, he is the kind of man who would neither deceive nor be deceived. Therefore, his utterance about the fossil age I accept as true.

Now, over and above the human, there is the Divine. As a scientist can reveal to me truths which are beyond my reason, so God can reveal to me truths beyond the power of my intelligence. Since I know Him to be One Who neither deceives nor can be deceived, I accept His revelation in faith.

How do men receive a scientific truth which is beyond their knowledge? Some deny it, some ridicule it, some are silent through indecision. The same reactions happen in the face of a Divine Revelation. Remember the time when Our Lord cured the man who was blind from birth? The miracle was worked to prove that He was the Son of God. The miracle was to be a motive for believing in Him, just as our associations with certain people give us an assurance of their trustworthiness. But some, refusing to recognize the miracle, denied that it was the same man who was born blind: "He looks like him." In other words, "There is a fraud." But the man born blind, now restored to vision, said, "I am he."

Now that the fraud had been eliminated, some inquirers asked how the change came to pass. When he answered that the Lord did it, the answer of those who saw the miracle was, "How can a man who is a sinner do such miracles?" Here is a new escape from belief. This time, deceit is no longer the excuse from assenting to belief, but rather an attack upon character. There was a latent consciousness that "this Man does many miracles," but they refused to draw the proper inference. The parents of the man were insulted; they verified the blindness of their son from birth, but no amount of proof could convince those who refused to be convinced. Poor mortals! So often on hearing a truth or discovering a fact which runs counter to their prejudices, they seek to disparage it. The man who had been blind could not convince them though he said, "Since the world began it has not been heard that anyone has opened the eyes of one born blind. If He were not of God, He could do nothing."

In answer, those who refused to accept this conclusion attributed an evil life to the one cured. He must be rotten, a liar, a thief, an adulterer, an idiot, otherwise he would not be so believing. Later on, when Christ saw the man, He asked him, "Do you believe in the Son of God Who speaks to you?" He answered, "I believe, Lord," and worshipped Him.

It will be seen that faith has nothing to do with expectancy, with prosperity, with fate; it is not even related to an abstract statement. It centers in a Person—a Person Who is truth itself. It becomes a dialogue between the human and the Divine, between a dark mind and a Light, between a weak will and a surrender, between Someone toward Whom we have a motive for believing and our poor self who eats the offered bread, though we know not all the mysteries of physiological digestion. Without that Someone, we all have an enfeebling sense of blindness; but when His truth is accepted, we no longer stumble, but walk—yes, run—into the ineffable Light of the perfect day.

[2]

The Absence of God

THE ONLY creature in the universe that is not satisfied with himself is man. He wants to be more than man, as every market tends to become a supermarket. What adds to this uneasiness is that when he tries to make himself less than man he becomes ridiculous, which an animal never does. We say to man in his stupid deeds, "Don't act like a monkey." But when we see a monkey doing crazy things, we never say, "Don't act like a thistle." The higher the reaches of which one is capable, the greater the depths to which one can fall. Man alone has the power of self-mutilation and self-destruction, but as with the mosaic image of Christ in the dome of St. Sophia, which could never be completely effaced, he who was meant to scale mountains can also dig caves, but he still retains the Divine Image.

On the positive side, man wants to be more than he is; he attains his true self only when he gets beyond self. When he rebels against God, he makes himself a god. To be a man, one must be a superman. When he refuses to ascend and to realize the deep cravings of his soul for truth and beauty and love without satiety, his failures all immediately register themselves in his conscience and even in his subconsciousness. Anxieties, rationalizations, excuses, psychoses, neuroses, and dread—all these are so many compensations for the refusal to be more than he is.

Even in his mediocrities and humdrum existence, he still dreams and hopes to get beyond the present. Women who have been jaded in many marriages hope to recover what they were looking for in novels which vicariously supply the romance which was never romantic. Teenagers substitute worship for Worship, forge new idols before which they prostrate with a religious fervor such as Samsons with long hair. But they would blow a fuse if Delilah used a scissors to shear away that all important attribute of juvenile divinity.

Man Ltd., or limited, is really unlimited in his desires. Even when he denies the Infinite there still come flashes, now and then, of that for which he was made and without which he cannot rest. It may be the sight of innocence in a child, or the vision of a beautiful young woman whose virtue matches her loveliness, or the chance meeting with a man who never sold his soul.

Our uneasiness even in the midst of thrills is a kind of pain. As Sir Almroth Wright has put it, "A pain in the mind is the prelude to all discovery." We generally do not strive to solve a problem unless it hurts us to leave it unsolved; many of us would not move unless the unsolved problem hurt us badly.

But too many of us just want enough money and stocks and property to heal the wounds of our humanity and the aches of our conscience, but these God has not for our giving. He refused to talk to the moral trifler, Herod, because it would only have increased his moral guilt.

God is known in two ways: by His presence in the soul which gives joy because by loving, one is walking toward Love. In this case, God is the Other which makes it possible for me to be myself. He is beyond me, and yet within me: He is the principle of my interiority, which permits me to live with myself, and the principle outside me from Whom comes light and power. But God is also present by His Absence—even atheists admit this. As the atheist Sartre put it, "God is dead, but man for that has not yet become an atheist." His companion for years, Mme. de Beauvoir, said, "One day when I renounced my belief in God, I knew I condemned myself to death. I was then fifteen years of age. I was alone in the apartment, and I cried."

For him who denies the existence of water, there is still thirst. Welcomed or rejected, recognized or ignored, God is in every fold of our nature. The Russian astronauts said that they did not find Him in the heavens; but they did not say that they looked within themselves. The prodigal denied the father until he "looked within himself." The self-blinded deny the sun, but the sun still shines for those who want to walk in the light.

[3]

Christ and the Cross

WE LIVE in an age of fission: the atom was split; the mind was split between the superego and the id; husband and wife were split, and so are the East and the West. Those things which should have been one were torn asunder, and if the Seamless Robe could be found, perhaps even that would be rent.

But the greatest divorce of all is the separation of what was meant to be one: Christ and the Cross. Only Christ on the Cross reconciles that shattering contradiction of life symbolized by the upright bar, and death symbolized by the horizontal bar. The Cross is the "yes" of God meeting the "no" of man. Christ alone pulls them both together by making death the stepping stone to life.

In this hour, however, the Cross and Christ have been divorced, and new partners come forward for each.

Who takes up the Cross? Communism! The Soviets have seen that the license of Western civilization leads to the chaos of an individual seeking his own, without regard for society as a whole. Socialism or Communism is the organization of this chaos, the introduction of discipline, responsibility, service, and dedication to the good of the state. But all this without love leads to concentration camps, cruelty, persecution, and the squeezing of individuals as grapes to make out of them the collective wine of the omnipotent Big Brother.

Who has picked up the Christ? Western civilization! He is paraded as a teacher of humanitarian ethics, one worthy to be compared with Buddha and Confucius, the one who blesses big gifts and inspires with pious platitudes. But the Christ without the Cross is an effeminate "do-gooder" who speaks only of soft things, can offer no hope to the suffering, and never picks up whips to drive buyers and sellers out of temples.

Could it be too that in the Church there is also, in a diminished way, that divorce between the Cross and Christ? St. Paul wept only three times, according to his writings, but one of them was when he thought of the "enemies of the Cross of Christ"—that is, those who would take the one without the other. This would be a better way to speak of mentalities within the Church than to call young priests, for example, "the new breed." If there is a "new breed," there is also an "old breed," but these are descriptions in terms of genes, rather than theology.

The Cross stands for sacrifice, dedication, enthusiasm, fire. Into this group of those who take the Cross without Christ, therefore, would fall those who have "zeal without knowledge," who feel they have a mission, spend themselves and are spent for it. But it is always done without Christ; for example, the priest who leaves his classroom where he is teaching catechism in order to protest the fluoridation of water in a city water supply has too much cross or mission, and too little Christ.

At the other extreme, there are those who embrace Christ without the Cross, who continue to prophesy in His name and say, "Lord, Lord," who carry on professionally—doing their duty and nothing more. Helping a neighbor nation with foreign aid, to proclaim the humanism of Christ, while permitting a softness in courts which consider discipline as a restraint of liberty, is the forgetfulness of the Cross.

There is this divorce of the Cross and Christ in the way parents teach children. Some lay a heavy cross on their children, forcing them to live under commands and Spartan rules, but they leave out the love which inspires rather than imposes discipline. No one ever wants to hurt another whom one loves, and that makes one restrain self in dealing with neighbor. The other extreme is to bestow affection, compassion, and gentleness on children, but never train them or teach them self-denial, under the false excuse that they would never love parents who disciplined them. This false love will never inspire sacrifice in children, but rather will make them egotists, loving only themselves.

[4]

A Quick Psychoanalysis

PSYCHOANALYSIS originally meant examination of the soul; *this* kind of psychoanalysis, conducted by the individual himself, is valuable. From examining his own soul, any one of us can learn five general truths about all human beings:

1. All of us are dual; we are conscious of a tension between our lofty ideals and their feeble realization—of conflict between what we ought to do and the way we act—of a struggle between our ego, with its longing for supremacy, and the curbs placed on our will by other egos with contradictory desires. There are conflicts between our desire to be free of every restraint, and the slavery to evil habits we suffer if we *do* throw off restraint; between the longing to be ourselves, and the fact that our best pleasures constantly take us out of ourselves. This state of tension is an endemic state in man.

2. Such a conflict is confined to man: animals know no such agonies of indecision between two apparent goods pulling them in different directions at the same time. This difference gives us a clue to the cause of all our tensions: for man has an immortal soul, and animals have not. We men are plagued with conflicts because we are suspended between the finite and the infinite; we are like mountain climbers halfway up, who aspire to the peak above, and shudder for fear of falling into the abyss below us.

3. Since we are all a composite of body and soul, each of us must make a choice between the two directions in which he can move: he can rise above himself or descend below his present state. He can surmount his human level by seeking God with all the passionate ardor of his soul; or he can slip down to the despair, frustration, mel-

ancholy of those who have ceased to seek goodness. For the boundaries of humanity can be crossed in either of two directions: upward
through faith, or downward to insanity. Every man at every hour
moves toward one condition or the other; he cannot remain normal
on the merely human level, for our own egos are too narrow and
squalid to serve as fitting dwellings for our immortal souls.

The men and women who, neglecting every effort to improve
their souls, assert that they are happy anyway are merely lying to us
and to themselves: their despair may be invisible, as yet, but it is latent and it is real. Let a crisis come upon such people, and the distress they concealed is evident enough. Suicides among those who
lose their money or who are crossed in love reveal that only a thin,
illusory substitute for the love of life saved them, until now, from
their deep despair of the goodness of the universe.

4. But if the only alternative for us is between pursuit of the
infinite God for whom we were made and the agony of despair, why
does anyone ever turn his back upon the Eternal?

There are two barriers separating men from a happy destiny, and
either one of them may cause a timid man or woman to hold back
and sink into despair. Some men are unwilling to make the intellectual effort to seek truth for its own sake, to try to discover what
this life is "all about," to humble their pride sufficiently to admit
that God may be other than their present conception of Him, and
that, to reach Him, they may still have many new things to learn
and believe. That refusal holds back the proud from happiness. But
there is another obstacle to belief: the refusal to admit Divinity because of the demands such a belief would make on us, and because
we dare not face life without the habits of lust and avarice and
selfishness which Faith would ask us to surrender.

5. The man who truly "enters into himself" is never pleased at
what he finds there: the inner emptiness can drive him to despair.
But there are two kinds of emptiness . . . the vast vacuum of a canyon which will never be filled, and the expectant emptiness of a nest
hollowed out in preparation for the birth of the birds. So there are
two kinds of despair: the Satanic despair, which refuses to give in to
God's mercy, and the creative despair of those who allow their
misery to be remedied by God. The first way of despairing was that
of Judas, who went out and hanged himself. The second way was

that of David, who cried, "Have mercy on me, O God; have mercy on me."

So long as such mercy is available for all who despair of their own confusion and conflicts and inner incompleteness, it follows that sin is never the worst thing that can happen to a man. The worst thing is the refusal to recognize his sins. For if we are sinners, there is a Savior. If there is a Savior, there is a Cross. If there is a Cross, there is a way of appropriating it to our lives, and our lives to it. When that is done, despair is driven out and we have the "peace which the world cannot give."

[5]

Making Up for Wasted Time

NEAR WHERE I live, there is a small park just off a main street. The other afternoon I saw five men spend about three hours there playing cards. They were city workers whose business it was to fix the potholes in the streets of New York. This "goofing off" from work was wasting the taxpayers' money. The scene evoked many thoughts concerning the pricelessness of time. An ancient Persian proverb says that there are three things that never return: the spent arrow, the spoken word, and the lost opportunity. No less impressive is the proverb of the sleepy African: "The dawn does not come twice to waken a man." Browning expressed it this way: "Youth once gone, is gone. Deeds, let escape, are never to be done . . . Nature has time, may mend mistakes, she knows occasion may recur . . . I must perish once and perish utterly."

According to a familiar Korean legend, a Sibyl came to the palace of Tarquin II bearing nine volumes for which she demanded a high price. Her offer being declined, she went away and burned three of the volumes. Returning, she offered the six, but demanded the same price as for the original nine. Again her proposal was rejected, and again she departed and committed three more volumes to the flames. Once more she returned, bearing the last three while demanding the same price as for the nine. Tarquin bought the three, but the chance of ever seeing the nine books of "Sibylline verses" was forever lost.

Each moment wasted means that life's precious treasures are diminished while the price for them becomes higher. Opportunities both rise in price and grow fewer every time we refuse to make use of them. The passions and bad habits we refuse to tame today will be harder to conquer tomorrow should we leave the hours of today unimproved. Time forges new links and the slavery becomes more harsh. It is easy to acquire a talent for foreign languages and music when young, but difficult later on in life.

Time opens opportunities. When Moses led his people out of Egypt, God spoke to him: "You have been going about this mountain country long enough: turn northward." The time of probation was paid; the time of opportunity had come. The emancipation of slaves waited for Lincoln; the open door of Ephesus for Paul. As Shakespeare put it: "There is a tide in the affairs of men which, taken at the flood, leads on to fortune; omitted, all the voyage of their life is bound in shallows and in miseries."

Though time is too precious to waste, it must never be thought that what was lost is irretrievable. Once the Divine is introduced, then comes the opportunity to make up for losses. God is the God of the second chance. Peter denied, but he had the second chance in which to become as solid as a rock. Jonah, who refused to accept a mission, was given the second chance and saved Babylon. There really is such a thing as a "second birth." Being born again means that all that went before is not held against us. The thief on the right side of the Lord on Calvary wasted a human life, but in accepting pardon won eternal life.

Speaking to a group of young drug addicts, I asked how many of them thought they were "hooked." Almost all hands went up. For them time held no promise but slavery to drugs. I took a rubber ball, and rolled it down the middle aisle of the hall. Naturally it went in a straight line. They all agreed it was a picture of their hopelessness. Time would not change them, but only deepen their addiction. Then I rolled the ball again down the aisle, and asked one of them to put out his foot in front of the ball. Immediately, the ball changed direction. So slavery to drugs would continue in a straight line of time unless a superior force intervened to alter its movement. So it is with grace or the extra power that comes from God when we ask it. No wasted life need be final. We may close the door on opportunity, but Divinity is still on the other side knocking, His hands full of gifts.

[6]

The Divine Psychology of Gossip

TRADITIONALLY, all gossips are women; but men are often guilty of the same offense. They call it "judging."

Our Divine Lord, in speaking of gossips, said, "Do not judge others, or you yourselves will be judged." His admonition not to "judge" demands that we make no wicked evaluations, do not look for the worst in others. God alone sees our neighbor's heart; we see only his face. In England the judges wear wigs in court, to show that it is the law which is passing judgment, and not their own personal views. This is done in recognition of the truth all men suspect—that there is something impudent in allowing even the wisest among us to engage in pigeonholing our friends or cataloging our enemies.

When we judge others, we also judge ourselves. Our Lord asked us not to judge, lest we be judged; and sometimes the judgment we make of others is in itself a condemnation of our own faults. When one woman calls another "catty," she reveals that she knows what cattiness involves. Jealousy can be a tribute paid by mediocrity to genius: the jealous person then admits the superiority of his rival, but since he cannot reach that level himself, he drags the other down to his. Other forms of criticism are equally revealing of the one who criticizes.

Our Lord told us that the gossip's faults are often greater than those he criticizes in his neighbor. "How is it that thou canst see the speck of dust which is in thy brother's eye, and are not aware of the beam that is thy own? By what right wilt thou say to thy brother, Brother, let me rid thy eye of that speck, when thou canst not see the beam that is in thy own? Thou hypocrite, take the beam out of thy own eye first, and so thou shalt have clear sight to rid thy brother's of the speck."

The "speck" was only a bit of chaff, a splinter of wood. But the beam was a sizable piece of timber. To set ourselves up as worthy of judging others is already to see ourselves as their superiors, to be guilty of the sin of pride, the huge "beam" that obscures our vision. We cannot gossip without either overrating ourselves or underrating our neighbors . . . and frequently we do both. For the gossip is prone to project onto another the fault he suspects within himself. No one gets angrier at being told a lie than a habitual liar. The incurable gossip flies into a rage when he hears that he, in turn, has been talked about behind his back.

Our Lord asked the gossips to examine their own right to condemn the faults of others. "He that is without sin among you, let him cast the first stone." The implication is clear: innocence alone has the right to condemn. But innocence will always wish to take on the guilt of the other, to atone for his failings as if they were his own. Love recognizes the sin, but love also dies for it.

We instinctively feel that the abuse of our neighbors is wrong, and we show it by the words we use when we are about to cut somebody's throat. For they are words of self-apology: "One doesn't like to be uncharitable, but . . . ," or, "Of course, we mustn't criticize, but . . . ," or "I always prefer not to judge anyone, but . . ." These words presage the knife . . . and the effect on him who has wielded it is always psychological darkness. "He that loveth his brother abideth in light. . . . But he that hateth his brother is in darkness."

God has offered a beautiful reward to those who do not judge: they themselves shall not be judged when they are brought before the heavenly court. Yet God's judgment—which they will escape—is sure to be more merciful than any that we make. David, when he had sinned, was asked whether he would rather receive his punishment from God or from man, and he wisely chose God's judgment as offering the greater mercy.

We men and women are not wise enough or innocent enough to judge each other. And the only decision we can rightly make about our brother who is doing wrong is to admit it and to say, "We will leave him to God."

[7]

Brother Atheists

ALL OF US who believe in God should regard atheists as our brothers —for they, too, believe in a god, and if they reject our God, we, too, as vigorously, refuse to believe in theirs. From their point of view, we are the atheists and they are the believers.

We believe in God, the Creator; God, the Law-Maker and the Savior—our Judge and our Supreme Love. The atheist denies the existence of a creator, and his only law is his own will. Such men deny that they have ever sinned; they therefore reject our Savior and say that they will save themselves. They repudiate the idea of an objective truth or morality outside their own consciousness, against which their conduct can be judged; and so they are their own lenient judges. The love they place in the highest height is self-love; and thus they make their egos supreme. The atheist has merely made himself into his god, and since it is hard for us to believe in his divinity, he may properly call *us* the "unbelievers."

But the atheist believes in *some* god; make no doubt of that. Every man has in his heart an altar, which is not empty. There are three possible kinds of God: the god of one's own ego, in which the atheist believes, and which is also the god of modern confusionism; the god of nature, of stone and gold and silver, which belonged to the old religions of idolatry; and the Supreme God, who made both man and nature, and redeemed them both upon the Cross.

Those who tell us that they deny the existence of God are merely substituting one god for another. A few people care so much for sensate pleasure that they make a god of sex, endowing it with mystery and depth so that it becomes their absolute. Others say that their god is happiness (and so do we). But those who pursue happiness for itself do not observe this strange thing: they can easily explain the sadness and unhappiness they meet in life—but they cannot explain their attachment to a happiness they want and cannot find, and have never realized. Their absolute is an ideal happiness which by themselves they cannot grasp or hold. And so is ours—but our God came to earth and, in His first Sermon, told us of eight ways we might attain this happiness.

Man cannot love anything unless he believes it is eternal; all our lives are spent in expecting something that never comes. This expectation of something better than anything we have yet known is an intuition of God. Even those who are most loudly atheistic cannot, therefore, escape from God.

God is very close to every human heart—closer than its dearest friend. If a man's life be evil, he has only to clear away the dross and God will come quickly to his consciousness. If he lives a virtuous life on the natural level—making a lip-profession of atheism, but obeying the moral law—he need only deflate his egotism and puncture his self-divinity a bit, and the True God will appear in all His love and mercy.

G. K. Chesterton once said, "God is more kind to the gods who mock Him, than men are kind to the gods they made." The True God forgives what little gods will not condone: insult and blasphemy and sin. It is because men worship little gods of self and nation that there are quarreling and wars. The small gods of the ego fight among themselves, criticizing and maligning every other god.

When a man throws out the little god of self and admits the True God, then the only character he judges is his own. He sees that inasmuch as he is worse than he had judged himself to be, others are probably better than he thought them. The true lover of God becomes like a child, who has no understanding of malice.

Nietzsche once boasted, "God is dead!" Yes, He is dead. Dead and buried. But buried in our hearts—even in the hearts of our atheist brothers—waiting for His Resurrection in their glorious discovery of His Truth.

II

The Pain of
Being Human

Are All Anxieties Abnormal?

SOMETIMES PEOPLE are described as "old prunes," but no one has given a reason for this description. It could be they are so called because a prune is a "worried" plum. In any case, as healthier and more normal civilizations sought to fly from sin, so now people seek to fly from worry. Anxiety is supposed to be the greatest affliction short of war and pestilence that can afflict humankind. Anxiety is a kind of feeling of apprehension that arises when the welfare of the body or mind or possessions is threatened. Most of the popular treatises on psychology further the wrong assumption that life should be without anxiety or tension; they hold that he who suffers from worry should immediately betake himself to a psychoanalyst to have his anxieties dispelled. The psychoanalyst, in turn, prides himself on being able to relieve all anxieties and thus restore the person to normal life.

Nothing is more destined to create deep-seated anxieties in people than the false assumption that life should be free from anxieties. Cabbages have no anxieties; the stones on the roadway have no worries, though people are always "walking over them"; pigs never have to consult the more Freudian-wise pigs in order to be relieved of their inner oversensitiveness; turkeys never develop a fear neurosis about a forthcoming Thanksgiving celebration. Only man has tensions and anxieties, and some of these are very definitely normal; if he were without them, he would be abnormal.

This does not mean that there are no abnormal anxieties and fears. There are, but most of them come from worrying about the ego: whether or not one is popular; whether he can increase his social or his economic position; whether another person is getting ahead over him, and so forth.

Ibsen in his *Peer Gynt* makes the superintendent of an insane asylum tell what is wrong with many of his patients; those whom he describes are all egotists—their anxieties are not about their neighbors, but about themselves.

> *"Beside themselves? Oh, no, you're wrong.*
> *It's here that men are most themselves—*
> *Themselves and nothing but themselves—*
> *Sailing with outspread wings of self,*
> *The cask stopped with the bung of self,*
> *And seasoned in a well of self.*
> *None has a tear for others' woes*
> *Or cares what others think."*

The egotist is one who cannot bring himself to cooperate or communicate with others; all his anxieties are those of sustaining his own ego, not those of striving for perfection.

Contrast this flight from anxieties with the Divine Mandate: "Take up your cross daily and follow Me." What is the cross but a contradiction—a tension between the upright bar of life and the horizontal bar of death. And again, the Divine Teacher says that His Father is the true husbandman who prunes certain branches of our ego that we may bear more fruit. Such mortification involves pain, tension, and anxiety, but it is the condition of self-perfection. In the Gospel of St. John after the evangelist had enumerated seven miracles to prove the Divinity of Christ, he finally said that people did not believe in Him. Then came the final and convincing proof when Our Lord said, "If I be lifted up, I will draw all men to Myself." In other words, when His life reached the supreme contradiction on the Cross, when the forces of evil would battle against the forces of good; when the normal desire to save a physical life would be surrendered in order to save men spiritually, then would come complete belief and victory.

Anxiety about soul-saving, tension between the body and the flesh, self-denial which implies the crushing of the ego for the sake of the emergence of the Divine image—all these are normal conditions of inner spiritual happiness. Abnormal anxieties indeed should be avoided, but normal anxieties particularly should be recognized and encouraged. The basic fact that human beings must face is this: either we are at war with our ego, or we are at war with others. He who does not fight his ego fights his neighbor. The cross at the center of one's own life is the assurance of peace of the individual and peace among men.

[9]

Fear

IT SEEMS probable that there has never been a period, in the history of Christian civilization, when fear was more general than it is today. This fear is largely of the unwholesome or earthbound type.

There is a good type of fear: filial fear, such as a child has for a devoted father—a fear which may also be called reverence or respect. There is a second fear which has a servile aspect: it is such fear as a slave feels for his tyrannical master, or a Soviet official for the dictator. But the third sort of fear—the kind which is causing immense distress today—is psychological fear, born of a faulty conception of the universe and arising without a rational, outward threat.

The psychological fears of our times come from the fact that so many men have ceased to fear God with a filial fear, with a fear of wounding Him; this wholesome fear has become corrupted into fear of their fellowmen. The mechanism by which this occurs can be easily studied, if we realize that all fear arises from love.

Sacred Scripture tells that where there is perfect love, there is no fear, and also that perfect love casteth out fear. As souls draw closer to God, their filial reverence increasingly loses the quality of fear for themselves and takes on a more self-forgetful note of reverent joy.

But when a man ceases to render to God any of the filial fear or reverence which is proper to his nature as a creature, then he develops unhealthy fears, which stem from misdirected loves. As St. Augustine said, "A man fears because something that he loves is in danger."

If a man's love is misplaced and rooted in his money, he will be filled with fear—either of losing it, or of being approached by someone requesting a donation. If a man loves himself in an egotistical way, imagining himself to be better than he is, he will fear criticism, for it might rob him of his self-complacency. If a person has an inordinate love of sensate pleasure, he will fear the day when his body grows old so that he can no longer enjoy these pleasures; that is the reason why some aging people lie about their ages in their talk, their manners, and their dress. Again, a love that is too much directed toward the self makes its possessor jealous—he fears that he may be dispossessed, not of what he loves, but of what he possesses of the loved one's attention. Such self-loving people also fear the loss of human respect in the community at large: they hurry and worry in order that others shall be impressed with their importance.

Fear is related to love in an even more profound way in the case of those with guilty consciences, particularly if the sins that trouble them have never been squarely faced within their own minds. This fear is of two kinds: the fear of deserved punishment, and the fear of having some day to admit to having hurt Love, which is, in this case, God.

There are many physiological and psychological reasons for fear which are commonly studied and discussed today. But few modern psychologists give due regard to this widespread type of fear: the one that springs from a repressed consciousness of guilt. The pathological effects of such fear have been wonderfully portrayed for us by Shakespeare, especially in *Macbeth*. Immediately after he has murdered Duncan, Macbeth is told by his wife not to worry. Modernists who deny the fact of moral guilt could find their views shared by Lady Macbeth, who says:

> *"These deeds must not be thought*
> *After these ways; so, it will make us mad."*

Her recommendation to "forget it all" is again expressed when she says, "What need we fear who knows it, when none can call our power to account?" She believes that guilt can be escaped, so long as it is not detected, and that "a little water clears us of this deed."

But such a denial of sin, by running away from it and refusing to repent of it, permits of no lasting satisfaction or peace. For Lady Macbeth, later in the play, suffers from what modern doctors would call a "compulsive neurosis," a state in which the sufferer feels forced to perform some useless action in his search for relief from inward tension. Lady Macbeth's compulsion is toward continuous washing of the hands, toward sleepwalking and toward a reversion of all her thoughts to the night of the murder.

"Who would have thought the old man to have had so much blood in him?" she asks, and, "Will these hands never be clean?" It seems likely that her profound sense of contamination of the soul forced her to seek cleanliness from the outside-in. Her attitude reminds us of the words of Our Lord, who spoke of guilty men as "whited sepulchers, outside clean, inside full of dead men's bones."

The guilt of Lady Macbeth finally reaches a point at which she cannot endure her inner guilt, and she attempts suicide. The mental self-punishment has turned into physical self-punishment, into the descent into Hell. But Hell begins on earth, when men begin to hate themselves, and seal that attitude by saying, "I can never forgive myself."

There was no rescue possible for Macbeth or for Lady Macbeth, because they kept their sins repressed. The moral conscience cannot operate in the cellar portion of our minds: the subconscious cannot repent. The sin must be brought up into daylight recognition and admitted to consciousness, as our own responsibility. But that recognition is still not enough; we cannot "forgive ourselves" without some greater forgiveness helping us. We need the Redemptive Power—whose mercy is without limits if only we are willing to receive it. Once the fearful soul has contacted this Divine Love in penitence and true contrition, fear vanishes: the released soul then has the ecstatic joy of being let out of prison into the light and sunshine.

The freed conscience is restored to the liberty of the children of God.

[10]

Loneliness

PASCAL SAID that there were two things that frightened him: one was his own heart and the other, the silence of the eternal spheres. Kant, the German philosopher, held that the two things which awed him were the moral law within his breast and the starry firmament above him. There has always been a tendency in literature to put these two together, and with a certain justice, for only a Power great enough to control the heavens could ever solace the individual heart.

The Hebrew psalmist was the forerunner of those who set in contrast the Providence of God, which was powerful enough to control the collective planets of the universe, and yet careful not to neglect the burden that weighed on a single heart: "He heals the broken in heart, and binds up their wounds. He tells the number of the stars; He gives them all their names." There is hardly any physician or psychiatrist or friend who, in the face of a broken heart, would immediately think of countless stars or, contemplating the starry encampment of night, would ever think of the loneliness of the human breast. These are the two extremes which only great minds ever fit into one thought—namely, the bleeding heart and the fiery stars.

In studying history we lose the sense of the hour, and we forget the rolling scroll of history in the problem of an hour. It is the nature, however, of Divine Love to assure man that He Who takes care of the great universe is the only One to Whom man can trust his life. The sovereign balm for every wounded heart comes only from Him from Whose fingertips there tumbled planets and worlds. Many a man has felt his helplessness and loneliness beneath the stars, and yet Scripture says that star-counting and heart-healing go together.

Today there is a tendency to believe that because the universe is far greater than we suspected, perhaps God is less perfect than we believed. This is part of the bad logic of Americans who judge the value of everything by its size. The true point of view is that the greater the universe, the more certain man is to have his fretful mind lifted up to the thought of God's eternal Presence and Power. Then, too, the fact that we unite the planets and the heart is proof that the sorrows of this life are not nearly as akin to earth as they are to heaven. Sadness of human hearts cannot be explained by any philosopher on this earth, but only by Him Who is powerful enough to make the stars, and Who holds the secret of healing in His own Divine Heart.

One finds the concretion and personalization of this relationship between stars and hearts in the contemplation of the Infinite God Who took upon Himself a human nature, and yet could be solicitous of one lost sheep, a woman taken in sin, a blind man, a thief, and a brokenhearted widow following the body of her only son. It is not just sympathy that we need, but the consciousness that we are in the strong hands of the Lord of all. God is not remote from the little life down here on earth. We may ask how He could miss us from the fold, when He is shepherding all the heavenly hosts. The answer is that God can find no room for His pity and no response to His love, nothing to bend over and heal and bless, except in our hearts.

He Who holds all the nations in the palm of His hand is, nevertheless, the God of "Abraham and Isaac and of Jacob." How often we say that it is very often the busiest person who is willing to help an individual. This is nothing but a confirmation that He Who made the heavens and lived for mankind spoke His tenderest love when His audience was one listener. Everyone else is too weak to heal a broken heart. He alone can do it Who counts the stars.

[11]

Despair

SNAILS, SNAKES, and scorpions cannot despair; neither can cabbages, camels, or centipedes. Only man, with the infinite and the eternal in him, can despair. The greater the expectation, the more keen can be the disappointment. The more there is to hope, the greater is the grief at not realizing it. Man alone, of all creatures, has a soul which is capable of knowing the infinite; he alone has aspirations beyond what he sees and touches and feels; he alone can attain everything in the world and still not be satisfied. That is why, when he misses the infinite and the eternal for which he was made and which alone can satisfy, he despairs.

The yearning within man for truth and love and beauty and perfection indicates that something is lacking for the fullness of life. This yearning is related to hope which, in its simplest form, is a gaze toward the future. A farmer cannot plant seed in the springtime, nor the mother press a child to her breast, nor the scientist conduct his research without hope. No spade would ever be dug into the earth, nor pen put to paper, were there not some expectation of good to come from it.

That hope for which we look may be in time, or it may be beyond time. If the ultimate and final hope is in this world, despair is inevitable. What peace is there in possessing, if death with its "shuffling of the mortal coil" means the breaking of all communication with what we hoped? There is then felt within the heart the radical tug between the infinite craving and the finite satisfaction between the sweet rind and the bitter pulp.

When, however, this desire for perfection and the infinite is placed beyond this life, there is no occasion for despair.

Those who are familiar with the thinking of the world for the last two centuries will recall how the world has swung from an unbounded optimism in human affairs to a despair which today engages and demands the attention of psychiatrists. Optimism today is at a discount. Men clamor less for happiness than they do for security. All the philosophers of the past argued to the existence of God and the moral law, from man's innate craving for happiness; today, man's deepest yearning is for some economic security.

This change in outlook may be likened to different attitudes of sea voyagers. In former days, man's first concern on taking a sea voyage was a port and a comfortable cabin; today, the first thing the traveler does is to look for a life belt. Many today are very uncertain as to whether or not there is a destiny to the voyage of life; in fact, they would rather not dwell upon the problem, for they know it makes ethical demands upon them which they are unprepared to make.

The age that expects a future life and the perfection of happiness beyond this life has a calm and peace which the turn of events cannot disturb. But when a man loses hope, and has no God to Whom he can turn, then he must be in a hurry to get something out of life. The believer can wait; the pagan must hurry. The gate threatens to close; then all is over. Hence the impatient scramble and scuffle to acquire as much as possible before the sun sets.

When the ultimate hope of personality is denied, then there are no longer any limits to crass earthliness which unleashes itself with boundless ferocity. The rapidity of wars, the almost incessant revolutions which disturb our modern world, are born of that frantic despair to salvage something before the world is taken away.

Those who have hope are like a boy with a kite. The kite may conceivably be so high in the clouds that it cannot be seen; but he who holds the string feels the tug of it. Once our hope is in God, we feel the pull and tug of it on earth. But as the heir must believe in his title to inheritance before he can hope in it, so there must be faith in things beyond, before we can hope. With such a strong basis for hope, despair fades away.

[12]

Grief

A CROCODILE has tear glands, but a crocodile never sheds tears; a
hyena has its mouth open, but a hyena never laughs. The tear ducts
in the animals are for the sake of lubricating the eyeballs, not for expressing grief. Beasts are divided from man by tears and laughter.
Both have to do with the soul rather than the body.

The dictionary defines a tear as "a drop of limpid fluid secreted
by the lacrymal gland, appearing in or flowing from the eye, chiefly
as a result of emotion, especially grief." A chemist would probably
define it as a solution of sodium chloride and calcium. A stoic would
say that it was a sign of weakness, for in the face of grief one should
bite his teeth and bear it; an epicurean would say, "Forget the grief;
man was made to eat, drink and be merry."

But somehow or other, just as the clouds portend the rain, so too
does grief issue in tears. Their laboratory is the heart; they are
merely the external and visible sign of something deeper and invisible, a kind of sublimation of woe, the predication of a grief, the dila-
tation of a loss which only the mind can conceive. Behind every tear
is an idea. The tears of an infant, which are hotter than the tears
shed later on in life, come from the broken toy, the pang of hunger,
or the thwarted egotism which the child has not yet learned to control. Then there are the tears of parting, as when the Ephesians
wept at the departure of Paul, "grieving over what he had said about
never seeing his face again"; tears of the lover when, having given
his heart away, he finds that it is not returned with garnished love,
but jilted and broken; tears of the mother who sees a young life

shipwrecked no sooner than it is launched on the sea of life, or else later on having a wayward son and wishing that the tears could have been shed earlier when an innocent life took its leave and departed; tears of penitents like Peter, who so wept for having denied Our Lord that his cheeks were furrowed with the tracks of grief and contrition.

Tears were consecrated and made sacred when Christ, the God-man, wept three times: once over death, in the case of Lazarus; once over the decay of civilization, when He wept over Jerusalem; and once for the sins of men as He crimsoned the olive roots of Gethsemane with tears of blood. In contrast to this compassionate love for the ills and woes of men which sin had brought, the ancient poet could fix no worse epithet on Pluto than: "He was a person who could not weep."

Tears are not without value, provided one sees a purpose beyond their shedding. As the morning rose is sweetest when embalmed with dew, so "love is loveliest when embalmed in tears." Many a person sees God through tears more often than in the sunlight; in fact, tears may leave the vision of the eyes clear for stars. There is such a thing as Crashaw described as "sweetness so sad, and sadness so sweet."

But not only do tears make hearts realize that the happiness for which we yearn is not here; they make us look beyond to another world where tears shall be wiped away when "He shall wipe away every tear from their eyes, and there will be no more death, or mourning, or cries of distress, no more sorrow; those old things have passed away."

But there is yet another value to tears in that they make us more sympathetic to the griefs and pain of others. In sorrow one should never go to a person who has not wept, nor in anxiety and worry should one ever consult a man who has not denied himself. Only those who have passed through the crucible of grief know how to make a rainbow appear in a tear. Why is it that children, when they have a grief, will run to the mother rather than to the father? It is because the mother knows trouble better than the father; she has companioned more with pain, has more often passed through its cycles, and in giving birth has gone down to the very edge of death.

That is why He Who promised to wipe away all tears is the One down Whose cheeks and body flowed those sacraments of compassion, those tokens of love which make Him the High Priest Who can have compassion for our griefs.

[13]

Shame

THE NINETEENTH-century concept of man failed because it ignored the spiritual discontent within man himself. A man is not an animal, as is proven by the fact that pigs and roosters have no complexes, but man has. Our modern man has three forces or fears: fear of death, fear of the meaninglessness of life, and the fear of being found out. As soon as wrong enters the heart of man, he begins to make fig leaves to cover his shame. Our secret dread is that we may be found naked—that is, in our true miserable condition. We try to replace nature by art, saying, "I am not fit for God or man to look upon." Thus the emotion with condemnation becomes mixed up with dishonor and blot.

The fig leaves we sew to cover up our shame are multiple. One of the latest fashions is to make it appear that society itself is wicked, and therefore it should not make one ashamed. The increased number of television programs about homosexuality is to destroy in the public domain any reproach for this perversity. By making it appear that every face is jaundiced, one need not blush at his own yellowness. If the mores of our time could be proven to be abnormal, then one need not be ashamed of his abnormality.

Another kind of fig leaf by which modern man covers up his shame is to attack religion. He thinks that by calling in doubt all moral standards such as guilt, conscience, sin, judgment, he immu-

nizes his conscience from reproach. Many of the slings and arrows against the churches come from the slingshots of an uneasy conscience and the bow of repressed guilt. It may be true in some instances that the churches are irrelevent to the modern world and give no resounding message to modern man. But a deeper analysis might reveal that they are entirely too relevant; that is why many do not want to hear their message. Throwing stones at the churches is a cheap way of escaping from one's own guilt. They may have all the failures of the poor woman taken in sin, but like her, they would be the first to admit it. Those who impugn the churches say they demand that they be pure and clean, but if they were as clean and pure as they want them to be, they could never find their way in.

What makes the sense of shame more galling is our denial of it, our covering it up with fig leaves which wither. The true way out is to face up to shame and realize that we can be accepted by God because we are unfit, and that we can be pardoned because we are guilty. It is the excuses which spoil us.

We have to have the courage to be ourselves. We are worthless. We do not have an inferiority complex; we are inferior. We are not just dumbbells; we are guilty. We have not just made a mess of things; we are sinners. Take off the mask!

We are blind to our own faults. That is why we say we need courage to sit down and to ask ourselves whether what we are doing is right or wrong, whether or not we are actually fostering passion, listening to our own wishes, seeking out others who will excuse our sins; whether we are not allowing self-love to blind us to our baseness.

There is need of some judgment outside of us. A light on the deck which rolls with the pitching ship is no guide. It must flash from a white pillar founded on a rock immovable among the restless waves. God can save this world, but He can save it only one man at a time. There must be individual access to Him for the reception of forgiveness, as if He and I were the only two beings in the world.

The people who are dragging their shame into a confessional box, with their feet hanging out from under a curtain like wiggling worms, have courage to face their own shame. It is the cowards who are running off to pillboxes, and to a thousand and one other escapes, who have not the courage to face that which has within themselves the possibility of great dignity.

Liberation comes when the message of forgiveness is accepted bravely and without excuse. Peter was a despairing man when he said to Our Lord, "Depart from me, for I am a sinful man, O Lord." Our Lord's answer briefly was, "I know it. That is why I want you."

[14]

Treasures in Darkness

THE GREATEST tragedies in life are not altogether in what happens to people, but rather how they react to what happens to them. Two thieves were crucified on either side of Christ; one asked to be taken down to go on with the dirty business of stealing; the other asked to be taken up in order to steal paradise with the gift of pardon. Both suffered equally, yet their reactions were poles apart. When St. Paul was troubled with some misfortune, one knows not what, and which he called a "thorn in his flesh," three times he prayed to have it removed. But the Lord answered him, "My strength finds its full scope in thy weakness." The suggestion is not that weaknesses and infirmities are to remain cherished. A child is not always to remain a child; a sick man should not remain weak when he should be strong. To be weak is to be miserable. But the weakness here in question is that which inspires strength and courage to overcome it.

Every man has his weakness; it is in struggling against it that he becomes strong. Moses was hotheaded; he worked on his temper and became the meekest man who ever lived. Paul was a bigot, and became an apostle. When a man admits that he does not know everything, he exposes himself to the receiving of faith; he who confesses a moral weakness and craves for a grace and power outside of himself makes himself receptive to grace and pardon.

The great ones of the earth have laid hold of some infirmity, and through it purchased strength. Raleigh wrote the *History of the World* in the Tower of London; Bunyan wrote *Pilgrim's Progress* in the Bedford jail; John Addington Symonds wrote his seven volumes on the Renaissance while suffering from tuberculosis in Switzerland; the Apocalypse of St. John was written while he was in exile. Elizabeth Barrett Browning said that she was always in ill health, and yet, propped up in bed with cushions and with her books on all sides of her, she wrote love poetry the world will never forget. Goethe in his old age wrote: "I will say nothing against the course of my existence. But at the bottom it has been nothing but pain and burden; and I can affirm that during the whole of my seventy-five years, I have not had four weeks of genuine well-being. It is but the perpetual rolling down of the rock that must be rolled back again."

"Adversity is the prosperity of the great." Instead of being cast down, noble souls, in adversity, rise to new heights. How often too it is that some people never look up until they are flat on their backs; they never think of God until they are face to face with some disaster. A great deal of rust requires a sharp file. Many a person would never think upon the meaning of life unless sickness had detached him from a too great love of the foibles of this life. Afflictions do not necessarily come as lightning to an oak to wither and to scar; rather they come like the repeated blows of the sculptor on a block of marble until the hidden form within is revealed. When the hidden Hand of the Divine Sculptor is felt, then no blow is hard. Nor can the believer ever despair in his adversity and say, "What does God know about suffering?" God answered that question by becoming man and bearing grief *for* us, and bearing grief *with* us and bearing grief *like* us. Having cleared the way through the forest of purposeless living, He made it easy to follow in His footsteps.

Treasures lie hidden in darkness. Only those who walk in the night ever see the stars. More men discover their souls in darkness than they do in light. This is not to invite darkness; it is only to be reminded that darkness need not go to waste when it is thrust upon us. When Paul was stoned at Lystra, there was a young man looking on, wondering why anyone who was so tortured for his faith should ever be so tranquil and peaceful. The youth carried the memory of that stoning with him, and later on became the friend of Paul, and his companion in his trials and stonings.

True, there are some whom affliction makes bitter. No one is ever better just because he has a trial. Without faith, affliction and darkness can burn and sear and cut the soul. But when trials are seen through the cross, then they fit into the Divine Plan. There is never a Good Friday without an Easter Sunday.

[15]

A Letter from Prison

COUNTLESS HAVE been the letters from prisons, some pleading innocence, others threatening vengeance, others complaining, or seeking release. None of these letters have, however, passed into literature and become inspiration more than the letters which Paul wrote from his prison in Rome. Most notable among them is the letter that he addressed to the faithful of Philippi, a city of Macedonia that was named after Philip, the father of Alexander the Great. It was there also that Anthony and Octavian defeated Brutus and Cassius in the year 42 B.C.

When his friends at Philippi heard of his imprisonment, they were much concerned, for would not his prison bars halt the spread of the gospel? The answer of St. Paul was:

> *"I hasten to assure you, brethren, that*
> *my circumstances here have only had the*
> *effect of spreading the gospel further."*

He had learned to turn awkward circumstances to the best account. If he had been a materialist, he would have thought of the restricted liberty as a galling chain. As Ezechiel among the captives of the Chebar yet saw the vision of God, so Paul saw three great advantages accruing from his imprisonment. The first was that through his imprisonment, the gospel became known to and through the Praetorian Guards. One guard told another until even "Caesar's household" heard the message he preached.

A second advantage accruing to his imprisonment, he said, was that those who were timid about their faith now became bold to speak without fear. His courage inspired courage. Probably because of the persecution, some in Rome were losing heart, but the faithfulness of Paul was like the sound of a trumpet in their souls. Example, then as always, was far more effective than precept. The sight of a suffering saint, patient and contented and happy, did more to influence the soldiers in the faith of Christ than a hundred sermons.

The third advantage the prisoner attributed to his chains was that harsh and baffling things can have their place in increasing the love of God. It may seem that an eagle is cruel in stirring her nest and driving out her young, but it is in order that they may use their wings and learn to fly. A man's biography is written in terms not so much of what he causes to happen, but rather what happens *to* him and *in* him. The difference between men is not in the adversity which comes to them, but rather how they meet the adversity. Imprisonment to Paul had its blessed result, for it sanctified him through the prayers of his friends at Philippi, and through the unfailing supply of the grace of the Master.

Now, as then, it remains true that the most happy, encouraging, and joyful things that have ever been said have come from lives that suffered, or have been falsely accused. They have never come from those whose lives are full of pleasure. From the latter comes cynicism; from the former encouragement.

As Stevenson wrote:

> *Two men looked out through prison bars,*
> *One saw mud, the other stars.*

[16]

Pain

I HAVE JUST been released from the hospital after open-heart surgery. It became necessary to replace a valve in the heart to ensure survival. Faced with the alternative of death within five days, I decided on the valve replacement in order to continue a life of usefulness in the Lord's vineyard. Many unexpected complications followed, all of which resulted in intense suffering over a long period of time. Perhaps it would be interesting to my readers to hear reflections on pain, which was so much a part of my life.

First of all, one quickly discovers that our capacity for pain is greater than our capacity for pleasure. In the intense throes of suffering one feels that it would be impossible to endure more. But another agony is added, or another day, and somehow we absorb it. It is amazing how much pain we can absorb. Despite the intensity, no pain ever turns into a pleasure. The opposite is true of pleasure, which can be converted into pain. For example, tickling may be funny at first, but it can become a downright displeasure. Drinking may give enjoyment at the beginning, but too much of it ends with nightmares of a "hangover." The same is true of drugs, which may exhilarate in the early stages, but then end in the degeneration of the brain or addiction and consequent slavery.

Why are we so made that there seems to be no limit to our ability to endure pain, but the boundaries of pleasure are quickly touched? I believe it is because pain was meant to be exhausted in this life. Joys are not, because they belong to another existence. True happiness is reserved for another world; in this one we but touch only its fringes and tassels. This world is not final. Pain was meant to have its last throb in time. Not so with true happiness; in time we have the sparks, but in future life alone we have the flame.

Another interesting fact about pain is that love, though it may not be able to kill pain, nevertheless makes it bearable. If I lose a purse containing money, the loss is softened by the knowledge that it was found and its contents used to feed a hungry family. A loving mother does not mind getting out of bed a dozen times in the night to care for a feverish child. What love supplies is a motivation for sacrifice. Price tags are taken off gifts because we do not want a proportion established between the giver and the gift. But this love cannot be an abstract ideal or a philosophy; to be effective, it must always be a person. I remember years ago Einstein wrote an article on adoring the cosmos as God. This struck me as rather naïve. I answered it saying that man could never love anything he could not get his arms around, and the cosmos is too big, too bulky. That is why the immense God became a Child that we might encircle Him in our arms and that as the Wounded Warrior we might lay Him on our laps to turn the wounds into scars.

Suffering, then, becomes bearable when we have someone whom we love. I believe the great tragedy of the world is not what people suffer, but how much they miss when they suffer. Nothing is quite as depressing as wasted pain, agony without an ultimate meaning or purpose.

Given my calling in life, who was the one whom I loved and for whom I tried to bear patiently a minor crucifixion? It was Christ on the Cross. I could offer up the pain to Him for a thousand reasons: to atone for my own sins and the sins of the world, for the sake of the spread of the gospel, for the conversion of sinners, and so on. We can never become like to God in our goodness, our nature, or our power, but we can become like to Him in our sufferings, which become a purification. Thus open-heart surgery is more than it seems; if understood aright, it opens the heart to sympathy with the pain of the world, and above all to greater love of God and neighbor.

III

The Quest for Holiness

Holiness

MINDS TODAY are no longer swayed by reason. As Newman said, the "syllogism makes but sorry rhetoric with the multitude." The eighteenth century was known as the Age of Reason. Descartes even went so far as to believe that he could discover one simple universal principle of medicine from which one could deduce every possible cure. It was also the custom of thinkers in those days to reduce all thought process to a digest of three or five or ten simple propositions which would serve as a guide for life.

Today reason has fallen into discard. No advertiser proves that his product is good; he merely affirms that it is. No automobile manufacturer argues that his car is better than any other; he has more ballet dancers floating around it in gossamer worshipfulness. Today cars are sold by men on horseback through the medium of television. A woman is seen doing dishes in a mink coat; no woman in a kitchen is ever over thirty; cigarettes are smoked only by boys and girls in love—all these inanities are part of the conspiracy against reason.

Applying this flight from reason to a higher plane, it is almost impossible to convince anyone of the truth of religion through reason —and yet a whole science of apologetics has been built up for this purpose and has been used for centuries. Shortly before he died, Ronald Knox pleaded for a new apologetic or an approach to religion which would suit our age of unreason and emotionalism.

This brings up another question: if the intellectual approach will not bring minds to the knowledge of God, what is left? Here a very extraordinary answer is to be given. Holiness. The modern man is not beyond being convinced, but he will be convinced only by those who bear the imprint of the truths in which he believes. He is very much like the original doubting Thomas who said that he would not believe until he saw the marks of the nails on the Hands and on the

Feet of the Divine Master. As Horace put it, "If you wish me to weep, you must weep first." The disciples of Emmaus, as they walked with the Stranger Who turned out to be the Risen Savior, said, "Did not our hearts burn within us as we talked on the way?" In concrete language, the saint is the only convincing argument in all the world.

If the Christian is no different in his thoughts, values, recreations, judgments, politics, and business methods from the non-Christian, how can the latter inspire what he has not? Holiness is like salt; its usefulness to others must begin with self. As only the wise man can impart wisdom to others, so only the saintly can communicate sanctity. A man can bring forth to others only those treasures which he already has in his own heart. The physician who is to heal others must not be a leper. The very sense of guilt which evil men feel before the innocence of a child is a reflection of their self-condemnation in the face of holiness.

If a thing reflects no light, it is black; if it reflects some light, it is blue or red; if it reflects all colors, it is white. This is probably the reason why the saints in heaven are pictured as wearing "white robes"—because they reflect the all-holy Christ. Arguments can be refuted, persuasions can be ignored, admonitions can be evaded, but the exhibition of moral piety exercises a persuasion which no half-decent man can resist. If a man is wholly bad, he will hate holiness and seek to kill it, or else will turn it to ridicule, as did Herod. But the man who is not possessed of evil will admit a force greater than reason in the presence of sanctity.

Sanctity is not mere morality. No man can be holy who is not moral, but a moral man is not necessarily holy. Holiness is the opposite of egotism and selfishness. The conduct of the holy man is a rebuke without word. St. Paul gives a list of things which proceed from egotism and which make news: adultery, impurity, luxury, feud, murder, drunkenness, and debauchery. And in contrast with those he sets the fruits of the spirit of holiness, which never makes the news: love, joy, peace, patience, kindness, generosity, forbearance, gentleness, faith, courtesy, temperance, purity.

[18]

The Seven Petitions of Life

THE GREATEST prayer of all—the "Our Father"—is a prayer of petition: when Our Lord taught these words to His disciples, He gave them the right to ask from God the things they wanted for themselves. But He also showed them, through this prayer, what things they *ought* to want.

The central petition of the "Our Father" asks, *"Give us this day our daily bread."* It is a practical plea: we may have our souls in the stars, but our bodies are in the dust of human living, and we need God's help in keeping body and soul together. Thus we ask to have our economic needs filled . . . but for this day alone; we are not encouraged to pray for security for the next twenty years. And it is only "our" bread for which we pray—bread that we have earned and have the right to eat. The racketeer does not eat his own bread. We pray, "Give us," not "Give me," for our desire for plenty is inseparable from the needs of those around us. We want no plenty while others starve.

The plea for bread divides the "Our Father" into two portions. The earlier half lifts the soul to God and the affairs of God—His honor, His kingdom and His will; the second half frees us from the specific frustrations of this life.

The phrase *"Hallowed be Thy name"* acknowledges the true shape of things and recognizes the grandeur of God in Himself, apart from His creation. We give Him glory, not because He needs this tribute from our littleness, but because we need to acknowledge Him for our own perfection, and because man, as lord of creation, may fittingly speak for all the things that God has made.

In *"Thy Kingdom come,"* the mind turns from eternity to time, to a prayer for grace enough to make our every act a service of this King. For "the Kingdom of God is not a matter of eating or drinking this or that; it means rightness of heart, finding our peace and our joy in the Holy Spirit."

"Thy will be done on earth, as it is in Heaven" is a plea that lesser wills shall be ignored, so that God's peace may prevail in us. There are many wills we can obey: our selfish will, which destroys our neighbor's rights and our own peace of soul; the dictator's will, which crushes individuality; the will of public opinion, which sends us through life with no more stability than a cork on the ocean; or, finally, the will of God, which ushers in the perfection of peace.

But we cannot follow God's will without subduing the world; the last three petitions of the prayer ask for help in doing that.

The first difficulty we must overcome is to free ourselves from the effects of past sins and from resentment against the injuries we have suffered. *"Forgive us our trespasses as we forgive those who trespass against us"* makes our reception of pardon conditional on our pardoning of those who have offended us. As we distribute mercy, so we shall receive it.

The second struggle in which we need God's help is that of avoiding future evil. *"Lead us not into temptation"* implores that we shall not lose our way. The way can be lost through egotism or lust or avarice: we pray for preservation from such temptations as are too strong for us, for victory over those which cannot be avoided.

The third and final fetter we must break if we are to live the lives we should is the sense of fear, frustration, boredom, ennui, despair, and melancholy which might weigh down the soul confined to a world of trials and sorrows. That is why we ask, *"Deliver us from evil."* The evil is inevitably around us; it is our task to keep clear of it. Our Lord said to God, speaking of His own followers, "I am not asking that Thou shouldst take them out of the world, but that Thou shouldst keep them clear of what is evil."

Character is decided by our choices; the man who chooses the seven values listed above is a good man. The "Our Father" is the perfect prayer; it petitions God to grant the gifts that would perfect our human natures.

Our Lord, Who gave us this prayer Himself, never in His life used the term "Our Father" of God, when He was speaking in His own name. He always made the distinction between "Your Father" and "My Father" to indicate the distinction in our status: for He was the natural Son of God and we are the adopted children. It was after He had spent a long time on the mountaintop in prayer that His disciples, asking Him how *they* should pray, were told, "When you pray, say . . ." And then He gave them this prayer which, when fully meant, has made men saints for the past two thousand years . . . the prayer that begins, *"Our Father Who art in Heaven,"* and ends with the confession of our helplessness to save ourselves from sin unless God Himself shall, of His Grace, *"deliver us from evil."*

[19]

Rest and Meditation

MODERN MAN would be far happier if he would take a little time off to meditate. As the Old Testament prophet said, "Peace, peace and there is no peace, but no man considereth in his heart." The Gospel tells us that Our Blessed Lord withdrew Himself from the crowds into the wilderness and prayed. Martha, who was too busy about many things, was told that only one thing was necessary. A life of faith and with peace of soul can be cultivated only by periodical isolation from the cares of the world.

There are various kinds of weariness: weariness of the body, which can be satisfied under any tree or even on a pillow of stone; weariness of the brain, which needs the incubation of rest for new thought to be born; but hardest of all to satisfy is weariness of heart, which can be healed only by communion with God.

Silence helps speech; retirement helps thinking. A contemporary of Abraham Lincoln tells us that he spent three weeks with Lincoln just after the Battle of Bull Run: "I could not sleep. I was repeating the part that I was to play in a public performance. The hour was past midnight. Indeed, it was coming near to dawn, when I heard low tones coming from the room where the President slept. The door was partly open. I instinctively walked in and there I saw a sight which I shall never forget. It was the President, kneeling beside an open Bible. The light was turned low in the room. His back was turned toward me. For a moment I was silent, as I stood looking in amazement and wonder. Then he cried out in tones so pleading and sorrowful: 'O thou God that heard Solomon in the night that he prayed for wisdom, hear me; I cannot lead this people, I cannot guide the affairs of this nation without Thy help. I am poor and weak and sinful. O God, who didst hear Solomon when he cried to Thee, hear me and save this nation.'"

One wonders how many of our public officials in the great burdens that are laid upon them ever cry to God for help. When the United Nations held its first meeting in San Francisco, fearful that we might offend the atheists, it was decided to keep a minute of silence instead of praying fearlessly to God to illumine and guide the nations. It was in the moment of Peter's failure in fishing that Our Lord said, "Launch out into the deep." It is in the times of our failures that the soul must draw away from the shores.

What the Savior promises in the retirement is "rest for your souls." Rest is a gift—it is not earned; it is not the payment for finishing a job; it is the dowry of grace. Greed, envy, wealth, and avarice think of rest in terms of the good things of the world; true rest is the stilling of passions, the control of wavering ambitions, the joy of a quiet conscience. There is no rest until life has been made intelligible. Most of the restlessness of souls today comes from not knowing why they are here, or where they are going, and they refuse to take time out to solve that problem. Until it is solved, nothing is solved. There is not even much sense in going on living unless one knows why he is living.

Driving power is always associated with inner repose; otherwise energy is explosiveness and imprudent action. They that *wait* upon the Lord shall *renew* their strength. The renewals of strength are less physical than they are spiritual. A tired soul makes a tired body more often than a tired body makes a tired soul. The rest which Christianity enjoins is less cessation from work than it is freedom from the anxieties that come from guilt and avarice. Spiritual refreshment in prayer, retreat, meditation are the most potent influences for restoring harmony to the thousands of nervous patients. Life, like music, must have its rhythm of silence as well as sound.

The rest which retirement and contemplation give is not just a rest from toil, but it is even a rest in toil. The peace of Christ is not a hothouse plant—it raises its head for the storms; it is peace for the battle and joy of conscience for those who assail conscience. The world cannot give it; the world cannot take it away. It is not given by outward circumstance; it rules in the heart; it is an inward state. To be spiritually-minded is to have rest.

[20]

Egotism—The Enemy of Inner Peace

HERE IS a psychological suggestion for acquiring peace of soul. Never brag; never talk about yourself; never rush to first seats at table or in a theater; never use people for your own advantage; never lord it over others as if you were better than they.

These are but popular ways of expressing the virtue of humility, which does not consist so much in humbling ourselves before others as it does in recognizing our own littleness in comparison to what we ought to be. The modern tendency is toward the affirmation of the ego, the exaltation of selfishness, riding roughshod over others in order to satisfy our own self-centeredness. It certainly has not produced much happiness, for the more the ego asserts itself the more miserable it becomes.

Humility which gives preference to others is not very popular today, principally because men have forgotten the greatness of God. By expanding our puny little self to the infinite, we have made the true infinity of God seem trivial. The less knowledge we have of anything, the more insignificant it seems. Our hatred of a person often decreases as we learn to know him better. A boy graduating from high school is generally not as humble as when he graduates from medical school. At eighteen he thought he knew it all; at twenty-eight he feels himself ignorant in the face of the medical science he has yet to acquire. So it is with God. Because we do not pray or contemplate or love Him, we become vain and proud; but when we know Him better we feel a deep sense of dependence which tempers our false independence. Pride is the child of ignorance, humility the offspring of knowledge.

A proud man thinks himself better than he is, and when criticized always believes his neighbor is jealous or has a grudge against him. The humble man knows himself as he really is, for he judges himself as he judges time, by a standard outside himself—namely, God and His moral law. The psychological reason for the modern fondness for news which deflates others, or brings out the evil in their lives, is to solace uneasy consciences which are already laden with guilt. By finding others who apparently are more evil, one falsely believes he becomes better. It used to be that the most popular biographies were the lives of good men for the sake of imitation, rather than scandals for the sake of making ourselves believe we are more virtuous. The pagan Plutarch said, "The virtues of great men served me as a modern mirror in which I might adorn my own life."

Humility as it relates to our fellowman is a golden mean between a blind reverence of others on the one hand and an overbearing insolence on the other. The humble man is not a rigid exacter of things to which he has no undoubted right; he is always ready to overlook the faults of others, knowing that he has so many. Neither is he greatly provoked at those slights which put vain persons out of patience, knowing that as he shows mercy to others so shall he receive mercy from God. Before undertaking a task great or small, before making decisions, before beginning a journey, the humble man will acknowledge his dependence on God and will invoke His guidance and His blessing on all his enterprises. Even though he be placed above others by vocation, or by the will of the people, he will never cease to recognize that God has made of one blood all the nations that dwell on the earth. If he is very rich he will not be a "defender of the rights of the poor" without unloading his riches in their aid. Our modern world has produced a generation of rich politicians who talk love of the poor, but never prove it in action, and a brood of the poor whose hearts are filled with envy for the rich and covetousness for their money. The rich man who is humble helps the poor, rather than the revolutionists who use the poor to bomb their ways to dictatorial thrones.

Another evidence of want of humility is in regard to knowledge. Scripture bids us "be wise unto sobriety." Humility moderates our estimate of what we know and will remind us that God gave to the wise more talents than others and more opportunities for developing those talents. But of him who has received much, much also will be expected. The intellectual leader has a tremendous responsibility thrust upon him, and woe to him if he uses his office of teaching to lead the young into error and conceit. Notice how often today authors will have their picture taken with their book in their left hand, the title in full view of the camera, so that the photograph may tell the story: "Look, Ma! My book!" Television commentators have books on their desks with the title toward the audience so that the audience may be impressed. No man who reads books at a desk ever has the titles turned away—but toward himself. Perhaps someday when there are diaphonous walls, the intelligentsia will keep the titles on their bookshelves turned toward the wall so that their next-door neighbor will know how smart they are.

In the face of Divine Wisdom, all that we have, or do, or know, is a gift of God, and is only an insignificant molehill compared to His mountain of knowledge. Well indeed, then, may those who enjoy any relative superiority ask with Paul, "What have you that you have not received? If so, then why glory as if you had not received?"

[21]

Humility

NOTHING HAS so much contributed to egotism as the false idea that an "inferiority complex" is a defect. The assumption is that we should have a sense of "superiority." How far we have departed from the virtue of humility! What is a humble man?

1. Humility is truth. A humble man neither praises nor belittles himself. Underestimation can be as false as overestimation. For a six-foot-tall man to say that he is only five feet tall is an offense against the truth, just as it would be to say that he was seven feet tall.

2. He recognizes that the gift of mind, or speech, muscle, talent, song or wealth, is something that has come to him. If he has received it as a gift from God, either directly or indirectly, he does not act as if he had not received it.

3. When the humble man receives praise, he looks into his own heart and wishes to God that he deserved heaven's praise.

4. He knows that he could never understand humility if it were not for the inspiration of all humility—namely, the God Who stripped Himself of His heavenly glory in order to walk among men and redeem them. That is why the Greeks and the Latins had no specific word for humility, in the noble sense, until Christianity gave it content.

5. Humility is humiliation and inferiority when men compare themselves only to other men who are greater; but it is the foundation of exaltation in him who considers himself as nothingness in the face of the Goodness of God.

6. The humble man makes room for progress; the proud man believes he is already there.

7. The humble man recognizes that titles, honors, position, glory are all external to himself, and could be lost in a moment; the only thing that is really his own is his will—that is why it is the perfect gift either to another person or to God.

8. The higher the building, the deeper the foundation; the greater the aspiration, the more rarefied the humility.

9. Pride is inflation, the swelling and puffing up of the ego which makes learning impossible. Humility is emptiness—not the emptiness of the Grand Canyon, which is unprofitable, but the emptiness of the nest which can be filled with song and new life.

10. Humility is not a want of enterprise, power, and dynamism. The man in the parable who shrank from doing anything with his talent was condemned. Paul was humble when he said that he had "labored more abundantly than all the other apostles," because he attributed it to the grace of God.

11. Humility is not a readiness to be trampled upon, nor a poverty of spirit which shrinks from the battle, nor an abandoning of responsibilities; it waits for the great battles and then drives buyers and sellers out of temples.

12. The humble man represses the tiny vanities of the day which exhaust spiritual strength; he waits in the desert, like a John the Baptist, until the hour of decision comes when power is seen as the other side of the coin of littleness.

13. Humility will accept a number of rebuffs and insults when no great cause is at stake, knowing that no one ever receives the just deserts of his misdeeds. But when not his own pride, but some principle is at stake, it is like a giant aroused from sleep.

14. The humble man is hard on himself and easy on others.

15. He is always dissatisfied with his writings, his works and accomplishments, but easily satisfied with the efforts of others, and never fails to give them encouragement.

16. He is ready to do favors for those who injure him, as Christ washed the feet of Judas, never cherishing revenge.

17. He is never discouraged, for discouragement is a form of pride.

18. He knows that the trees that bear the most fruit have branches that bend downward and hang lowest to the ground.

19. He never courts to be seen by men.

20. The humble man knows that there are two things said about him that are untrue: things that are too good to be true, and things that are too bad to be true.

[22]

Modern Hair Shirts

LENT IS a penitential season, a time when men once put on hair shirts, sacrificing any hope of bodily ease for forty days. G. K. Chesterton once said that St. Thomas à Becket wore a hair shirt under his purple, so that the people might have the benefit of the purple, and he might have the benefit of the penance.

Those whose lives are a constant search for sensate pleasures find it hard to understand why anyone should ever have worn a hair shirt. But in ages of universal faith, everybody knew that the hair shirt, like fasting, was a form of penance; it was to be what St. Paul called a "thorn in the flesh," a sacrifice of comfort in order to tame a man's errant desires and rampaging instincts for self-indulgence. Although it is probably impossible to buy a hair shirt in America today, it does not follow that modern men have less need for asceticism—or that they are not given penances as severe as those of medieval men.

As many people wear "hair shirts" now as ever before in history, but they are not called by that name, and they are not always assumed in the sacrificial spirit appropriate to Lent. The modern "hair shirt" is the sum of the trials, annoyances, and criticisms which surround one in the tense and nervous world of today. A hair shirt may take the form of rising early to get to work on time; of taking dictation from a man whose voice is so low that he can hardly be heard;

of answering an endless series of foolish questions at the information desk; of a gum-chewing assistant, or a colleague who blows smoke rings in your face, or—commonest of all—the hard grind of working to make both ends meet.

Any of these trials is an occasion for penance, if one chooses to accept it and offer it up to God. A hair shirt of this sort is not one we put on ourselves; it is our neighbor who puts it on us. And he usually puts it on to stay.

The old hair shirt could be taken off, if the suffering became too great; the new one sticks to us like a plaster. The old hair shirt was made to measure; the new one takes our measure. The older ascetic risked losing all the benefit of his hair shirt if he became proud of the fact that he wore it. But the new hair shirt is always humbling: no man can be proud of the fact that he knows a bore, or that his car got stuck half an hour in traffic. The older penitents were expected to take off their hair shirts on Holy Saturday, but the new hair shirt outlasts every Lent.

The tragedy is that most modern wearers of the hair shirt get no spiritual benefit out of it. Their trials and frustrations irritate and annoy them, making them complain, making them only rebellious and "difficult." Because they do not use their trials properly, they have the pain but miss the merit.

Pain and sacrifice are vastly different things—but the difference lies in the will, and not in the degree of suffering. Pain is sacrifice without the love of God. Sacrifice is pain combined with love of God. There is an enormous difference between the woman who diets and the woman who fasts, although they may both lose fifteen pounds. But one does it for the sake of her body, and the other for the sake of her soul. There is no material difference in the hair shirts they wear, but the formal difference is very great indeed.

To gain merit from our inescapable hair shirts, two basic beliefs are needed. One must first acknowledge the fact that man is a composite of body and soul, and that a real effort will be required to keep the body the servant of the soul. The second essential is a belief in the Redemption which shows us how, by penance, we may make up for our own past failings, and even for the faults of others.

In earlier days, when life was less difficult and there was less egotism and more charity abroad, the literal hair shirt had its place. But nowadays hair shirts are everywhere we turn. Perhaps if we examined our conscience, we should discover that we ourselves were the worst hair shirt our neighbor had to bear. Because the good Lord knew this, He told our neighbors how to wear us patiently, when He said to them, "Take up your cross."

[23]

How to Find Out What Is Ailing You

WHAT ARE the three possible attitudes of a mind in the face of something which we have freely done, and which we ought not to have done? After a fault, there can be either regret, remorse, or repentance.

Regret has no moral or ethical implications; it generally expresses itself as "What a fool I made of myself," or "How stupid I am," or "How could I ever have done such a thing?" Regret always looks to the past, wishing that one could undo it. The regret can be for various psychological motives—for example, because it diminished the good opinion others may have had of us, or because of the consequences, such as "Now I will have a lawsuit on my hands."

In regret, the past is regarded as something which one would like to capture again in order to do things differently, but there is a deep sense that the past is untouchable. Hence the sterile reflection made by the regretful "The past is past; what is done is done." What is tragic about regret is that those who have that psychological experience regard the fault as irreparable; nothing can be done to make amends.

Remorse is different. It does not regard the past as a broken egg which cannot be pieced together again; it desires a future where one can undo the past. Remorse has an element of expiation, and blotting out the past, which is not present in regret. It would like to hold the egg a second time; it would never be dropped again. Remorse is always a prisoner of the past; it does not shrug its shoulders and forget it. The past is present; the fault is ever before the eyes, but there is no way to undo it.

Remorse quickly leads to despair, because there seems no road of escape. The large number of souls who are stretched out on psychoanalytic couches are suffering from this remorse. They feel an inner contradiction within them, between what they want to be and what they are. They believe that a psychoanalyst can explain this conflict away in terms of parents and grandparents. But the fault lies not in the stars nor in the parents, but in the heart itself. Because contradiction or inner conflict is the consequence of remorse, which often leads to suicide, it is falsely believed that it is easier to die by contradicting life with death than to live with both.

Finally there is repentance, which is a higher kind of remorse. St. Paul spoke of both of these:

> *Supernatural remorse leads to an abiding and salutary*
> *Change of heart, whereas the world's remorse*
> *Leads to death.*

Repentance is also self-reproach, like the other states, but it is never sterile; it lays hold of the past by undoing it through penance. Both Judas and Peter denied Our Lord, but Judas repented unto himself, which was regret and remorse, and took his own life; Peter repented unto the Lord, which produced a new man. God alone, through the redemptive merits of Christ, receives the sinner as the sea receives the bather—to clean him and restore him to the shore more refreshed than ever. In taking a human nature and becoming a new Adam, Christ undid the sin of the first Adam. Then the sin of Adam became a "happy fault," for it ended in a greater gift than that which was lost.

Only the Divine Who is outside of time can lay hold of the past and make it serve the future in a different way. Godly sorrow makes a man grieve because he has sinned and hurt someone he loves; worldly sorrow or remorse makes one wish that he never had to suffer from an Oedipus complex. The remorseful man considers himself as stupid; the repentant man considers himself as a sinner. Sin can be redeemed; but the past, as past, cannot be recaptured by man alone. As Spenser wrote of the remorseful soul: "It is dying each day with inward wounds of dolor's dart."

The particular brand of psychoanalysts who deny guilt are farther away from the truth than was Cicero who, looking into the future, wrote of those who are passive on a couch instead of active on their knees:

"Think not that guilt requires the burning torches of the Furies to agitate and torment it. Frauds, crimes, rememberances of the past, terrors of the future—these are the domestic furies that are ever present in the minds of the impious." Nothing in this life need be wasted; even the faults of the past can be turned into goodness—but it takes more than a man on a couch to do it; it takes a Man on a Cross.

IV
Tranquillity of Soul

Pleasure and Joy

EVERYONE WANTS to be happy. But few find happiness because they fail to distinguish whether it will consist in pleasure or in joy. The latter alone gives true happiness. But what is the difference between pleasure and joy?

Joy is inward; pleasure is outward. Pleasure depends on something external to one's self—for example, a cocktail, a dance, or a fancy car. When the external pleasure fails or satiates, happiness ends. Joy, on the contrary, is inward. Our Blessed Lord said, "These things have I spoken to you that My joy might remain *in you.*" Joy is not disturbed by external circumstances; it may exist under the most adverse circumstances, even suffering.

Pleasure is changeful; joy is constant. Because the things upon which pleasure depends change, there is a constant vacillation of ups and downs, moments of depression and moments of exaltation. Joy, on the contrary, is permanent, hence Our Blessed Lord said, "My joy might *remain* in you."

Pleasure is a seeking; joy is a finding. He who thinks happiness is pleasure must incessantly run from one stimulus to another, which is an indication of the fact that he has not yet found pleasure. If ambulances were running through a city street, one could be certain that men had not yet found health. If gold prospectors were running up and down mountainsides, one could be sure that they had not yet found gold. Joy, on the contrary, is something that is found; it gives mental peace and repose, hence the Divine assurance that no one on earth can take away joy.

Pleasure is built on self-seeking; joy is built on self-sacrifice. The worldling gets his pleasure by getting, and the more he gets, the more he feels he needs, for the simple reason that the more he gets, *the less he really has.* It is peculiar how the outward increase of things deepens a sense of inner poverty; that is why the less one has

on the inside, the more one has to cover it up with external pomp
and exaggerated luxury. It is not so much that one wants more outside of himself; it is rather because one feels a greater emptiness on
the inside.

Pleasure cannot survive a crisis; a joy survives crisis and is unfailing. Lord Byron wrote a pathetic requiem as he lie dying:

> My days are in the yellow leaf,
> The flowers and the fruits of life are gone;
> The worm, the canker, and the grief
> Are mine alone.

Joy, on the contrary, because its basis is not getting but giving,
reaches its peak when there is the greatest sacrifice of self. The only
recorded time Our Lord ever sang with joy was the night He went
to give His Life as a ransom for mankind.

The secret of joy is the following:

> God first
> Others next
> Self last.

[25]

Joy from the Inside

EACH OF US makes his own weather, determines the color of the
skies in the emotional universe which he inhabits. We can, by a creative effort, bring such sunlight to our souls that it makes radiant
whatever events may come our way. We can, on the other hand,

permit ourselves to slump into a state of inner depression so deep and filled with gloom that only the most intense outward stimulations of the senses are able to rouse us from our apathy.

Everyone must have pleasure, the philosophers tell us. The man who has integrated his personality in accordance with its nature and oriented his life toward God knows the intense and indestructible pleasure the saints called joy. No outward event can threaten him or ruffle his happiness. But many men look outward for their pleasure and expect the accidents of their lives to provide their happiness. Since nobody can make the universe his slave, everyone who looks outward for pleasure is bound to disappointment. A glut of entertainment wearies us; a realized ambition becomes a bore; a love that promised full contentment loses its glamour and its thrill. Lasting happiness can never come from the world. Joy is not derived from the things we get or the people we meet; it is manufactured by the soul itself, as it goes about its self-forgetful business.

The secret of a happy life is the moderation of our pleasures in exchange for an increase of joy. But several contemporary practices make this difficult for us. One of these is the type of merchandising which tries to increase our desires in order that we shall buy more goods. Allied with this is the spoiled-child psychology of modern man, which tells him that he is entitled to get anything he wants, that the world owes everyone the satisfaction of his whims. Once the ego has become the center around which everything else revolves, we are vulnerable: our peace can be destroyed by a draft from an open window, by our inability to buy a coat made of some exotic fur so rare that only twenty women in the world can wear it— by our failure to get invited to a luncheon, or our failure to pay the biggest income tax in the nation. The ego is always insatiable, if it is in command; no indulgences and no honors quiet its craving, either for "madder music and for a stronger wine," or for the heady delights of testimonial dinners and glaring headlines.

The ego-centered men view as calamities the denial of any of their wishes: they want to dominate their world, to pull its puppet strings and force those about them to obey their will. If such an ego's wishes are crossed and checked by another ego, its owner is in despair. Occasions for despondency and sadness are thus multiplied, for all of us are bound to be denied some of the things we want. It is our choice whether this loss shall be accepted with a cheerful good grace or taken as an outrage and an affront to us.

Today millions of men and women consider that their happiness is destroyed if they must get along without a few things of which their grandfathers had never dreamed. Luxuries have become necessities to them; and the more things a man needs in order to be happy, the more he has increased his chances of disappointment and despair. Whim has become his master, trivia his tyrant; he no longer is self-possessed, but he has become possessed by outward objects, trumpery toys.

Plato in his *Republic* wrote of the man whose life is run by his whims and fancies; his words were written 2,300 years ago, but they are still pat today: "Often he will take to politics, leaping to his feet, and do or say whatever comes into his head; or he conceives an admiration for a general and his interests turn to war; or for a man of business, and straightway that is his line. He knows no order or necessity in life; he will not listen to anyone who tells him that some pleasures come in the gratification of good and noble desires, others from evil ones, and that the former should be fostered and encouraged, the latter disciplined and chained. To all such talk, he shakes his head and says that all enthusiasms are similar and worthy of equal attention."

Pleasures must be arranged in a hierarchy if we are to get the greatest enjoyment out of life. The most intense and lasting joys come only to those who are willing to practice a certain self-restraint, to undergo the boredom of a preliminary discipline. The best view is from the mountaintop, but it may be arduous to reach it. No man ever enjoyed reading Horace without drilling himself with the declensions of his grammar first. Full happiness is understood only by those who have denied themselves some legitimate pleasures in order to obtain deferred joys. Men who "let themselves go," go to seed or go mad. The Savior of the world Himself told us that the best joys come only after we have purchased them by prayer and fasting: we must give up our copper pennies first, out of love for Him, and He will pay us back in pieces of gold, in joy and ecstasy.

[26]

Does Happiness Consist in Riches?

THERE IS NO ONE who does not want to be happy. To seek happiness is a proof of our imperfection. As Pascal expressed it: "All men have happiness as their object: there is no exception. However different the means they employ, they all aim at the same end."

> O happiness! our being's end and aim,
> Good, pleasure, ease, content! whate'er they
>   name.
> That something still which prompts th' eternal
>   sigh,
> For which we bear to live, or dare or die.
>   ALEXANDER POPE

Nor do we want this happiness through another man's eyes; we want it as something peculiarly our own. The difficulty is where to find it. The fact that we feel happy when we receive something we want, and that we feel unhappy when we are deprived of it, proves that happiness has something to do with the objects of our desires or purposes. For that reason, at the end of every human activity there are pleasure and joy or sadness and pain, just as at the end of every human life there is a heaven or a hell.

Does happiness consist of riches or wealth? There are indeed many advantages to riches. Herodotus claimed that they allowed a man to indulge his passions. George Bernard Shaw said that money gave power: "Money talks; money prints; money broadcasts; money reigns." But wealth can never constitute happiness, because it is only a means to happiness and extrinsic to oneself. This is what Our Lord meant when He said, "A man's life does not consist in the abundance of his possessions." If you put a penny close enough to your eye, you can shut out the light of the sun. Want of wealth is not necessarily the cause of unhappiness. There are more divorces, more frustrated lives, more inner misery among the rich than among the poor. "A golden bit does not make the better horse."

Riches in great abundance have a peculiar quality; they make men more greedy. As Thomas Jefferson said, "I have not observed men's honesty to increase with their riches." No matter how much money a rich man has, he hates to lose what he has, just as no matter how many hairs he has on his head, it hurts to have one pulled out. This spirit of covetousness hardens the soul, and drew from Our Divine Lord the warning: "It is easier for a camel to pass through the eye of a needle, than for a rich man to enter the Kingdom of Heaven." "But woe to you rich! for you are now having your comfort."

There is a peculiar paradox about riches: the more covetous the rich man is, the poorer he is, for there is always something he wants. But the consecrated souls who have taken the vow of poverty are richer than all the rich, for there is nothing they desire; therefore they possess everything.

In any case, how foolish to make happiness consist in that which one day we must leave. If riches are really ours, why can we not take them with us? The only things we can carry with us at death are what we might carry away in a shipwreck. As Shakespeare said, "If thou art rich, thou art poor; for like an ass whose back with ingots bows, thou bearest thy heavy riches but a journey and death unloads thee." On the last day, relatives and friends will gather around the deathbed of the rich man and ask, "How much did he leave?" for wherever there is a will, there is a lawsuit. But the angels will ask, "How much did he take with him?" "The land of a certain rich man brought forth abundant crops. And he began to take thought within himself, saying, 'What shall I do, for I have no room to store my crops?' And he said, 'I will do this: I will pull down my barns and build larger ones, and there I will store up all my grain and my goods. And I will say to my soul: Soul, thou hast many good things laid up for many years; take thy ease—eat, drink, be merry.' But God said to him, 'Thou fool, this night do they demand thy soul of thee; and the things that thou has provided, whose will they be?' So is he who lays up treasure for himself, and is not rich as regards God."

Next, we will answer the question: does happiness consist in glory, reputation, and honors?

[27]

Does Happiness Consist in Glory, Reputation, and Honors?

REPUTATION AND honors are witnesses to excellence or prominence, but they do not constitute it. Making honor the goal of life is to make our happiness dependent upon others, and happiness should be something no one can take away. Furthermore, if honor is the ideal of life, then disgrace is the only sin.

It is really not honor based on virtue which men seek today, but rather reputation, which is measured more by its width than its depth. Reputation is often only popularity, and, like a breeze, it cannot be kept. You must enjoy it while it blows. It is like a ball—men generally start kicking it about when it stops rolling. The greatness of any age is to be measured by those whom it holds in high repute. The youth of today is not in danger because of its love of pleasures, but because it worships the wrong kind of heroes. Many of the present century who have reputations will be quoted in the next century to prove how barbarous was the thinking of this century.

Anyone who enjoys the world's repute, if he is honest with himself, knows that he does not deserve it. The world is saying things about us that are either too good to be true or too bad to be true. As Charles Lamb put it, "I am accounted by some people a good man. How cheap that character is acquired! Pay your debts, don't borrow money, nor twist your kitten's neck off, nor disturb a congregation, etc.; your business is done. I know things about myself, which would make every friend fly me as a plague." St. Philip Neri, seeing a condemned man led to the guillotine, said, "There goes Philip Neri, except for the grace of God."

How unstable is happiness based on "being well-known"! How many go up like skyrockets and come down like sticks! Applause is contagious. Let two or three applaud in a theater and everyone follows. As Shakespeare said:

> Glory is like a circle in the water,
> Which never ceaseth to enlarge itself
> Till, by broad spreading, it disperse to nought.

The truly happy person does not really care what others may think of him, for true glory consists in the judgment of God rather than in the judgment of men. St. Paul said, "It is a very small matter to be judged by you or by man's tribunal." The most lasting reputations are those that are achieved after death when the tinsel of empty glory fades away. The greatness of Lincoln is posthumous. The glory of Christ came after His Crucifixion. And from Him has come this warning: "Woe to you when all men speak well of you."

No stronger words escaped the Divine Lips than those directed against popularity seekers, who sought to have their names publicized in the market places then, as they do today in the newspapers: "All their works they do in order to be seen by men; for they widen their phylacteries, and enlarge their tassels, and love the first places at suppers and the front seats in the synagogues, and greetings in the market place."

[28]

Happiness

HAPPINESS DOES NOT consist in the abundance of things a man possesses, nor does it reside in the satisfaction of different specific desires—for example, pleasure at one moment, publicity at another. Rather, happiness is conditioned on two things: an overall purpose in life and, second, the crushing of egotism and selfishness.

The goal of life must satisfy the highest reaches of personality, namely our desire for life, our craving for truth, and our lust for love. Life is not satisfied by three more days of living, but by unending immortality; truth is satisfied, not by knowing all geography to the exclusion of science, or all art to the exclusion of philosophy; the mind can come to rest only when it possesses a knowledge of all truth, not in an abstract form, but personalized in Him Who says, "I am the Truth." Finally, the will is satisfied not by a love that grows cold or has phases like the moon, but by a love that is a continuous ecstasy without hate or satiety. This Perfect Life, Perfect Truth, and Perfect Love is God, the Father, Son, and Holy Spirit.

The second condition of happiness is crushing egotism and selfishness which stands in the way of attaining that ultimate goal or purpose. Hell is the ego affirmed in time, in isolation, and in eternity in conflict with other egos who are constantly negating our ego. Hell is composed of completely egotistic persons! Those who presently live with such people now have a foretaste of hell. The reason the ego has to be naughted is because unless a "for sale" sign is hung on it, neither God nor neighbor can move in. Only when the glass tube has had all the air removed and becomes a vacuum can it become the medium for X rays which can penetrate the flesh and brain though we see it not. So long as there remains the ego or selfishness by which we affirm our pleasure over others, we are consumed by an inner unhappiness. In hell, nothing burns but the ego—a sensation that egotists dimly feel in the gnawing that goes on inside their conscience.

Because it is so hard to get rid of pride and lust, covetousness and anger, gluttony and sloth, the business of achieving happiness below is very slow. Inner peace is rarely attained in one stroke; we have to inch ourselves through the door of happiness. There are no plains in the spiritual life. We do not just climb a few paces through rough roads and then finally come to a land of contentment. Rather, we reach only a momentary clearing; the brushes, thorns and briars still lie ahead to cut and bruise the flesh; the occasional danger of slipping back a few feet now and then is ever present. As Our Divine Lord said, "Take up your cross daily." The struggle for happiness is even conditioned upon having a wrestling match with ourselves; it is not easy to get the lion and the lamb to lie down together; the retriever has a hard time catching his quarry, the wild beast within us; if it does happen, it is by the skin of one's teeth.

But even though it be difficult, there is a peace and a joy about the pursuit of Divine Happiness which the egotist cannot understand. Each trial and struggle has its strength as grace pours in from heaven above. The more the balloon of our egotism is shot full of holes, the more apertures are made for the influx of light and love. Our own individual resources never have to be budgeted against the daily crosses. Others wonder whence come strength and patience, never suspecting that such souls are no longer self-contained cisterns that quickly run dry; rather they are great reservoirs into which the sluice gates of heaven open. Everybody wants to be happy. The reason most people are not happy is because they want to be happy in their own way and without any purchase price. Paradoxical as it may seem, happiness begins when the ego dies.

[29]

Is Modern Man Far from Peace?

No ONE IS dangerously unhappy except the individual who does not know what happiness means. Life is unbearable only to those who are ignorant of why they are alive; men in such a condition of soul equate happiness with pleasure (which is a very different matter) and identify joy with a tingling of the nerve endings (which it is not). But things which are external to us never bring us inner peace. The more persistently anyone looks for satisfaction and a goal to serve in something outside of his control, the less stable he will find it, the more subject he will be to disappointments.

There are two movements toward happiness. The first of these is our withdrawal from the outside—from too great an absorption in the things of the world. The second movement is far more profound: it is an ascension from what is inferior within us to what is its superior, from our egotism to our God. Modern man has experienced the first movement; exterior things have become so many sources of misery to him. Wars, depressions, the insecurity and emptiness of life have so terrified men that they have tried to close off their contacts with the outside world and have begun to seek for satisfactions in their own limited selves. That is why psychiatry is having such a field day: the modern soul, alarmed at what it finds without, has drawn down the shades and begun to look for contentment in analyzing its own unconsciousness, anxieties and fears, its doldrums and frustrations.

But such self-containment can prove a prison if one is locked into it with his own ego alone, for there is no more confining straitjacket in the world than that of the self left *to* itself. The cure never lies in using a psychoanalytic scalpel to release the inner moral pus and watch it flow; that is a morbid act for both the patient and the doctor. The cure, rather, consists in discovering why one is lonely and afraid of solitude—for most people have a dread of being alone, without knowing why the prospect frightens them.

The problem of our day is this problem of finding interior peace, and it is in this that the twentieth century is marked off from the nineteenth. A hundred years ago men looked to the exterior world for the answers to their problems: they worshipped science or nature, expected happiness to come from progress or politics or profits. The twentieth-century man is worried about himself: he is even more concerned over the problem of sex than by sex itself—interested in the mental attitude he should take toward it, rather than in its physical satisfaction and the begetting of children. His own values, moods, and attitudes absorb him.

Although a great deal of nonsense has been written about the interior life of men in our day, it is still true that the twentieth century is closer to God than the nineteenth century was. We are living on the eve of one of the great spiritual revivals of human history. Souls are sometimes closest to God when they feel themselves farthest away from Him, at the point of despair. For an empty soul, the Divine can fill; a worried soul, the Infinite can pacify. A self-contented, proud soul, however, is inaccessible to Grace.

Modern man has been humiliated: neither his proud expectations of progress nor of science have turned out as he hoped. Yet he has not quite reached the point of humbling himself. He is still imprisoned in the self, and able to see nothing else beyond. The psychoanalysts may be allowed to bore into his thoughts for a few years more; but the time is not far off when modern men will utter a frantic appeal to God to lift them from the empty cistern of their own egos. St. Augustine knew it well; he said, "Our hearts are restless until they rest in Thee."

That is why—although a catastrophic war may threaten us—the times are not as bad as they seem. Modern man has not yet returned to God; but he has, at least, returned to himself. Later he will surpass and transcend himself with God's grace, which he is seeking even now. No one ever looked for something unless he knew that it existed; today the frustrated soul is looking for God, as for the memory of a name he used to know.

The difference between those who have found God in faith and those who are still seeking Him is like the difference between a wife happy in the enjoyment of her husband's companionship, and a young girl wondering if she will ever find a husband, and perhaps trying to attract men by the wrong approach. Those who search for pleasure, fame, and wealth are all seeking the Infinite, but the seekers are still on the outskirts of the Eternal City. Those with faith have penetrated to their real home within the Infinite and have found the "peace which the world cannot give." As one can see a figure far off and not yet recognize him as a long-lost friend, so one can sense the need of the Infinite and desire the endless ecstasy of love, but not yet know that it is God.

It makes no difference how wicked a soul may be, there is no one subjecting himself to illicit pleasures who does not have a consciousness of his subjection and his slavery. Perhaps that is why alcoholics are often liars: their lips deny a slavery which their lives so visibly witness. Such individuals, unwilling to admit themselves mistaken, still refuse to be convinced of Divine Truth; but their sadness and their emptiness will eventually drive them to the God of Mercy.

Our exterior world today is in desperate straits, but the inner world of man is far from hopeless. The world of politics and economics lags behind the psychological development of men themselves. The world is far from God, but human hearts are not. That is why peace will come less from political changes than from man himself, who, driven to take refuge within his own soul from the turmoil without, will be lifted above himself to the happiness for which he was made.

[30]

Contentment (I)

AMERICANS LOVE to be comfortable. "Comfort" is a lovely word, but in the Greek original it is found in only one place in the entire New Testament, and that is when St. Paul states that he is satisfied or in comfort in whatever condition he happens to find himself. This is indeed a queer kind of comfort, particularly because he found himself so often in perils of the sea, in perils of false brethren, in storms and stonings, shipwrecks and imprisonment. Comfort to him, therefore, was a kind of contentment rather than a lounge chair. And what a great distance it was from the stoicism of those days, which gritted teeth in the face of trial and trouble and then boasted of insensibility to pain.

To be content when one abounds and when one wants is rather an inner than an external comfort such as our civilization praises, and that is the difference between Pauline and American comfort. After all, the rich man who has millions can never be content in the real sense of the word, because there is still something outside him which he does not yet have. So he has to build bigger barns to lessen that area between his "much" and "everything." On the contrary, a missionary who commits a kind of social martyrdom to succor the afflicted in needy lands, or the holy man or woman who takes the vow of poverty has more than the rich man. This is because they have nothing in the material order that they desire; since there is nothing they desire, in one sense, they have everything.

Our American problem is that of an affluence which, instead of being satisfied with what one has, strives to keep on multiplying it.

Advertising is geared to turning luxuries into necessities, and to the increasing of wants. This is the inverse of a condition of happiness which consists in diminishing wants. Affluence, at its best, is only external contentment—the mink coat that is kept in mothballs has no affluence value unless it is worn and seen. One wonders how many women would make so many sacrifices to get a mink coat if everyone else in the world were blind. It has reached a point now in the prosperity of our civilization where it is almost impossible to get a thing repaired. When one brings an auto, a radio, a television set, a toaster, or a carpet sweeper to be repaired, the usual retort is, "Throw it away; buy a new one." Be discontented with anything but "next year's model." One wonders, too, as regards weather—if the modern man does not grumble far more about the weather than did his grandfather. He is able to make comparison with other climates because of his travels. But the older generation, which never had a suntan in January, was more satisfied with each day's weather as it came. As the Irish say when it is raining, "It is a good day to save your soul."

The gloomy old Schopenhauer once asked, "Is there a man alive who is content with his lot?" Paul was, and there are millions and millions of others, because the contrarieties of life can all be reconciled since each day, in its own way, contributes to our eternal perfection. Prosperity contributes because it draws from the grateful soul an act of thanksgiving and a sharing of the blessing with others. Trials, sufferings, the enmity of others are no less functional, but even more so, in the developing of a spiritual character. "All things contribute to good in those who are called to be saints." The widest range of circumstances and experiences can become the warp and woof of a moral life.

A consecrated love is the secret of contentment; on the contrary, a want of an overpowering love is the reason for unhappiness. The mother loving a child is content, and for that child she will even forsake pleasures. The giddy girl gives up her frivolities when she finds one to whom she can sacrifice herself. Beyond all these lesser loves is the supreme love of God, for whom we are made. When everything that happens is seen as coming from His hand, one is content knowing that an all-wise and loving Lord prompted it. Then, too, shall not the Christian know that Christ, Who bore so much and rose to glory, is the pattern upon which his life is to be modeled? Nothing is so transforming to blessings and to trials as the secret of contentment and working out His purpose toward us. Contentment is the manna that is laid up in the ark that contains the Presence of God.

[31]

Contentment (II)

RESTLESSNESS IS the opposite of contentment. Greater is the number of the restless than the contented, and yet contentment is not impossible in any situation of life. Contentment is the virtue of being satisfied with whatever state or condition in which we find ourselves. It consists not so much in adding fuel to the fire as in taking some fire away; not in multiplying wealth, but in diminishing desires, in realizing that thirst can better be quenched out of a cup than out of a river. Velvet slippers do not cure gout, and a bed of gold does not ease sickness more readily than a mattress of straw.

There is no psychological road to tranquillity of soul, only the spiritual. Those who lack the spiritual are always discontented. As Isaias put it, "Rebellious hearts like the tempestuous sea can never find repose; its waters must ever be churning up mire and scum. For the rebellious, the Lord says, there is no peace." Contentment never comes with the mere *having*, regardless of its proportion, because having is external of our being, and peace resides within. Unless we are happy on the inside, nothing on the outside can reach the depths of the soul. It will be found that most discontent is over material things, which proves that they are sought more ardently than the goods of the soul.

This does not mean that contentment is incompatible with an earnest desire to enlarge our provision of earthly things, in order to give blessings to those around us; nor does contentment mean sloth in business or neglect of worldly interests. Contentment is not the opposite of thrift and industry, but of covetousness and unbelieving anxiety.

Contentment is a gracious disposition of the mind, arising from absolute trust in God, so that the scales of our heart are equally poised in both prosperity and adversity. We become content as we realize:

1. The goodness of God. When we say that God is good, we do not mean that He is good like some grandfathers who care not if their grandchildren tear the house to pieces; rather God is good after the manner of the father who tempers justice with mercy to bring his children to perfection of character. God does not always give us what we want, but He gives us what we need. If He multiplied thousand-dollar bills instead of loaves and fishes in the desert, no one would have said that he received enough. But the Gospel tells us that "each had his fill." When manna was given to the Jews in the desert, it was a sufficiency for each day; those who would have stored up in an avaricious fashion found that it could not be used.

2. Contentment also comes from a steady recognition of God's omniscience. A deep sense of His unsearchable wisdom is well calculated to allay our fears and compose our spirit. What we know in relation to Him is less than the mouse knows in relation to us. A child is given bitter medicine, cries and protests against it, but the parent knows that it is, at the moment, best for the child and will result in ulterior good. So it is with the trials of life; we may not understand them for the moment, but in the Divine Mind they all cooperate unto good to those who love Him.

3. A realization of our ill deserts. A diabolical pride lurks in the heart of anyone who complains, saying "What did I do to deserve this?" as if our lives were so blameless and so innocent as to merit no reproof or correction, or as if we were not part of a fallen world. If God the Father did not spare His Son and the Son did not spare the mother, then shall we, in the face of what innocence suffered for the guilty, repine against the absence of those things which the heart covets? The more humble we are, the more we see that we have forfeited all rights to goodness and deserve far more purifying

correction than we have received. "His be the thanks, if we are not extinguished." Nothing more quickly composes the mind in the face of adversity and prevents it from being puffed up by prosperity than the cry of the Roman centurion: "Lord, I am not worthy that thou shouldst enter under my roof." Two things are incompatible: trust and fear. He who trusts, loves, and where there is love there is no undue worry. Much of this contentment is lost by not putting ourselves outside the Divine area of love as a waif of the street is outside the care and the blessings of a home. *"Trust Him when dark doubts assail thee; trust Him when trust is small. Trust Him when simply to trust Him is the hardest thing of all."*

V
Love

Love Is Infinite

THERE IS a profound difference in quality between the possessions that we need and use and actually enjoy, and the accumulation of useless things we accumulate out of vanity or greed or the desire to surpass others. The first kind of possession is a legitimate extension of our personalities: we enrich a much-used object by our love, and it becomes dear to us. We can learn about the two kinds of ownership in any nursery: a child who has only a single toy enriches it with his love. The spoiled child with many playthings spread out for him quickly becomes blasé and ceases to take pleasure in any one of them. The quality of his love diminishes with the number of objects offered for his love . . . as a river has less depth the more it spreads over the plains.

When we visit a large mansion inhabited by only two people, we feel the coldness of such a house, too vast to be made a home by human love. Each of us by his presence can ennoble a few cubic feet, but no more. The more people own beyond the limit of things they can personalize and love, the more they will suffer boredom, ennui, and satiety.

Yet, men and women are forever trying to add to their possessions far beyond the limit of enjoyment. This is because of their mistaken belief that their hunger for Infinity can be satisfied by an infinity of material things: what they really wish is the Infinity of Divine Love.

Our imaginations are easily misled into desiring a false infinity, when once we begin to long for wealth. For wealth and money are things that appeal to the imagination, which is insatiable in its wishes. Real goods, such as those our bodies need, have not this quality: there is a narrow limit to the amount of food our stomachs will hold, and when that is reached we do not wish for more. Our Lord fed the five thousand in the desert with fish and bread, and all of them had their fill. But if He had given them, instead, $20,000 savings bonds, no single person would have said, "One is enough for me."

Credit-wealth, stocks, bonds, bank-balances, have no set limit at which we say, "No more." They have in them a caricature infinity, which allows men to use them as false religions, as substitutes for the true Infinity of God. Like money, love and power can become *ersatz* religions: those who pursue these things as ends will never find satisfaction. Such men are all in pursuit of God, but they do not know His name or where to look for Him.

Since every increase in quantity among the things we love brings a decrease in the quality of love, there are two ways by which we may hope to keep love pure. One is to give away in proportion as we receive; this habit reminds us that we are merely trustees of God's riches, not their rightful owners. Yet, few people risk doing this: they are afraid to touch their capital, and every cent they add to it becomes part of the sacred pile which must not be disturbed. They become identified with what they love; if it is wealth, they cannot bear to part with any portion of its accumulated burden.

The second way of preserving ourselves from an unseemly greed is the heroic way—the way of complete detachment from wealth, as practiced by St. Francis of Assisi and all those who take the vows of poverty. There is a paradox in such a renunciation, for the man who has given up even the hope of "security" is the richest man in the world; he is the most secure of all of us, for he wants nothing—and that is a boast that no millionaire can make. Everyone's power of renunciation is greater than anyone's power to possess; no man can own the earth, but any man can disown it.

The misers may fill their wallets, but never their hearts, for they cannot obtain all the wealth they are able to imagine and desire. But the poor in heart are rich in happiness. God gave us love enough to spend in getting back to Him so that we could find Infinity there; he did not give us love enough to hoard.

[33]

The Mystery of Love

THERE COMES a moment in even the noblest of human loves when the mystery has gone. One has now grown "used to" the best, and has come to take it for granted, as jewelers may casually handle the most precious stones without troubling to admire them. What we completely possess, we can no longer desire. What we have already attained, we cannot hope for. Yet hope and desire and, above all, mystery, are needed to keep our interest in life alive.

When wonder has vanished from our days, then they become banal. Our minds were made to function at the stretch and to reach out, forever, toward the solution of some lofty problem that forever eludes us. It is possible that the popularity of mystery novels in our day is occasioned by the fact that so many people have ceased to dwell on the mysteries of faith and are looking, in any cheap substitute that comes to hand, for something to replace what they have lost. Readers of mystery stories spend all their wonder on the method by which someone was killed; they do not, as the contemporaries of Dante and of Michelangelo would have done, wonder about the eternal fate of those who die.

Man cannot be happy if he is satiated; our zest comes from the fact that there are doors not yet opened, veils not yet lifted, notes that have not been struck. If a "love" is only physical, marriage will bring the romance to an end: the chase is ended, and the mystery is solved. Whenever any person is thus taken for granted, there is a loss of the sensitivity and delicacy which are the essential condition of friendship, joy, and love in human relations. Marriage is no exception; one of its most tragic outcomes is mere possession without desire.

There is no love left when one hits bottom, or imagines that he has; the personality we have exhausted of its mystery is a bore. There must be always something unrevealed, some mystery we have not probed, some passion that we cannot glut . . . and this is true even in the arts. We do not want to hear a singer constantly reiterate her highest note, or to have an orator tear a passion to tatters.

In a true marriage there is an ever deepening mystery and, therefore, an ever enchanting romance. At least four of the mysteries of marriage can be tabulated. First comes the mystery of the other partner's physical being, the mystery of sex. When that mystery has been solved, and the first baby is born, a new mystery begins: the husband sees in his wife a thing he never saw before—the beautiful mystery of motherhood. She sees in him the sweet mystery of fatherhood. As other children come to revive their strength and beauty, the husband never seems older to his wife than on the day they met, and the wife appears to him as freshly beautiful as when they first became engaged.

When the children reach the age of reason, a third mystery unfolds: that of mother-craft and father-craft—the disciplining of young minds and hearts in the ways of God. As the children grow to maturity, this mystery continues to deepen; each child's personality is something for the parents to explore and then to form closer to the likeness of the God of love.

The fourth mystery of the happily married involves their social living, the contribution that they jointly make to the well-being of the world. Here lies the root of democracy, for in the family the individual is not valued for what he is worth, nor for what he can do, but for what he is. His status, his position in the home, is granted him by virtue of merely being alive. If a child is dumb or blind, if a son has been maimed at the war, he is still loved for himself and for his intrinsic worth as a child of God. No parent mitigates his love because of changes in a child's earning power or worldly wisdom, or troubles about the class to which his offspring may belong. This reverence for personality for its own sake in the family is the social principle on which the wider life of the community depends, and is a potent reminder of the most important of all political principles: the state exists for the person, and not the person for the state.

[34]

True Love

THERE ARE two kinds of love: love for its own pleasure, and love for the sake of another. The first is carnal love; the second is spiritual. Carnal love knows the other person only in a biological moment. Spiritual love knows the other person at all moments. In erotic love, the burdens of the other are regarded as impairing one's own happiness; in spiritual love, the burdens of others are opportunities for service.

Somewhere along the line, the modern world has been duped and fooled into giving the name of love to some vague obsession which parades itself in every billboard advertisement, reigns in the film industry, puzzles dramatists who must solve triangles short of suicide, makes novels best-sellers, perfumes so exotic as to be unfit for a tyro's concupiscence, and humor more spicy. Love has become so vulgarized, so carnalized, that those who really love are almost afraid to use the word. It is used now almost exclusively to describe one of the opposite sex, rather than a person; it is made to revolve around glands, rather than a will, and is centered in biology instead of personality. Even when it disguises itself as infatuation for another, it is nothing else than a desire to intensify its own self-centeredness.

Purely human love is the embryo of the Love of the Divine. One finds some suggestions of this in Plato, who argues that the purpose

of love is to make the first step toward religion. He pictures love for
beautiful persons being transformed into love for beautiful souls,
then into a love of justice, goodness and, finally, God who is their
source. Erotic love is, therefore, a bridge which one crosses, not a
buttress where one sits and rests; it is not an airport but an airplane;
it is always going somewhere else, upward and onward. All carnal
love presupposes incompleteness, deficiency, yearning for completion, and an attraction for enrichment, for all love is a flight for
immortality. There is a suggestion of Divine Love in every form of
erotic love, as the lake reflects the moon. The only reason there is
love for creatures in human hearts is that it may lead to the love of
the Creator. As food is for the body, as body is for the soul, as the
material is for the spiritual, so the flesh is for the eternal. That is
why in the language of human love there can often be detected the
language of Divinity, such as "worship," "angel," "adore."

The Savior did not crush and then extinguish the flames that
burned in Magdalene's heart, but transfigured them to a new object
of affection. The Divine commendation that was given to the
woman who poured out the ointment on the feet of her Savior
reminded her that love which once sought its own pleasure can be
transmuted into a love that will die for the beloved. For that reason
He referred to His burial at the very moment her thoughts were
closest to life.

Because it is in the Divine Plan to use the love of the flesh as a
stepping stone to the love of the Divine, it always happens in a well-
regulated, moral heart that as time goes on, the erotic love diminishes, and the religious love increases. That is why in true marriages the love of God increases through the years, not in the sense
that husband and wife love one another less, but that they love God
more. Love passes from an affection for outer appearances to those
inner depths of personality which embody the Divine Spirit.

There are few things more beautiful in life than to see that deep
passion of man for woman which begot children as the mutual incarnation of their love, transfigured into that deeper "passionless
passion and wild tranquillity" which is God.

[35]

Love Is Not Automatic

LOVE IS NOT automatic. One does not find it like a glittering jewel, which from that point on would shed its luster without any effort of our own. Rather, it is like a seed that is planted, which grows with constant and daily care, renews itself amidst storms and winds, rejoices in its blossoms, thrills to its fruits, dies to itself in the winter of its discontent, and arises again to the freshness of a higher life in the Easter of its glory. Love must undergo a continuous transformation, under penalty of sinking otherwise into dullness and monotony. Without its alternative beats of the cross and the empty tomb, it has only the continuing cold identity of the stone.

Love must have crises or it dies. It thrives on what seems, for a moment, like its death. These transformations of crises happen in the birth of a child, and particularly the first, when a husband is made a father and a wife a mother; they also happen in sickness, sorrow, quarrels, and mutual pardons, and even follow the death of one of the partners. Love is not like a plain, but like a succession of valleys and mountains, for even the mountains have their height purchased by the depths of the valleys. Love, even in the spiritual order, is not one constant ascent in joy to God; instead, one passes first through brambles and thorns to a clearing where such trials are left behind. Temptations to sin against love never cease, though their character varies with the years. In all love, human and divine, there is nothing lost, but something is always being re-created, something lost being found, like the father with his prodigal son. There would never have been an Acension without a Crucifixion, and there never will be a glorification of human love without its crisis.

When Peter, on the Mount of the Transfiguration, saw Our Lord's face shine like the sun and His garments white as snow, he wanted to make that glory captive and permanent. But the Savior spoke of death and reminded Peter that such transcendent glory would come only after He had passed through the winepress of Gethsemane and the darkness of Golgotha. No love ever mounts to a higher level without death to a lower one.

If love by its nature were to be void of crises, then there should have been none in the woman whom Our Lord chose as His Mother. But actually we find two great moments of love: the one reaching from Bethlehem to Cana; the other from Cana to Calvary. In the first she appears only as His Mother; in the second, she appears as the Mother of all whom He would redeem. In the first she is the Mother of Jesus, for she calls Him "My Son." In the second, she appears as the Mother of men as He addresses humanity, saying, "Behold thy Mother." Cana was the turning point, for there she was given the choice of keeping Him solely for herself or of delivering Him to His public life and ultimate death, by working His first miracle.

In human love, too, there comes a moment when something seems to be lost, but actually if one survives that "death" one rises to new heights of joy. Many married people do not live together long enough today to know they love one another. They mistake a crisis for the end of love, when it is actually only the beginning of a deeper and wider love. They are like the marble which, on seeing the chisel, refuses to sustain the blow by which a new image might be chiseled and revealed in it. Divorce is cowardice and surrender. It is love's refusal to submit to the law of love; it is the seed refusing to die to itself in the earth so that it might bring forth new life; it is the violin protesting against the tightening of its strings, that it may produce a sweeter melody.

Our modern life seems geared to a discontinuity. Life is snuffed out in birth control; love dies in the refusal of sacrifice. But in the meantime there will always be the remnant of true lovers, who will see that as gold is purified by fire, so love is enriched by sacrifice.

[36]

Love and Being in Love

THE ONE WORD which, if blotted out of our vocabulary, would destroy advertising and our justification for anything immoral is the word "love." But, like "freedom," its meaning is not fixed. "Freedom" can mean, for example, "freedom from," which would deny all law, discipline, and restraint, and "freedom for," which is the goal or purpose that is unattainable if there be undue restraint. In like manner, "love" can mean either one of two things. Love can mean either freedom of concupiscence or freedom of benevolence. Freedom of concupiscence is the right to pursue anything that gives one pleasure or profit or enhances the ego. "I gotta do my thing" is one of the lowest forms of freedom of concupiscence. Its more legitimate expression would be the right to knowledge which perfects the mind, the right to food which is necessary for health, and the right to property which is the economic guarantee of human liberty.

The other kind of love is love of benevolence, which is not directed to self but to others. For example, serving the neighbor in need . . . doing without some luxury to supply a necessity of a neighbor . . . disciplining the ego to prove a deep concern for a friend. It almost always involves sacrifice or the surrender of the selfish for the sake of compassion and charity.

These two loves are like the extremes of a rainbow with its infrared at one end and the ultraviolet at the other. They are rarely distinguished in any discussion of love. A young woman who justifies her living with a boyfriend by saying, "I love him," is miles apart from the young woman who goes to a missionary land to serve lepers. Unfortunately, we have only one word in English for love—the Greeks had three. Hence, its indiscriminate application to justify adultery on the one hand, and to motivate the self-denial of a young woman who believes in chastity. Unfortunately, lust and pornography today monopolize the sacred word which is the definition of the all-Holy God.

The basic reason why there is so much anxiety, fear, depression, and neurosis in mortals is because of this identification of love with lust. As C. S. Lewis put it, "We use an unfortunate idiom when we say of a lustful man prowling the streets that he 'wants a woman.' Strictly speaking, a woman is just what he does not want. He wants a pleasure for which a woman happens to be the necessary piece of apparatus."

Every pimp that walks the streets of New York soliciting young girls for immoral purposes convinces the stupid young things that he "loves" them. He does not love them; he hates them. What he loves is the money he makes on her ruined life. The selfish ego is projected into the other person and what is loved is not the body and soul of that person, but the pleasure the body gives. That is why even marriages last only two years or more until the well runs dry or the novelty disappears. Sex is transferable; love is not.

There is no such thing as a substitute for a father or mother or sister. Sex has a role in life as important as eating: one sustains social life and deepens the love of the unity which is the basis of society—namely, the family; the other supports physical life. To devour food and then tickle the throat to disgorge that food in order to go to the table again is a perversion of a natural appetite. The disgorging of human life to have sex without love is equally unnatural.

True love is also distinct from "being in love." "Being in love" is an emotion, the battery that starts the engine, the frosting on the cake that urges the beholder to eat the cake. Love, on the contrary, is not in the glands nor in the feelings, but in a decision; it is not a thrill but an act of will, not a desire to have but to be had, not to own but to be owned, not to possess but to be possessed. "Being in love" is the spark that moves a person to make a promise. Love is the keeping of the promise: for better or worse until death does the parting. It is much better to learn how to walk than to return to the infantile thrill of taking the first shaky steps.

[37]

A Nobler Love

CHARACTER BUILDING should not be based solely on the eradiction of evil, for it should stress even more the cultivation of virtue. Mere asceticism without love of God is pride; it is possible to concentrate so hard on humiliating ourselves that we become proud of our humility, and to concentrate so intently on eradicating evil as to make our purity nothing but a condemnation of others. The difference in the two techniques—pulling up the weed or planting good seed—is illustrated in the ancient story of the Greeks: Ulysses, returning from the siege of Troy, wished to hear the Sirens who sang in the sea, tempting many a sailor to his doom. Ulysses put wax in the ears of his sailors and strapped himself to the mast of the ship—so that even if he wished to answer the appeal of the Sirens, he would be saved from doing so. Some years later, Orpheus, the divine musician, passed through the same sea; but he refused to plug up his sailors' ears or to bind himself to a mast. Instead, he played his harp so beautifully that the song of the Sirens was drowned out.

A positive and not a negative goodness is the Christian ideal. A character is great, not by the ferocity of its hatred or evil, but by the intensity of its love of God. Asceticism and mortification are not the ends of a Christian life; they are only the means. The end is charity. Penance merely makes an aperture in our ego into which the Light of God can pour. As we deflate ourselves, God enters. As we empty ourselves, God fills us. And it is God's arrival that is the important thing.

When a Christian character is motivated by love alone, it finds much more goodness in the world than before. As the impure find the world impure, so those who love God find everyone lovable, as being either actual or potential children of God. This transformation of outlook takes place not only because love moves in an environment of love, but principally because, in the face of the love diffused by the saint, love is created in others. As jealousy in A begets jealousy in B, so generosity in A begets generosity in B. Love begets love; if we are kind, we get kindness back. The lover gets much more out of the world than the man who is cool or indifferent; he has not only the happiness of receiving, but the happiness of giving as well. Even when his love is not reciprocated by the wicked, the barbed word or the insult never hurts him.

Love makes us loathe the faults that hold us back from love. But we are not disheartened over them—for our failings are never insurmountable, once they are discovered and recognized as such. It is excusing them or labeling them falsely—calling egotism an "inferiority complex" or self-indulgence "gracious living"—which prevents spiritual progress. Most important of the rules for attacking evil in ourselves is to avoid direct in favor of indirect assaults. Evil is not driven out; it is crowded out. Drunkenness and alcoholism are not mastered by saying, "I will not drink," but through the expulsive power of some contrary good. When the soul begins to love God, it no longer has such morbid fears that they must be drowned in drink. The joys of the spirit also crowd out the pleasures of the flesh; we must have happiness, but the man who has found it on the high road of the spirit will no longer need to pursue it on the low road of carnality. If I raise my fist against a man, he will throw up his arms in self-defense; and so it is with evil under a direct attack.

"But I tell you that you should not offer resistance to injury." The little, illicit loves of the egotist are driven out by the larger loves of things beyond the self. Basically, there is no cure for selfishness until one learns to love others more than the ego; there is no cure for sex until the soul is loved more than the body; no relief from avarice until the treasures which rust does not consume are loved more than those which thieves can break through and steal. Sustaining all these efforts to develop character, there is a memory of the Divine plea: "Come to Me, all you that labor and are burdened; I will give you rest." Not until a nobler, finer love is found can a man master his vices or overcome his mediocrity. In a complete conversion, souls which were formerly addicted to vice, like Augustine, no longer feel any desire for their old sins, but rather a disgust. As the eye blinks at dust, so the soul now blinks at evil. Sin is not fought; it is, rather, no longer wanted. Love casts out sin as well as fear; the great tragedy of life is that so many persons have no one to love. As a man in love with a noble woman will give up all that displeases her, so a soul in love with God gives up all that might wound that Love.

[38]

The Greeks Had Three Words for Love

IN ENGLISH there is only one word for love; if there are synonyms they do not have very definite shades of meaning. For example, "I love Paris in the springtime," "I love crepes suzette," "I love Mary" all use "love" indifferently. Rightly has it been said that the Greeks had a word for it—in fact, they had three.

The first word for love was *eros*, which is generally what is meant by sexual love; it is something biological, glandular, instinctive, emotional. It does not always distinguish between the pleasure and the person. Too often the wine can be drunk and the glass forgotten. The illusion is created that there is deep affection for the other person, but what really happens is that the ego is projected into the other person. What is actually loved is the pleasure which the other person gives. The frosting on the cake is eaten but the cake is ignored.

This erotic love sometimes turns to hate. This could never be if the other person were really loved, because love would exist whether the other person reciprocated love or not. When the ego feels that it no longer is receiving the pleasure it expected, there develops a contempt on the grounds that one has been "cheated." This is a very immature kind of love and that is why its sponsor, Cupid, is generally pictured as a child that has never quite grown up. When one reads of divorces after a few years of married life, one can be sure that it was an erotic love which was at its basis. As a Russian writer has so well put it, "If unreciprocated love is hard on the heart, sometimes reciprocated love can be worse."

Another Greek word for love is *philia*. This is the kind of love which exists both in friendship and in marriage. In erotic love, the other person is replaceable; in philia, the other person is irreplaceable. No one can take the place of an intimate friend, of a devoted wife or a consecrated mother. Philia is based on some kind of community of feeling, interest, or service; the intellect rather than the glands dominates the affections. The relationship existing is that of I–Thou rather than I–it; affection is based on the responsibility of the "I" for the "Thou." This was the kind of love that Damon had for Pythias, that made Jacob serve seven years to win the heart of Rachel, that a wife has for a husband such as is expressed in the poem of Elizabeth Barrett Browning, the last lines of which read:

I love thee with the breath, smiles, tears of all my life!
And, if God choose, I shall but love thee better after death.

The third word for love was not much used in classical Greek; it was a love so noble and divine that Christianity alone made it popular—that word is *agape*. It was used only ten times by Homer; it is found only three times in Euripides; later on, it was used a bit in the popular Greek which was spoken throughout the world after Alexander conquered it. The Greeks did not need such a word because Plato held that there could be no real love between God and man, inasmuch as the gods, being perfect, desired nothing; therefore, they had no love for man. Aristotle argued in the same way. He said that there was too great a disproportion between man and God to express the existence of any love between the two.

When God sent His only Son to this world to save it, and when His Divine Son offered His life on Calvary to redeem it, then was born a love between God and man which the Greeks could not and did not understand. That kind of love was best expressed by agape. In contrast to it, the word "eros" is nowhere found in the New Testament; the word "philia" in all its forms is found forty-five times, but the word "agape" is found three hundred and twenty times. Once this agape began to exist, then it flowed down to illumine even the eros. Eros became the sensible expression of the Divine Love; fraternal and friendly love was also sanctified by the agape, inasmuch as we were to regard everyone else as better than ourselves. The only true lovers of friends are those whose love is explained by the agape of Him Who so loved the world, He sent His only begotten Son to redeem it.

VI
Sex

The Infinite and Sex

OF ALL THE things man knows, the thing he knows least about is himself. He is forever trying to solve the riddle of himself, to prove the meaning of his nature. Some modern writers attempt to find a shortcut solution by reducing man to a single one of his many instincts: sex. Appalled at the difficulty of understanding the whole man, they blot out of consciousness all of him except one tiny area and, by studying that, pretend that they have charted man. This "answer" gains popularity with those who have lost an understanding of the true goal of life: not knowing their proper end, they cling to the intensity of sensual experiences and use them as a drug by which they may escape from worry over the ultimate meaning of their lives.

Sex is a small part of men, but it always affords a bridge to the infinite, the supernatural: if it is not divinized by selfless love, it becomes diabolically perverse. Man cannot be a "mere animal," as the animals are. To the young, whose sexual desires are strongest, infinity is the normal climate of the mind. Young men live in dreams and hopes of the future, and all their desires are infinite in their scope, so that false mysticism is very close to every youthful urge: whatever the young man feels is so intensely felt that he can set no bounds to it. "Calf love" is no exception to the rule.

Even among those who deny God, sex remains one matter which can never be taken for granted. Their very shame, or denial of shame, implies that this instinct is one which involves the spirit, as other instincts do not. No one ever blushes over his desire to eat, even when his hunger is intense—yet all men blush if they are accused of being secretly in love. They intuitively feel that there is something sacred and secretive about this passion, so that it should not be bruited about too carelessly: it involves secrets only Heaven should know. That is why marriage, even among savages, has always been surrounded by religious rites.

The spirit cannot be banned from sex. The human wish for fidelity and love that lasts, for loyalty and for true devotion, does not spring from the flesh but from the spirit of man. Sex thus acts as a link between the worlds of spirit and of matter. Shame enters in to protect the spiritual aspect from being detected by the coarse hands of the world. And it is through the spirit that men are allies of infinity.

Love, which properly is both the origin and goal of sex, is infinite in another way: it is meant to be outgoing, radiating from the small center of self to limitless distances. Love is centrifugal; it flees the ego and seeks its object in God and all His children who come our way. Love is something we can never hoard, something that must be spent to be possessed. In the family this is splendidly exemplified, for the love which first exists between husband and wife alone grows greater as it is further expended by both upon their children and one another.

Once given, love should never be taken back, according to God's scheme. It is meant to push out from us, farther and farther into His infinite, until we love all things because we see them as His Own. But if sex is separated from love and made mere means of self-gratification, the process is unhealthily reversed. The other person is now seen as a mere means to pleasure, not as a person commanding love. The "affair" becomes a mere exchange of egotistical delights. And, since love was never meant to be recalled, to summon it back upon the self in such a way turns it to poison, makes it a burden on the heart, transforms its energy to hate. The centripetal movement of love—from the neighbor and God toward the ego—means frustration, hate, and worry. God can come to us through anyone we love, so long as our love for him is outgoing, is concerned with his best interests and not our own. But sexual activity that is egotistic destroys our relationship to God and neighbor. The infinite is always entered through the gate of self-forgetfulness by means of love; to turn back toward self again is to revert to the discontentment that accompanies all efforts to find happiness by self-indulgence.

Sex is the most "psychosomatic" of human functions: there is nothing else in which body and soul, finite and infinite, flesh and spirit are so closely intertwined. When sex is allowed to link the two, peace and joy result; when the flesh and spirit are divorced, and sex is sought alone, boredom and ennui result. It is life's long task to keep the relationship of soul and body in its proper order. A sex philosophy which, ignoring this necessity, encourages one to love the *body* of another, dooms love; for it is only if the object of our love is *body-plus-soul* that love can last. It is the Infinite beyond them both which enables a man and a woman to remain in love. If they attempt to leave the spirit out—to limit their love affair to a mere Thou and I—there is no love. For either the Thou becomes absorbed in the I (which is power and seduction) or the I is surrendered to the Thou (which is idolatry). Two full and loving personalities can love only if they invite the blessing of the Infinite, of God.

[40]

Liberation of Sex

IT IS AMUSING to read letters to the press and releases from high-powered advertising agencies that at last sex has been liberated. No longer, it is said, is sex kept in dark closets, but brought before the public for its gaze and study. From the frequent use of such words as "liberation" and "freedom," one would think that sex was like Livingstone in Africa who had just been found by the free world.

If sex has been so shackled, why has there been such an increase in the world's population? Why is marriage still a day of feasting and why do women weep with joy at the sight of a beautiful bride? Discussion of sex has no more been in bondage than has discussion of appendicitis. To say that is to forget the enormous amount of literature that has been piled out in the classical language of Latin alone on the subject *De Sexto*. Those who talk about "liberation" of sex forget a very important distinction between things which a person must do (a) for himself alone, (b) with one other person uniquely, and (c) with a crowd.

There is a natural and right tendency in human nature not to speak of those things which a person does absolutely alone—for example, blowing his nose. It is a purely individual, not a social act. In fact a child begins to be a boy when he resents his mother putting a handkerchief to his nose and saying, "Blow hard." The moment he resents making social what is so individual, he has become a man. There are no treatises on "belching" or reports on "picking one's teeth at table" or "stomach growling" and other related subjects, because these purely individual actions are not the subjects of general conversation. Would one help the cause of "liberation" if he wrote a treatise on the "Liberation of Burping"? It has not yet been discussed publicly, hence should one deduce that it has been enslaved up to this point and that it needs some Great Gaseous Emancipator?

In addition to certain things which every person must do for himself, there is also something which he does uniquely with one other person. Those things he does with many other persons, such as eating or drinking or playing games, are social by nature. But making love is not public by nature; it is personal, unique, and incommunicable. No one is scandalized by seeing the French eat their meals at tables on sidewalks in Paris, but everyone is shocked when one sees a husband and wife embracing each other in public. There is nothing ethically wrong about it. What disturbs one who sees it is not the action, but the making of that which is personal *profane* or vulgar or common. By their very nature such actions are incommunicable except to another person who shares the secret. To speak of that couple as "liberating marriage" is to completely miss the distinction between sex in pigs and love in humans.

This innate regard for the sacredness of love explains timidity in a woman which makes her shrink from a too precocious revelation and surrender of the secret of her creative power. If she does like to talk about it publicly, she has lost the mystery of life. It also explains chivalry in man toward woman, not because he believes her to be physically weaker, but because of the awe he feels in the presence of the mystery.

People are not prudes because they keep the uniqueness of the secret to themselves; monkeys are not "liberated" because they do not keep the secret. Monkeys are not persons and therefore they lack the communication not of a glandular reflex, but of the secret of a heart. The stud farm is not the same as the hearth and home.

It is very likely that people will one day say that the flag has no mystery or meaning in our American life, nor is it a symbol of a piety or sacred loyalty. Then someone will write an article on the "Liberation of the American Flag" and plead that it should not only be flown above our heads but trampled beneath our feet; otherwise it is enslaved to one attitude. To call that day "liberation" will be to take a worm's-eye view of America; the same tragedy could happen to love if one took a worm's-eye view of it.

[41]

Sexual Revolution (I)

"SEXUAL REVOLUTION"—such is the description of the new society in which youth boasts that it will no longer be troubled by "taboos, myths and morals," and the thousand and one fences which keep them from poaching on others' property. We may have, by the same logic, other kinds of revolution—e.g., a "traffic revolution" when everyone runs through red lights, or a "murder revolution" in which the muggings and murders of today will become so general that we can invoke the same law: "Everybody's doing it." With the corruption and dishonesty in business and in politics, our "dishonesty revolution" cannot be far around the corner.

True, the Victorians said too little about sex, but are not we saying too much? It was said that if we did away with prudery, we would banish all problems about sexuality. But doing so has increased our problems, and to such an extent that sex has become "intellectualized." Now we wallow in it, as it becomes a flat surface. As Robert Fitch wrote, it is "like a cock crowing on a dunghill, not to salute the dawn but to glorify in an apotheosis of carnality, the filth on which he stands."

It is affirmed that we are no worse than in other days of erotic excesses. This is a half truth. People indeed were bad, even in the days of great faith; in the Middle Ages, the stones burst forth into Gothic cathedrals. But there was this difference: in those days, they knew they were immoral. They admitted both the law and the fact that they broke it. Today, we not only break the law, but we deny the law. In those days when men had a cancer, they called it a cancer; today we call it health. Every criminal knew he was a criminal. Louis XIV, Richelieu, and others did not claim that their actions were moral. That was one of the reasons why civilization stood, while some individuals fell. The few in former times who broke the moral laws were considered off the reservation; today those who break the moral law are considered on the reservation, and those who keep it are considered off.

It is wrong to call it a revolution in morals; it is rather a revolution in culture. The upheaval in morals is merely the tip of the iceberg; the four fifths hidden beneath the surface of life represents culture. Life today is full of frustrations. The soul has no home. The flesh gives an immediacy of release to this emptiness, and makes us forget the loss of the meaning of life, while the promiscuity acts as a kind of opiate to the emptiness resulting from excesses.

It is not a sexual revolution as such. There have been many of those in history in the past, such as at the close of the Middle Ages. The reasons why it is not a sexual or moral revolution are the following:

First, sex today is intellectualized and thought about, dreamed about, advertised. It has moved out of the glands into the brain; it has lost its natural expression and turned into a kind of mania or obsession. Its devotees are like those who say of television, "I hate it," but go on looking at it.

The perverse forms which the so-called sexual revolution has taken proves that it is not natural, but rather abnormal. The glorification of homosexuality, the turning of love into dread drudg-

ery of constant searching and trysting, the murders which are associated with it in plays and novels, is almost like talking about food in terms of garbage, and health in terms of leprosy.

Furthermore, girls in college relate it often to status—hence the contempt and the ridicule of other girls because they have not trafficked away their virtue. Boys, too, pride themselves on the number they have ruined. Sex has thus become snobbery. It is almost like stealing fruit from another's garden not to eat, but to boast at a robbers' convention of how many rotten apples are in your barrel.

The justification that is given for immorality is often psychological—namely, to escape repression which is harmful. Sex is sought as a kind of prophylactic: your mind has 32 percent less cavities. In other words, sex is wanted for nonsexual reasons. It would be very much like a man entering religion for the sake of the money he could make out of it. As love of God and neighbor, in this instance, would not be the primary reason, so sex is not the primary reason for this so-called moral revolution. It is the cultural emptiness, banality, frustration, and meaninglessness of life in which we live.

[42]

Sexual Revolution (II)

IN THE LAST article, we brought out the fact that the so-called "Sexual Revolution" is really a cultural revolution and an escape from the frustrations and emptiness and meaninglessness of life. Not knowing why one is here or where one is going, some seek to escape from the so-called culture of our time with its atomic bomb, its mass civilization, its hangovers, psychoses, and neuroses, through something primal, basic, elemental, and primitive. It is a curious twist of human nature that it should fill up the emptiness of the soul with the husks of flesh. Sex is not wanted primarily; something else is wanted, and sex is the substitute for that other thing. It is not the other person who is wanted, but some fleeting seconds of escape, thanks to the other person.

This relation between frustration and sex madness was manifested in economic depressions and political revolutions. It is a way out—a search for security. As Georgina H. Seward put it, "People in our competitive individualized society have an exorbitant need of affection and reassurance. It is this need for human response, rather than genuine sexual desire which leads them into the tense, clutching types of relationship so prevalent among us. Sexual possession of another somehow assures an individual and bulwarks his ego defenses, taking the place of a partnership based on mutual love."

Why is sex so difficult to talk about, and why does not sex education completely solve the problem? The argument for giving youngsters sex education is that it will keep them from harm. It is pleaded: If you knew the effects of typhoid fever and you saw a quarantine sign on a house, would you not stay away from that house? Well, youngsters will avoid dangers and pitfalls of sex once they are told about them.

The analogy is not sound. First of all, no one has a typhoid attraction, but everyone has sex attraction. No one is inclined to break down the door and invade the privacy of such a diseased person; but the same cannot be said of the erotic appetite.

Furthermore, sex is not digestion or any other body function. It rightly is called a mystery. And what is a mystery? A mystery is something which has two sides: one that is known and another that is unknown. One is visible and the other invisible, one physiological, the other spiritual. The physical, visible side of the mystery is that every person is either male or female. The spiritual, invisible side is that this difference in sexes also implies love.

If the biological fact of eating and the biological fact of mating are the same, why is it that we do not mind seeing people eat in public, but we shrink from seeing lovemaking in public? It is because lovemaking is something reserved by one person for another, and involves secret communication. To expose the personal to the public, the secret to the "vulgus" or crowd is to render it "vulgar."

A boy becomes a man the day he resents his mother, in the presence of other people, putting a handkerchief to his nose and saying, "blow." He has come to a personal stage where he knows that there are certain things every man must do for himself, such as blowing his own nose and making his own love. To take that which is reserved for the sanctuary of human life and to placard it at the crossroads of the world is to profane the sacred.

Herein lies the essence of the obscene: the divorce of sex and love, the physiological from the spiritual, the biological from the mysterious, the common from the personal. Because of this double element, parents have difficulty in communicating a true knowledge of sex to their children; this difficulty is inherent in all sex education. What is communicated is only the scientific, the physical, the corporal. But what cannot be communicated to children is how this common fact is hidden in love, and how it is used to express love in those deeper moments when words fail; sex is then a breath in the atmosphere of an abiding love and a lifelong bond in which soul communicates with soul as well as body with body. Plato, speaking of knowledge, compared it to a man in a cave. What he saw were the shadows of figures passing in the daylight, leaving their shadows on the wall. In sex, the shadow or the biological is often seen, but the spiritual escapes.

[43]

Sexual Revolution (III)

In the last article we dealt with the difference between the physiological and spiritual sides of sex. When only the physiological is considered, it is only natural for the young to think that sex is an animal function, for does not exactly the same act prevail in the animal kingdom? Since pigs and roosters and goats have sex, and we have sex, are we not to do what comes naturally? Why introduce morals? What difference is there between a pigsty and a bedroom of a husband and wife?

The first difference is that the animal mates when in season; man, however, has not just biological urges. He always has reason and will. Endowed with human freedom, he lives not in a barnyard but in a universe where there is a respect for the dignity of other persons and where love is bound up with liberty. It is the tremendous power of the word "no" which gives so much thrill to the word "yes." The more instinct rules, the greater the promiscuity and the less relation there is with a person. One of the reasons boys look down on "pickups" is because there is wanting that deliberate choice which is the mark of the person. Girls resent having attentions forced upon them, because they have been deprived of the power of choice which is essential to love. Even prostitutes develop a completely detached attitude from those whom they serve because they know that they are only in an animal relationship without any love. They sometimes come to justify their lives saying that they just fulfill a biological function, and hence they are not doing wrong to any person because there is no love involved.

Animals fulfill functions and when persons do the same, they are like batteries that can be substituted one for another, or face tissues which can be thrown away when used. One even finds this absence of the respect for persons in professions: some doctors have no personal interest in patients—they love only the disease; some social workers and even clergymen are interested not in the afflicted person, but in "the case."

Why is it that girls who were so close in college are so far apart when they come back to an alumni meeting? Each one brings out the picture of her babies and tells about her home. No one else is interested, except through politeness. While in college, the relationship between them was personal; now the relation between them is functional. It is what they are doing, not what they are. That is why alumni meetings can become so boring—the common bond of sharing trials and tests is gone; there is nothing left to talk about to each other except the role they play apart from one another.

A further proof that the relationship is not zoological is the storm that a brother will put up if any boy abused his sister, "Hey, lay off, she's my sister." But is not the animal with whom he has had biological relations someone else's sister? What a storm of protest would go up from a family of children if the mother were attacked on the street! If we are animals, why protest? If we protest, then it must be that somewhere inside of each of us is an image of God; we are persons, each with the right of self-determination, so much our own that no one else in all the world is like to us.

Another reason why human sexual relations are not animal and that we are not justified in doing what comes naturally is our sense of shame. How many a young man after having plucked an unripe rose and trampled it underfoot will say, "I forgot myself." Forgot what? To be an animal? Or did he forget to be a person? What was automatic and physiological, as in seduction and rape, is not human at all. Animals do not have this remorse, nor does it exist in marriage because in marriage the atmosphere of love is kept up for a lifelong relationship. Outside of it, one wanted to be lost in the other person, but one finds himself thrown back on self, more lonely than before. No dog ever had a psychosis from being a sex maniac, nor a rooster a psychosis from running after chickens. Why not? Because there is no spirit in them as there is in man; because being made for the physical alone, the physical is natural. It takes eternity and the destiny for eternity to make a man despair. Because he has wings, man becomes frustrated when he wallows.

VII
Persons and
Neighbors

Our Neighbors in Distress

IN THE parable of the Good Samaritan it is said that a priest and a Levite passed by the wounded man and help was given him by one of another race—namely, the Samaritan. We do not know whatever happened to the priest and the Levite, but it is very likely that they went into Jerusalem and reported the condition of the dying man to a social service agency. The point of the parable is that some neighbors have to be helped in their emergency at the cost of our convenience. The neighbor is not the one who lives next door, nor the one with whom we have a nodding acquaintance. What makes a man a neighbor is love in the heart. When this is wanting it avails nothing that a man lives in the same block, or belongs to the same club, for none of these external bonds can supply the place of love.

No doubt those who saw the Samaritan aid the wounded traveler would have said that he was a neighbor or an old friend, but the truth of the matter is that the Samaritan did not know the wounded man at all; it was his genuine compassion and affection that made the Samaritan his brother and his neighbor and a friend.

The story of the Good Samaritan was told in answer to the question of a lawyer, "Who is my neighbor?" The answer of the parable is. "Every man in distress is your neighbor." Sometimes that neighbor is the one who is least capable of making known his condition. Not long ago one of the nationally known picture magazines had a photograph of a man prostrate on subway stairs. For thirty minutes many people passed him by without ever a helping hand. The editorial comment was about the coldness of the modern man in the face of distress. What was forgotten was that the photographer of the picture magazine did nothing for thirty minutes for the afflicted individual except to snap pictures and make his own living. The unfortunate traveler on the road between Jericho and Jerusalem could make no importunate supplications for relief, could not even ask for help. The need is often greatest where the least is asked. How many forms of misery are there lying within our knowledge as we journey through the bloodstained road of life. We pass them by because they do not bar our progress or because it is possible for us to put them out of our mind and live as if they were not in it.

The best way to help a man is by identifying ourselves with his affliction, getting into him and feeling his pains as our own. It is not enough merely to have an intellectual understanding of another man's difficulty; we need to go a little farther to feel it as our own burden, as the Samaritan put the wounded man upon a beast of burden and took him to an inn. On the other hand, if we have a trial and want to get mastery over it, the best person to go to is the one who has gained a victory over the same temptation. If one has marital difficulties and is inclined to leave the spouse, the worst person to go to is a psychiatrist who is already divorced and remarried. The best man to convert a drunkard is a converted drunkard. Power to appreciate temptation is the fine condition of being able to help others out of temptation. The first step God took toward making us become like Him was to become as far as He could like us.

The powerful are always under obligation to the weak. Advantage of any kind is not a personal possession but a trust. St. Paul said, "I am a debtor both to the Greeks and the barbarians; both to the wise and unwise." He owed the Greeks nothing—they had persecuted him; the barbarians he had never seen, but Paul was conscious that God had conferred upon him great gifts and he was bound to make others partake of them.

It is such willing generosity that marks the true lover of mankind. There are two kinds of liquors and juices, those that pour themselves out and drop of their own accord, and those that have to be squeezed and pressed out by violence. The latter give but grudgingly; the former are generally found more sweet. Those who help others reluctantly are like the reluctant juices. It is a long time before the purse can be found and before the hand can get in it to find change; when they give they do it in such a manner as if to indicate that the hand had stolen from the heart unaware, and that the eye was displeased with the discovery of the theft.

Love that desires to limit its own exercise is not love. Love that is happier if it meets only one who needs help than if it met ten, and happiest if it met none at all, is not love. One of love's essential laws is expressed in the words of Our Lord that the Apostles fondly remembered after He ascended: "It is more blessed to give than to receive." Our nation will be happier and our hearts will be gayer when we discover the true brotherhood of man, but to do this we must realize that we are a race of illegitimate children unless there is also the Fatherhood of God.

[45]

How Much Do We Love the Poor?

THE ATTITUDE toward the poor differs vastly between a man born rich and a man born and reared in poverty. A man born rich, reared in luxury with every whim and instinct satisfied, never knowing want or hunger, will in our modern civilization often pose as a defender of the poor and the downtrodden, particularly if he is in politics. Several generations ago, the rich espoused the cause of the rich; today they sponsor the disinherited and the needy. In the case of many, this is done because their consciences bother them when confronted with poverty; they assuage their sense of guilt by raucous and loud proclamations in favor of every law, policy, and plot to raid public treasuries for the downtrodden and the needy.

While it is commendable to see those who possess great wealth speak in favor of the socially and economically disinherited, one wonders how sincere really is the profession of love. If they favor using public funds, why should they not favor using their private funds? If it is well to give drink to the thirsty from the public reservoirs, why is it not commendable to give them water from their own tables? Really, no one can lay claim to being a liberal in favor of the moneyless, the unemployed, and the indigent, until he himself has felt their want by a surrender of at least some of his own possessions.

Recently we received a letter from a little girl, aged seven, whose father had deserted his wife and family, returning only occasionally to abuse and maltreat them. The little child sent us twenty-five cents for the poor of the world, and added that the other three cents was given by her little sister. Those who have been pinched by poverty are most conscious of the poverty of others. When one is tempted to do wrong, the only person to whom one can go for advice is to one who has suffered temptation and overcome it; but never to the one who gives way to every impulse and appetite. He who has never won a battle cannot give advice to a general on how to conduct a campaign.

Thousands who have allowed their marriage to become shipwrecked through selfishness often consult those advisers and counselers and psychoanalysts who themselves are living with a second or a third wife. Can one who has not been a patriot in one country be counted on to be a true patriot in another? Can he who has failed love expect to be an expert on advising others on matters of love? Businessmen do not normally seek out counsel on how to make profits from those who have gone into bankruptcy. Boys do not ask baseball players whose batting average is .182 how to hold the bat. A man with razor scars over his face is not the one to ask concerning the right way to shave. Should not the scarred, the strikeouts, the bankrupt on the subject of marriage be scrupulously avoided when one has a marriage problem? One would not only save much money, but one would be better advised by going to the next-door neighbor who has raised a family and weathered a thousand storms on the matrimonial sea.

In another domain too, those who suffer will find the sweetest consolation from those who have suffered, not from those who bear no wounds. I believe that every nurse should have an incision—if not a physical incision or scar, at least a mental one, in the sense that she should have an appreciation of pain. A surgeon in a recent letter said that he has just had two operations within a few weeks, and he does not like being a patient. He confessed also that from this time on, he will have a deeper appreciation of the suffering of those on whom he lays a scalpel. Physical suffering is not always the condition of being able to bring solace to others; it is sufficient that the one who consoles at least knows the value of self-discipline and self-restraint. He who takes up his cross daily is already conditioned to speak to others on how to bear a cross. A fat woman appeared on television and said that her profession was that of a diet expert. Everyone in the audience laughed. Why? Because if she gave advice on diet, why did she not diet? And so on, down the line. When a politician boasts that he loves the poor, find out how much of his capital he has given to the poor. When a psychoanalyst tells you to get a divorce, find out if he himself has not failed in his own marriage. The reason why such questions are reasonable and should be asked is because He Who came to this earth to ask us to die daily, to take up our cross, Himself embraced a cross and overcame it by a resurrection. The reason He bears His scars is to show that all things borne in His Name can be overcome, thus finding a joy and peace which the world cannot give.

[46]

Saints

THE TWO GREAT characteristics of our days are secularity and sensuality; secularity is the exile of the Divine from education, international law, politics, economics, and the social life; sensuality is the reduction of love to glands and epidermic contact. Over and above these two degenerations, there are yearnings in the heart of every man for something more than wealth and the pleasures of the flesh. Not many ever get close to it because it costs quite a bit.

Our Lord Himself said that "narrow is the gate and strait is the way that leadeth to love," and few there are who find the way. And yet despite all of His superhuman demands, He gently turns to His followers with all their weaknesses and foibles, their weariness and their despair of relief, and says, "Come to Me, all you that labor and are burdened; and I will refresh you. Take My yoke upon you, and learn of Me, because I am meek and humble of heart, and you shall find rest for your souls. For My yoke is sweet and My burden is light."

Here is a tangle of seeming contradictions—yokes that are not yokes, crosses that do not get crossed up. These words have been realized in millions of souls, like Ignatius of Antioch who could hardly wait until he was ground up between the teeth of lions as wheat to be made the bread of life, or like Maximilian Kolbe who sang hymns to fellow prisoners and gave them joy in the midst of the tortures of a dictatorship. What begins as asceticism and a detachment from the world ends in a wild tranquillity of joy that is of heaven's making, not the earth's.

Take, for example, Augustine. If there was ever a Freudian before Freud, if there was ever a man who believed that man is to be understood in terms of sex instead of sex understood in terms of man, it was this university student and world traveler, playboy, and psychologist. But with the help of God's grace he takes himself in hand and becomes a saint, summing up the first thirty-three years of his sinful life in the words: "Late have I loved Thee, Beauty so old yet so fresh, late have I loved Thee."

During the years of his youth he lived in a sex-mad world and for secular purposes. But as the psychological struggle between his sensuality and his desire for inner peace became more acute, he began to pray in the all too human words, "Give me chastity and continence, O Lord—but not just yet." Then, worn out by the pull between what he was and what he ought to be, he prayed differently, "Let it be now—now." Then, in his treatise on psychology which is the greatest treatise ever penned, he wrote of carnality speaking to him: "And they moved the garment of my flesh and murmured softly: 'Are you really going to get rid of us? And from this moment we shall never be with you . . .'"

But another voice—the voice of all the good and pure people in the city—spoke to him saying, "Can you not do what they did? Or can they do it by themselves, or do they not rather do it in the Lord their God? . . . You cannot stand by yourself. Cast yourself on

Him, and be not afraid; He will not let you fall." It was at this moment that he picked up the Scriptures and read the verse from Romans: "Not in rioting and drunkenness, not in chamberings and impurities, not in contention and envy. But put ye on the Lord Jesus Christ, and make not provision for the flesh and its concupiscence."

As he put it: "I did not want to go on reading, for all the darkness of doubt fled away." From that moment on, he tasted the sweetness that comes to those who are on the royal pathway to sainthood. Many are on the verge of it, but many miss the joys because they will not take the first step of giving up their ego. Men are not saintly because they do not want to be saints. They ask, "Why give up the field for the pearl of great price?" As Léon Bloy wrote, "One step beyond mediocrity and we are saved."

[47]

Farmers

A FINANCIAL DEPRESSION can empty half the apartments on Park Avenue, in New York City, but it fails to touch the man who owns and tills a few acres of land. The farmer owns *real* wealth as distinguished from *fictional* wealth in the form of stocks and bonds. Productive land as a solid basis of economy has not been highly regarded by our modern acquisitive society, but its rediscovery is the condition of national peace.

It has hardly been noted by either the so-called defenders of democracy or their enemies the Communists that the farm, or productive land, is one of the keys to security. European and American civilization, while praising the tiller of the soil in the abstract, nevertheless look upon him patronizingly, either as a "peasant" as is the case in Europe, or as a "farmer" in America. Peasants are considered either backward, because uneducated in the same way as a city dweller, or else antisocial because they dress badly. But the city slicker with his shirt of many colors, the tail overhanging the trousers like limp sails and his hirsute open neck, can hardly lay claim to being "the glass of fashion and the mold of form."

The Communists have been slightly more considerate in their propaganda than the Western world, inasmuch as they promise the break-up of large estates. But their emphasis is principally on the proletariat or the factory worker rather than on the peasant. Mao, the Communist former leader of the Chinese tyranny, was at one time under suspicion by the Kremlin because of his favoritism toward the farmers rather than the factory workers.

The unrealistic attitude toward the productive landowner is due in large part to the industrial revolution with its stress on machinery. Even Marx, in his *Communist Manifesto* believed that "peasant property" would eventually vanish. "We do not need to do away with it. The evolution of industry has done and is daily doing away with it." Whenever Marx had his eye on the ultimate destruction of anything through his iron socialism of confiscation, he said it would "devolve" into disappearance. He did this for marriage and religion as well as for farmers' property. Communism has no doctrine for the peasant except the confiscation of his land, for Communism, being a military and industrial ideology, cannot endure a population whose security is tied to the land rather than to the handouts of a totalitarian state. The liquidation of fifteen million kulaks, or farmers, in the beginning of the Soviet system was planned destructiveness of the individual freedom that belongs to ownership of land. Communism first promises the division of large estates, then taxes the tiller of the land to a point where he submits to collectivization so that in the end landlord ownership becomes state ownership and "the last state of the man is worse than the first." The transfer of all land to the state and the turning of farmers into "statecroppers" from sharecroppers reduces them to the subproletariat class, or the hewers of wood and the drawers of water for the factory workers.

Because even the Western world has given more social approval to the city worker than to the farmer, it has not seen the land as the potential for cracking Communist propaganda in its orbit countries.

Instead of promising the enslaved people of Europe deep freezes, bigger automobiles, pushbutton tuning, and electric light bulbs washed in distilled water, it might be well to promise the people the return of their own land and a return to the land.

The vast majority of the Communist-tyrannized peoples are rural, and the Voice of America that promises them the blessings of an industrialized civilization will not appeal nearly as much as a pledge to restore them to their land.

The factory worker with all his boasted "social security" is fundamentally insecure. He works on someone else's property, uses someone else's tools, procures increased purchasing power through becoming depersonalized in a mass movement, and in the end has nothing to pass on to his children. The man with a little bit of land is the stable element in society; he is his own boss, has the joy of seeing a seed planted by his own hands grow to fruit, and above all has that sanity and peace that come from being able to put his hands into God's own earth.

The specter of hunger haunts the earth, because there are not enough humans on land. Half the people now living have never eaten in their lives what we Americans call a "square meal." An acre and a half of good ground yields enough to keep a person on a balanced diet, but nine tenths of the total land mass of the earth is still unused. A man is free on the *inside* because he has a soul. This soul infused by God is the source of his rights. Because he is dependent on God, he is independent of an absolute state. But man must have some guarantee on the *outside* that he is free. That guarantee is property.

To be able to call something his own is the external side of his internal freedom by which he calls his soul his own. Property thus becomes the economic guarantee of human freedom. Communism had to destroy private ownership of land before it could destroy human freedom. Democracy must work the other way around and sustain liberty by enabling as many citizens as possible to own land which they labor, as the guarantee against a totalitarian state. The farmer is not a survivor of the past; he is the token and promise of a better future.

[48]

The Importance of Persons

ARE WE PERSONS or individuals? Is our government a government of the people, or is it a government of the masses? In answering these questions one learns the basic principles of politics and government. But in order to understand them better, a little history of what has happened in the last two or more centuries will be helpful. Human personality has been submerged or forgotten through several successive stages:

1. The first stage was the emphasis on humanity during the eighteenth century. Humanity is indeed sacred, but those who glorified humanity often used it as a cloak for the gravest injustices and cruelties to certain humans. A Dostoevski character said that he loved mankind in general and could give learned discourses on the necessity of loving mankind, but that if he were left in a room half a day with a man who had a peculiar way of blowing his nose, he began to despise him. Humanity was loved but not always the human. Rousseau, who glorified humanity in his politics, also deserted each of his children immediately after birth.

2. The second stage is Communism, when humanity degenerates into the masses. Masses is the Communist word; it signifies the absorption of persons into the collectivity of the state. The masses are made up not of persons but of ants; not of self-determined individuals but of those totally determined by propaganda and dictation; not of men and women enjoying freedom and conscience, but of a stony unit with no other conscience than state conscience, and no other morality than the dictator morality, and no other freedom than the freedom of the whole.

3. The tremendous influence of the false humanitarianism which did not love each human, and the rise of Communism, which absorbed humanity into a dictatorial mold, have had their effect even on democracies in which not humanity, not the masses, but the group becomes all-holy. The same basic principle runs through all three: namely, the person is subordinated to the collectivity. In the democratic group, personal creativity is submerged; every man must fit into a kind of mold. He reads the same news, hears the same newscasters, listens to the same television programs, reads mostly the same books. No one knows who is responsible for group opinion; the authoritarianism is anonymous—it is always "they." They say, "They are wearing." In education, professors will be less interested in teaching truth than in improving group reactions; in business, he who shows creativity is knocked on the head until he is down to the level of the uncreative majority; machines have been invented in which everyone pushes a button hidden near the chair, and a meter registers not individual votes, but the group reaction.

The "humanity" of the French Revolution, the "masses" of the Communist revolution, and the "group" of modern socialism of the democratic societies have all conspired in varying degrees to destroy personality and creativity and true leadership. The reaction will come when society reintroduces the following basic considerations:

1. The unit of society is not the individual, but the person. An orange, a cow, a stone are all individuals, but an orange, a cow, and a stone are not persons. Individuals are replaceable; persons are irreplaceable and unique. When one buys lemons, one can say to the storekeeper, "Take this one and give me another." But one cannot replace a mother or father, or any person in the world.

2. A government is solid when it is not of the masses, but of the people. Masses are made up of individuals; "People are made up of persons." Hence, the Constitution of the United States is the constitution of "people" . . . "We the people . . ." Masses are determined from the outside by propaganda and fear and force and terror; people are persons determined from the inside by freedom and an enlightened conscience.

3. A person does not belong to the state in the totality of his being. He has certain relationships which transcend the state. That

is why a truly democratic government recognizes freedom of religion and worship. A person is the key to the future political developments of the world. Our Lord made a person more important than the universe.

[49]

The New Slavery

THERE ARE three ways in which a man becomes a slave. He may be born into slavery, or forced into it, or he can deliberately accept his servitude. All three forms flourish in the modern world. Men are born and forced into slavery in Russia and her satellite states. Men in the free world invite slavery when they ask the government to provide complete security, when they surrender their freedom to the "welfare state."

The slave states of the Western world are an outgrowth of monopolistic capitalism—an economic system which is opposed to the wide distribution of private property in many hands. Instead, monopolistic capitalism concentrates productive wealth among a few men, allowing the rest to become a vast proletariat.

Some representatives of monopolistic capitalism, sensing this evil in their system, have tried to silence criticism by pointing to the diffused ownership of stocks in the great corporations. They advertise, "No one owns more than 4 percent of the stock of this great company." Or they print lists of stockholders, showing that these include farmers, schoolteachers, baseball players, taxi drivers, and even babies. But there is a catch to this argument, and it is this: although it is true that individuals of small means *own* shares in the company, it is not true that they *run* the company. Their responsibility for its policies is nil.

Possession properly has two faces, two aspects: we all have a *right* to private property, but this is accompanied by our *responsibility* for its righteous use. These two things (which should be inseparable) are frequently divided today. Everyone admits that the farmer who owns a horse is obliged to feed and care for it; but in the case of stocks and bonds, we often forget that the same principle should prevail.

Monopolistic capitalism is to blame for this; it sunders the right to own property from the responsibility that owning property involves. Those who own only a few stocks have no practical control of any industry. They vote by postcard proxy, but they have rarely even seen "their" company. The two elements which ought to be inextricably joined in any true conception of private property—ownership and responsibility—are separated. Those who own do not manage; those who manage and work do not control or own.

The workmen in a factory may have a shadowy, unknown, absentee "employer"—the thousands of individual owners of stock—whom "management" represents and tries to please by extra dividends. The workman's livelihood is at the disposition of strangers who make a single demand of their representatives: higher profits.

Faced by such insecurity, labor unions seek a solution in demands for higher wages, shorter hours, pensions, and such things. But this approach takes monopolistic capitalism for granted, and accepts the unnatural division between property and responsibility as permanent. A much more radical solution is apt to come, and this may take either of two forms.

One way of remedying the situation would be through a profound alteration of our political and economic life, with the aim of distributing the means of production more widely by giving every workman *a share in profits, management, and ownership, all three.* The other alternative (which is not a constructive solution) is confiscation: this may take the violent form of Communism, or the less noticeable form of bureaucratic encroachment through taxation, as favored by the welfare state. Confiscation is an unhealthy solution for a real disease. It amounts to telling men that because they are economically crippled, they must abandon all efforts to get well and allow the state to provide them with free wheelchairs.

The denial of the right of ownership to a man is a denial of his basic freedom: freedom without property is always incomplete. To be "secure"—but with no accompanying responsibility—is to be the slave of whatever group provides the security.

A democracy flirts with the danger of becoming a slave state in direct ratio to the numbers of its citizens who work, but do not own; or who own, but do not work; or who distribute, as politicians do, but do not produce. The danger of the slave state disappears in ratio to the number of people who own property and admit its attendant responsibilities under God. They can call their souls their own because they own and administer something other than their souls. Thus, they are free.

[50]

Man Is Dead

SOMEONE OUGHT to write a book entitled *Man Is Dead* in order to help us think clearly on the books shrieking *God Is Dead*. The two should go together, as they do in this true story told me by the one who actually experienced it. When he was a boy, he and another boy went into some thick woods in Canada. They decided to amuse themselves by having a contest as to which one could use the worst "cuss words." They finally ended by taunting God for being dead. Then, as it got dark, they became frightened because they could not find their way out of the woods. So they both knelt down and prayed to God to get them out. One of the boys who told me the story later became a priest.

One-sided books on the funeral of deity are apt to be a projection of one's own want of spiritual life. Thieves generally believe that "honesty is dead"; adulterers readily concede that "love is dead"; he who has read little history says that "history is bunk"; and they who have had little genuine theological experience are apt to deny Divinity but in more abstruse language than their real sentiment: "The hell with it."

We live in the "Time of the Great Divorce"—i.e., the separation of the sacred and the secular, the rupture of the worldly and the heavenly, the tension between the love of God and the love of neighbor, the pull between the service of the Lord and the service of humanity. That which God joined together, man has separated.

The children of this divorce break up into two groups: those who see that some religious people do not concern themselves with the world write books on "God is dead." On the other hand, those who see that men engaged in the pursuit of the secular neglect the aspirations of the soul for Life and Truth and Love should write books on the subject "man is dead." There they lie on a psychological couch, having everything they ever wanted and yet being still unsatisfied. They would deny that there was any such thing as bread, but they hunger; they sneer at the fountains of refreshment, but they still thirst.

It is the irreligious people who write obsequies about Divinity, and the religious people who turn up their noses at suffering humanity who write death notices about humanity. Only the world exists for the former, and only God exists for the latter. The suffocated spirits of the one and the inhuman hearts on the part of the pious are both equally to be condemned. The only true, sensible perspective is the one which sees that love of God and neighbor go together.

In the parable of the Good Samaritan, the priest and the Levite who were dedicated to religion passed by a wounded man on the highway without offering any help. They later authored the bestseller "Man Is Dead." The Good Samaritan, who might have been scandalized at the inhumanity of religion to humanity, probably gave to the innkeeper a copy of his latest release: "God Is Dead." I know of a pious woman who goes to church every day, has a prayer book bulging with holy pictures and her bedroom plastered with them, and yet out of her vast wealth she has never given a cent to the poor. Humanity does not exist for her, but only Divinity.

A rich young man came to Our Lord Who bade him sell all he had and give to the poor, and then come and follow Him. The rich

man could not do it, "because he had many possessions." His avarice
and love of riches blinded him to the higher instincts of love. To
him "God was dead." There was another rich man who apparently
was guilty of nothing wrong except to clothe himself in fine purple,
eat well and ignore a beggar, Lazarus, at his door. To him, "man was
dead."

Too often neglect of human service is mistaken for Christian self-
denial, and more often the embalming of Divine service is mistaken
for love of humanity. Actually both are dead. Dead are the professors of theology who see only the sons of men and forget that they
have a Father—otherwise they would be a race of illegitimate children. Dead too are the so-called religious people who see only God
in the abstract and forget that He came into the dust of human
lives, washing feet, touching white leprous sores, hugging little children, and leaving a beloved disciple who wrote, "If we do not love
men whom we see, how can we love God Whom we do not see?"

VIII

Giving

Taking on Burdens

Two OPPOSITE ways of regulating life are to be found in these thoughts: "I have enough worries of my own without taking on the worries of others." The other is to be found in a letter St. Paul addressed to the Galatians: "Bear ye one another's burdens and so fulfill the law of Christ."

The first and egotistic philosophy of life would not be so popular if it did not have seeming logic behind it, and it is this: such people think that taking on the burden of the neighbor doubles their own load just as, if I had a sack of fifty pounds on my back and took on my neighbor's sack weighing equally as much, I would have to carry one hundred pounds. This is true indeed in the physical order, but mental burdens are not like sacks of potatoes or stones; they have no "weight" in the sense that they are material. Rather, worries and troubles are of the mind, and hence the law of measures and weights does not apply to them.

Because worries are mental and spiritual, the opposite can be the truth. Help someone in distress and you lighten your own burden; the very joy of alleviating the sorrow of another is the lessening of one's own. If we dig someone else out of a hole, we get out of the hole we are in. There could be no burden bearing without the inspiration of love. That is what is meant by fulfilling the law of Christ which is the law of love.

Running through the universe is the law of interdependence: "All are but parts of one stupendous whole." Every particle of matter in the universe attracts every other particle according to the relation of mass and distance. The universe would fall apart if there were no interest in one another's burdens. The same is true of the human body. The eye cannot say to the ear, "I can live without your services," or the heart say to the bloodstream, "I do not see why I should be pumping all day just to help you." "Each cell for itself," if put into practice, would invite death. In like manner, the greatest happiness of nations is to be attained, not by each hoarding up its resources, but by exchanging them or giving them to other nations as the United States has done. Burdens of others are to be our concern whether they be burdens of want, burdens of ignorance, burdens of care, burdens of doubt, or even burdens of sin.

He who does not love does not share. The need to give is born of the need of love. If two people associate with each other because of what they can get out of each other, or because of the pleasure which each gives the other, there is no true friendship or love. When a person clutches his own burden of sorrow to his heart and expects another to bow down to it, he thereby makes others feel their inferiority. But when we accept the burden of another, all superiority is done away with, and when egotism vanishes, unhappiness disappears.

Those who look only after themselves are generally found to be sullen and sulky. The word "sulky" is derived from a horse-drawn vehicle which had two wheels and room for only the driver. He carried no one else. Those who worry about themselves not only increase their own burdens, but add to the woes of those around them. To them can be applied the words of the poet Manfield: "The harm I have done by being me!" As the Russian Turgenev put it, "It seems to me to discover what to put before oneself, in the first place, is the whole problem of life." Once it is deeply engraved in the heart that Divine Love so much loved the burdens and cares of mankind that He became man, and took them on Himself as if they were His own, and did not leave them until they were done away with—even by a crucifixion—then the believing heart has a motive and an inspiration for carrying the burdens of others. The Lord did it first, and to love Him above all else is to desire to prolong that love in our life —even by being Simons of Cyrene and helping others bear their cross. This is happiness and peace!

[52]

The Best Gifts in Life Are Free

MANY IN HEAVEN once were alcoholics, adulterers, thieves, racketeers, but there is no one in heaven who did not become humble. But the mere mention of humility conjures up, in many minds, the idea that humility means allowing other people to walk all over you, or a self-abasement, or that it turns one into that perfect example of mock humility, Uriah Heep. Because the poet Keats understood it as such, he said, "I hate humility."

Humility is not self-contempt, but the truth about ourselves coupled with a reverence for others; it is self-surrender to the highest goal. A man who is six feet four is not humble when he says, "Oh, no, really I am only four feet four"—because that is not the truth; neither is an opera singer humble when she says, "Oh, I really am nothing in the singing profession"; neither is a beautiful person humble when she says, "I am really ugly." Such protestations against the truth are marks of pride, rather than humility. Humility in such cases consists in the acknowledgment of the truth that we have received the gifts for which we are praised: "What have you that you did not receive, and why do you glory, as if you had not received?" The humble person is embarrassed with praise because he knows that his voice, his talents, or his power come to him from God. In his heart of hearts, he passes the thanks on to God when the lips of men exalt him. He takes praise as a window receives light, never to possess it and hoard it unto himself, but to pass it through with thanksgiving to God Who so endowed him.

All good things that men possess are in constant peril of running into exaggerations, once it is forgotten that they are gifts. A man on the strong side may become self-willed and push his weight around; one who has intellectual power may look down on the ignorant, forgetful that they have moral gifts which far surpass his mental powers; the self-reliant may become corrupted into self-conceit, and those who have self-confidence may be so sure of themselves as to fall into the pit because of a refusal to listen to the counsel of others. Those who can watch often despise those who cannot watch, and who sleep; the strong may try to force the weak to walk at their pace, and become angry with them because they cannot. Life has to be toned down with that moral quality which recognizes that wealth, health, wisdom, and above all faith are gifts of God which grow and intensify with a spirit of thanksgiving.

We strive for what is best, but "the best gifts of life are free," or bestowed. Spring is a gift; music is a gift; a rose is a gift; air is a gift; grass is a gift; the silver stream, the blazing horizon, the purple of the dawn are all gifts. As the poet Lowell put it in "The Vision of Sir Launfal":

> At the devil's booth all things are sold,
> Each ounce of dross costs its ounce of gold;
> For a cap and bells our lives we pay,
> Bubbles we buy with a whole soul's tasking:
> 'Tis heaven alone that is given away,
> 'Tis only God may be had for the
>   asking;
> No price is set on the lavish summer:
> June may be had by the poorest
>   comer.

Love itself is a gift; forced love is rape; forced patriotism is tyranny. What is true of the love of man and woman is true of the love of God; it is free on His side and first; it is free on our side and a response. "If any man will open the door, let him come in and sup with Me."

Because we are the recipients of gifts, the humble man is reverent and thankful to God. Daniel Webster was once asked what the greatest thought was that ever entered his mind; his answer was,

"Personal accountability to God for His gifts." President Garfield, in a similar vein, once said, "It is above all things necessary that in every action I should have a good opinion of James Garfield, for to eat and drink and sleep and wake with one you despise—though that one be yourself—is an intolerable thought, and what must it be as a life experience?" The proud man counts his newspaper clippings —the humble man his blessings!

[53]

Trumpets and Broadcasts

MULTIPLIED APPEALS for relief in our grief-stricken always find a ready response in the hearts of generous people. It is interesting to note how many appeals are based on human vanity, such as "the largest donor during the week will receive such and such a prize." These are but enlarged reactions of the beggar who knows enough to use a tin cup in order that the giver will always have the "reward" of hearing the "clink" at the bottom of the cup. The tin cup is not in order that the blind man may hear the gift fall, but in order that the giver may know that his gift has fallen.

To such promised rewards of praise, notoriety, and publicity, the words of the Savior are in striking contrast: "When you give alms, do not sound a trumpet before thee as the hypocrites in the streets, to win the esteem of men." The trumpets have now given way to broadcasts and telecasts, but the purpose is the same: to let other men know of our generosities. It was a custom of great personages in the past to blow trumpets as they passed through crowds, and then scatter coins to gain the good will of the poor. Now the trumpet has been succeeded by broadcasts or telecasts or the press, but the purpose is ever the same: to gain honor among men. It is not the publicity itself which is bad, but rather the ungodly motive for which it is sought.

Everything evil in the world is a perversion of something good. Evil is either an excess or a defect of the good. The goodness associated with all charity and benevolence is twofold: first, that righteous and good actions ought to be rewarded; second, that the prospect of reward is a legitimate stimulus for giving. Every man knows in his heart that there ought to be some blessing following his gift, and that this blessing ought to be an encouragement of his goodness. But though these aspirations and instincts are good, they become evil when the blessing one wants is the praise of men through the soundings of announcements over television, radio, or pictures in the paper.

The point that Our Blessed Lord made was that our overanxiety about public approval disqualifies us for receiving His reward. This is an advertising age: the flowers that He made to grow and waste their perfume on the desert air are now in exhibition halls. It is hard, therefore, in the face of a world spirit, to avoid publicity and the receiving of our reward from men rather than from God. Of those who court praise, Our Lord said, "They already have their reward." They sought human ostentation, and they received it; they get exactly what they hoped for, and thereby they lose the rewards which God stores up for them. Thus the greatness of the gift is spoiled by the littleness of the motive.

Actually those who seek applause for their gifts do not really give at all—they buy. They are not surrendering—they are purchasing. They are less impressed with the need of others than they are with the heed that will be given to them. Their gift is a kind of a speculation. They made an investment in publicity, and they look for their adequate returns. It is so easy for the eye to wander from the hungry person to whom the offering is made, to the bystanders that they may notice what we have given.

That generous souls may not be overinterested in trumpets and broadcasts, Our Divine Master followed with the counsel: "When thou givest alms, thou shalt not so much as let thy left hand know what thy right hand is doing, so secret is thy almsgiving to be; and then, thy Father Who sees what is done in secret will reward in secret." This means that the giver will not dwell on the greatness of his gift, nor on the observation of others. He is to be like the harp whose vibrations are unseen when it gives out the note.

There is another blessing than the praise of men. To love the poor because we gain something is not to love them, but to love ourselves. The reward contemplated should be nothing else than growth in likeness of the Father and the increase of our filial consciousness. Then our giving will always be in the spirit that we are perhaps more needy than those whom we have helped. They need only a roof over their heads, or clothes for their backs; we need, however, the crushing of our egotism and the blessing of God in our hearts.

[54]

The Problem of Giving

"To HAVE" is the opposite of "to give," yet each of these things is good in its proper place. To have is to extend our personalities: we do not contain within ourselves all the essentials for human living, therefore our "being" must be completed by also "having." Existence implies the right to have sufficient food and clothing and a place to live; it does not, however, imply the right to have a seagoing yacht. Our rights to own property, to have things, decrease as the objects are farther and farther removed from personal necessities.

The virtue of giving is dependent upon having, for unless we possess something we cannot give it away. (This is true even of our time.) But having does not, to most people, appear as an opportunity for giving—they look upon giving as a loss, because having is, in itself, so dear to them. This is shortsighted; if you give away half a loaf, another half loaf remains to you, and you have had the happiness of being a donor too.

Many people, especially among the rich, estimate the value of their own personalities in terms of owning more and more unessential things. They refuse to cut into their capital, increasing it each year until it seems to them another self without which they would not be complete. To slice off a portion of this capital through alms would seem to them like cutting off an arm or a leg.

One woman has lived in history because she did not fear cutting into her capital. The story is told in the Gospel: "As He was sitting opposite the treasury of the temple, Jesus watched the multitude throwing coins into the treasury, the many rich with their offerings; and there was one poor widow, who came and put in two mites, which makes a farthing. Thereupon He called his disciples to Him, and said to them, 'Believe me, this poor widow has put in more than all those others who have put offerings into the treasury. The others all gave out of what they had to spare; she, with so little to give, put in all that she had, her whole livelihood.'"

Our Divine Lord was interested in studying the almsgivers, and it was the quality of their giving which arrested Him far more than the quantity they gave. He had once said that where our treasure is, there our heart is also. Now He tells us that where the heart goes, there the treasure follows. Few of us have His attitude toward alms; we do not trouble to read the list of donors in fine type under the heading, "*Amounts less than . . .*" But probably that would be to Him the most important section of the list; on that occasion in the temple He immortalized a gift of two of the smallest coins in the ancient world.

Probably the poor woman at the temple did not see her Judge or know that she had pleased Him, or guess that, in the scales of Divine Justice, she gave more than all those others who put offerings into the treasury. They gave of their superfluity: she gave all she had, "her whole livelihood." She was poor, yet she gave to the poor. She emptied herself to fill the emptiness of others. The jingle of her two small coins as they fell cried out to refute the whole base philosophy of materialism, which would teach men to acquire as much as they can—as if this earth were our only home.

And the widow's tiny gift has another meaning: it reminds us that Our Lord wants *everything* from us. He was the first "totalitarian" of the spirit: He asks that we hold nothing back from Him. He demands total love: "with thy whole mind, thy whole heart, thy whole spirit, and thy whole strength." Only those who have given their whole hearts to God can give Him their whole capital as well.

Nothing that is given in such a spirit of generosity is ever lost. In the materialist's reckoning, what is renounced is lost forever. In the realm of the spirit, this is not true. For what we give to God is not only recorded to us for eternal merit—it is even returned in this life. One of the most practical ways of assuring that we shall always have enough is to give and give and give in the Name of the Lord. Similarly, the most rapid increase in love of God can be obtained by being totally generous to our neighbors. "Give and the gifts will be yours; good measure, pressed down and shaken up and running over, will be poured into your lap; the measure you award to others is the measure that will be awarded to you." (Luke 6:39.)

The use to which we put what we have is closely related to what we are, to our "being," and to what we will become. He who keeps everything he has for himself must lose it all at death; he who has given it away will get it back in the coin of immortality and joy.

IX
Freedom

Two Keys

To BE ABLE to say "yes" is a mark of human freedom; but the power to say "no," particularly to a gift of love, is a stronger sign of freedom. Nature, which is the field of science, never says "no" to the gifts of the Creator. The beauty of a sunset looking like "a host in the golden monstrance of the west"; the flower in the crannied wall that tells of the past and forecasts a future; the seed that dies and rises again like a Good Friday and an Easter—all reflect the majesty, power, and beauty that were put into them when they fell from the creative Hand of God.

But nowhere does the offer of beauty for the soul, truth for the mind, and the noblest of all love for the will go for naught and be met with the frozen negative, except in the heart of man. The earth does not make sterile the seed that falls on its good ground, but the spirit of man can freeze the seed that falls from heaven. The ego has the power of freedom given to it by God which makes possible the refusal of any other gift. It is hard to believe that if there were some universal remedy discovered that would cure mankind of all diseases and ills to which the flesh is heir, anyone who was prostrate from sickness would refuse its healing balm; but in the order of morality and truth, millions there are who refuse forgiveness for their wounded souls, a harbor for their searching minds, and an abiding love for their tortured hearts. Grace, which is the illumination of the mind to see a truth which it never saw before, and the strengthening of the will to do something about it, which it could never do before, is a growth to perfection which man often rejects; but the acorn would never fail to use the external gifts of sunlight and moisture to become the oak.

Many graces come to the soul, for example, to give up an evil life, to intensify the life of the spirit, to cultivate an inner peace through love of God; when they are rejected, they become like undigested

food in the stomach, or perhaps even like ground glass in the digestive tract. What was meant to be a nourishment becomes, by its
very rejection, a hindrance and an uneasiness. If an acorn could
voluntarily stunt its growth by refusing the nutriment of light,
chemicals, and rains, so that it always remained a crooked sapling,
one would have a picture of what happens to a human heart when it
spurns those graces which should contribute to its perfection.

Psychologists and psychiatrists are constantly dealing with unhappiness, and the wisest of them see that there are some deep roots
which escape analysis. Just as a theologian knows that there is such a
thing as "white grace" or the presence of God in the soul, so a wise
psychiatrist knows that there is such a thing as "black grace" or the
absence of God in the soul. The latter is a gnawing void, a harrowing sense of futility after the most sensate of pleasures, a discontent
with having what one thought would bring happiness, after "one
drank every cup of joy, heard every trump of fame, drank early,
drank draughts that might have quenched common millions, then
died of thirst because there was no room to drink."

Each human heart is a garden, a secret garden which God has
kept uniquely for Himself. That garden is locked like a safety vault
—it has two keys. God has one key; hence He can keep out anyone
but Himself. The human heart has the other key; hence not even
God can get in without man's consent. Here is the great difference
between nature and man. The vault of nature has only one key and
that is in the Hand of God; but since man has the gift of freedom,
he has the other key and, with it, the power to turn his back on the
Flame of Love while admitting only the sparks. When the two keys
of God's love and human liberty, of Divine vocation and human response meet, then Paradise enters the heart. God is always at the
garden gate with His key. Man pretends that he has lost his key, or
that the key does not work, or that the garden is not beautiful anyway. But all the while it is in his hand, if he would only use it.

[56]

What Is Freedom?

IT HAS OFTEN been said that many crimes are committed in the name of liberty. This is possible only because such a noble gift has been misunderstood or perverted. Actually, it is easy in our modern world to study the true nature of freedom, for the extreme errors are so clearly visible. It would not be true to say that these extremes are Western civilization on the one hand and Russian on the other, but it would be true to say that the extremes are certain groups in Western civilization and the Communist Party in the Soviet Union. Some in the Western world identify freedom with absence of law or restraint; hence any kind of discipline, punishment for crime, obedience to authority, is shrieked down as the destruction of the individual rights and liberty. Here there is a confusion of freedom *within* the law with freedom *from* the law.

In the Communist world one meets the other extreme, which suppresses individual freedom for the sake of the law of the Party. If it be asked how such a regime could ever be called "free," the Communists answer with the example of their patron Engels. He said that a stone dropped from the hand is "free" because it obeys the law of gravitation; in like manner, a man is free whenever he obeys the Party dictates. Freedom is thus placed outside man in the controlling group or party.

Because of the confusion about the word "freedom," a summary of the philosophy of freedom would be helpful. Man has a free will in search of liberty. Free will is a gift; liberty is a conquest. First, free will is a gift: every human being has been endowed by the Creator with the inalienable gift of choice to be master of his judgments and his acts. Sticks and stones, sealing wax and electric ranges are not free because they are material; only where there is a spirit is there a free choice. Ice must be cold and fire must be hot, but a boy ought to be good and a man ought to be good. Free choice is the essence of personality. Not even God Who gave that gift would destroy it, for the gift itself was the effect of a free choice on the part of God Himself. Choice is a free act of man in search of the end or purpose for which he was made; some mistake this end, and think it is money or flesh instead of the attainment of perfect life and truth and love.

Now we come to the second principle, that though free choice is a gift, freedom is a conquest. No man wants freedom just for the sake of freedom. In one sense, every man wants to give away his freedom for what he believes is his perfect happiness. A man is free to love a woman. In proposing, he may even tell the woman that to him his greatest freedom is to be her slave for the rest of his life. Freedom is ours to give away.

Obviously, some give their freedom away and become slaves in the most disastrous sense of the term. An alcoholic became such by a free act of choice multiplied a thousandfold. Finally came the surrender, and he became the "slave of drink." He sold his choice, but in a way to destroy his personality. Now take another example in which one gives away freedom of choice to attain a true spiritual freedom. The husband in love with his wife acquired by a free choice on the part of both is an example of the highest kind of liberty in the order of human affection. True spiritual liberty exists when two essential values are acquired: *self-mastery,* by which one is liberated from external constraint such as excessive drinking or smoking; and the *complete and total gift of self* to justice, truth, and love, which are rooted in God. Such are those who dedicate themselves to the person of Christ in serving lepers to make reparation for sins. Others use their free choice to attain what is to them the maximum of spiritual liberty. As Kafka wrote, "Christ is such an abyss of light that before Him one must close his eyes to avoid throwing oneself to Him in total dedication." At this peak of freedom, one has quite surpassed the first stage of freedom which is identified with the power to choose evil as well as good; one enters into the spontaneity of love in full clarity. The truth is that man is not so much free as freeable; he makes himself free by choosing those goals which give his spirit the maximum room for joy. On this earth, it is only the saints who are the true liberals, inasmuch as they are the most free.

[57]

Freedom

MEN TALK MOST about freedom when they are losing it, as they talk most about a Depression when they have lost their money. Freedom is both internal and external. Internal freedom is the right to choose what we ought for the perfection of our personality. External freedom is the absence of constraint and force. This is the kind of freedom that was envisaged in the slogan of the "Four Freedoms" during the last world war.

External freedom is lost through the police state, such as is found in Russia, China, and behind the Iron Curtain. Internal freedom is lost by the denial of responsibility. Democracies boast that they alone have freedom, because they do not force their people to submit to a dictatorship. But there are psychologists, psychiatrists, philosophers, dramatists in democracy who deny that when a man does anything wrong he is guilty. "Compulsion" is the polite word to cover up the denial of inner freedom.

This point has been covered before in other articles, but here we touch upon the value of this inner freedom from heaven's point of view. Hell is one of the eternal guarantees of human freedom, for it admits the right of a free man to cry out *non-serviam* through all eternity. Heaven, too, is freedom because no one ever gets there without a very conscious effort. But apart from these ultimate guarantees of liberty, there is another very interesting proof of it that affects our daily life. The best introduction to it may be told in the story of a painting. It is a picture of Christ standing at the side of an ivy-covered door and knocking. Holman Hunt, its artist, was criticized because there was no latch to be seen on the outside of the door. The answer of the artist was that the latch is on the inside—we open it. Heaven knocks down no doors.

There are two incidents mentioned in the Gospel which illustrate this point of how much responsibility is involved in human freedom. One was a scene on a lake; the other, a scene on a roadway. The apostles were rowing in the dark against the winds and the seas. Suddenly the Lord came walking toward them on the waters, but He made it appear as if He would pass them by—until they called to Him. The other scene was on the road to Emmaus. The Lord conversed with the strangers on that Easter Sunday late afternoon, and made as if He would move on from their presence until they beckoned Him to remain.

In both instances, the latch is on the inside. God will not stop unless He is bidden to do so. There must be the outstretched hands, the pleading voice, the aspiring heart. He is not like the man who came to dinner. He will pass by unless he is asked to stay. All the responsibility is on the human side. Grace makes no assault; revelation does not compel; the rich young man who departs because he has great possessions is allowed to move on; those who cannot accept His word about the Bread of Life are allowed to leave and "walk no more with him"; Judas who betrayed is not bound, nor is Peter's sword used to restrict his freedom to betray. How little do those who accuse religion of being authoritarian understand that the only authority is love. No one is compelled. Even the chief and head and the all-important Rock of the structure was asked, "Will you also go away?"

Freedom is so all-embracing that Divine benefits of graces are given not on the basis of merit, but on the basis of free acceptance. A man does not need to be worthy before the Divine Wayfarer stops. He need only want it. Freedom, therefore, has tremendous responsibilities. Because so many have abused their freedom and suffer from false choices, they are ready to throw it away—some to Communism, others to alcohol, others to dope, and others to couches which blame guilt on grandmothers. Others, however, knowing its full responsibility in the greatest act of freedom there is, say, "Abide with us, the day is far spent."

[58]

How to Be Free

THE SAD AND tragic fact of our day is that many people in the world no longer want to be free. At first this sounds contrary to fact, but there are three high-powered evidences to support the view that many are in flight from liberty.

Freedom is a burden and a responsibility, because it means we must answer for our choices and decisions. As many want to look for truth rather than find it, because the discovery of truth demands decision, so many like to talk about freedom rather than enjoy it. By throwing the responsibility off their own consciences, they hope to avoid the remorse, anxieties, and fears that follow from its misuse.

There are three principal escapes from true freedom today:

1. *Communism*, which is the transfer of political liberty to the dictator and the death of personal conscience through being devoured by the state-conscience.

2. *Sociologism*, or the affirmation that murder, crime, juvenile delinquency, immorality, and all social orders are due to bad economic environment rather than to the abuse of personal freedom through evil choices.

3. *Bad Behavior*: The enslavement of the human will through giving way to evil passions, such as lust, alcoholism, avarice, pride, to the extent that personality becomes other-possessed rather than self-possessed.

The wise old Socrates, who lived several centuries before Christ, brought this out in one of his dialogues. "Tell me," said Socrates, "do you believe that freedom is one of the greatest possessions both for the individual and the state? Certainly! But do you think a person is free who is a slave to bodily passions, such as one who is sex-mad? Not at all. Is it not true that he who is hindered from doing what is pure and is constrained to do what is foul, is a slave to the worst master? Yes. The incontinent therefore are enslaved to the worst slavery," concludes Socrates. "Yes, I agree." A man has as many lords as he has vices, for each of them chants to the soul in chains: "Thou art mine."

There are few basic principles which will help man achieve true liberty, which is the right to do whatever he *ought*, and the *ought* is determined by what is best and highest in good for his personality. This *ought* is conscience in the natural order, and Revelation in the supernatural.

We are more *freeable* than *free*. Freedom is not just something with which we are born; it is something we achieve. America did not receive a perpetual endowment of freedom; it has had to struggle and fight to preserve it. Freedom is not an heirloom or an antique; it is a life that must fight against the corrosive powers of death and nourish itself on the daily bread of goodness and virtue. What is true of political freedom is true of the individual. Parents realizing that a child is not yet in possession of perfect freedom say, "Now you must go to school and learn truth." Up until that time the child was "free" to believe that the moon was made of green cheese. But now the child is given the restriction of a scientific truth which ushers it into a true freedom. The child begins to think freely as he thinks truly about the moon. As Our Blessed Lord said, "The truth will make you free." What is true in the realm of science is true in the order of morality; stand fast in the possession of those true principles which clear your mind from false conceptions. As a man can be wrong about the nature of the moon, so he can be wrong about the purpose of life. A savage who thinks the purpose of a thermometer is to devour will do harm to his stomach, as a man who thinks the purpose of life is to eat, or to enjoy himself sensually, will do harm to his mind.

We make ourselves free by knocking off all those hindrances and obstacles to the development and unfolding of what is highest in us —namely, the pursuit of Truth and Love and Goodness which is basically the definition of God. Freedom is not attainable at once, but by leaps and bounds. It is not a cradle from which we cry and pout, shriek and clamor for the satisfaction of our biological wants, but rather a hurdle race in which we surmount obstacles to win the race of being free on the *inside* where no hammer can destroy and no sickle cut.

Another principle is that freedom is increased most in service of fellowman. No one really belittles himself in aiding his neighbor, even the one whom he considers beneath him on the social ladder. The most popular boy or girl in college is always the one who is most interested in others, who uses freedom to become a "slave" and in the end finds love. In the natural order, a grain of wheat struggles first for bare existence, and then at the moment of harvest it reaches a condition where service is imperative to it. It grew to be used at the table of man. In the moral order, no human being is to be destroyed for another as the grain of wheat, because each person is autonomous and of eternal value. But as soon as he reaches maturity he thirsts to use his powers for the betterment of fellowman. "I am among you as one who serves," said Our Divine Lord. All this is another way of saying that the free man is one who loves God and therefore knows what is right, and who loves neighbor and therefore spends himself and is spent in the betterment of the world.

X
Obedience

Obedience

ONE OF THE rarest household words is "obedience." It has fallen into a discount like many of the other passive virtues, such as humility and resignation. Obedience is said to belong to older social conditions of monarchies, feudalism, but is unsuited to democracy and to liberty.

But liberty is not the enemy of obedience. Liberty is most secure not when it chooses evil, but when it moves within its own sphere which is that of a moral good. Moral good is to the soul what air is to the bird and water to the fish. The fish can leap out of the water and die upon the bank, but the liberty of the fish is complete without this added capacity for self-destruction. So it is with man. To choose evil is to do violence to his highest nature.

Liberty derives strength from obedience. A driver is free to steer his car in traffic, because he is obedient to the civil laws. An aviator is free to fly, provided he obeys the laws of gravitation and aviation. It is only through obedience that one learns to command. He would be a poor general who had never served in the ranks.

The relationship between strength, freedom, and obedience is found in that very area where we might expect obedience to be dispensed with, and that is when the Divine Master went down to Nazareth and was subject to His Mother and foster father until the beginning of His public life. The Holiest of all learned obedience not by the things which He did, but by that which He suffered.

There is no obedience worth anything which is not the child of love. Obedience which is mechanical and forced is dread.

Obedience is easy when it is dictated by love or, better, inspired by it. The more respect there is for the one who gives the command, the easier it is to comply. Where there is little respect, obedience is difficult. Love is like wings to a bird, like sails to a ship. When love cools, obedience slacks and drives heavily, because it lacks love on it, which acts as a kind of oil.

Napoleon's soldiers achieved extraordinary exploits under the influence of fervent attachment for him, which no law could have required them to attempt. Cold-blooded orders by a domineering officer would have offered little encouragement to bravery.

The law says you shall do this or you shall be punished, but Divine Love says, "I have loved you with an everlasting love. I have forgiven your sins. Now My Love shall sweetly constrain you. The influence of My inward Spirit shall guide you in your ways."

Parents, therefore, are not to be like a herder with a stick and a dog who herds the cattle to market, but rather as a shepherd going before his sheep, lovingly leading the way.

[60]

Sweet Obedience

OBEDIENCE DOES NOT mean the execution of orders that are given by a drill sergeant. It springs rather from the love of an order, and love of him who gave it. The merit of obedience is less in the act than in the love; the submission, the devotion, and the service which obedience implies are not born of servitude, but are, rather, effects that spring from and are unified by love. Obedience is servility only to those who have not understood the spontaneity of love.

Our Lord spent three hours in redeeming, three years in teaching, and thirty years in obeying, in order that a rebellious, proud, and diabolically independent world might learn the value of obedience. Home life is the God-appointed training ground of human character, for from the home life of the child springs the maturity of manhood, either for good or for evil. The only recorded acts of Our

Blessed Lord's childhood are acts of obedience—to God His Heavenly Father, and also to Mary and Joseph. He thus shows the special duty of childhood and of youth: to obey parents as the vice-regents of God. He, the great God Whom the Heavens and earth could not contain, submitted Himself to His parents. If He was sent on a message to a neighbor, it was the great Sender of the Apostles who delivered the message. If Joseph ever bade Him search for a tool that was lost, it was the Wisdom of God and the Shepherd in search of lost souls who was actually doing the seeking. If Joseph taught Him carpentry, He Who was taught was One Who had carpentered the universe, and Who would one day be put to death by the members of His own profession. If He made a yoke for the oxen of a neighbor, it was He Who would call Himself a yoke for men—and yet a burden that would be light. If they bade Him work in a little plot of garden ground, to train the creepers or water the flowers, it was He Who was the great Dresser of the vineyard of His Church Who took in hand the waterpot and the gardening tools. All men may ponder well the hint of a child subject to His parents, that no Heavenly call is ever to be trusted which bids one neglect the obvious duties that lie near to hand.

There is an Oriental proverb which says, "The first deities which the child has to acknowledge are his parents." Another says that "obedient children are as ambrosia to the gods." The parent is, to the child, God's representative; and in order that parents may not have a responsibility that will be too heavy for them, God gives each child a soul, as so much clay which their hands can mold in the way of truth and love. Whenever a child is given to parents, a crown is made for it in Heaven; and woe to those parents if that child is not reared with a sense of responsibility to acquire that crown.

The flower that is planted in the right place to absorb out of the earth and atmosphere the nutritive forces that it needs will grow. It toils not, neither does it spin, and yet its invisible machinery captures the sunbeams and converts them into flowers and fruit for the welfare of man. So, children placed in the right environment grow in age, too. Place a water wheel in a stream and it turns; place it in the rocks and it does not move. As long as we are in the wrong place, we cannot grow. The secret of the growth of Our Lord is that He started in the right place; He was bathed with the warmth and the light and refreshment of a home that was dedicated to God. One cannot put a bomb under a child and make it a man. Each thing has its own appointed law of growth, provided its roots are properly fixed. All growth is silent, and there is not a word out of the home of Nazareth in these eighteen long years between the finding in the temple and the marriage feast. Thus when nature is baptized in the fullness of the powers of spring, there is hardly a rustle. The whole movement takes place secretly and silently, for the new world comes up like the sound of a trumpet. The greatest moral structures grow from day to day without noise; God's kingdoms come without observation. So Our Lord stayed in His place, did His carpentry, was obedient to His parents, accepted the restraints of His position, met His cares with a transcendent disdain, drank in the sunlight of His Father's Faith, possessed His soul in perfect patience, although urged by deep sympathy and a throbbing desire to save man. It is in His human nature that Our Blessed Lord gives us a perfect example of obedience.

[61]

Necessity of Obedience

THERE IS A forgotten aspect of obedience to law—namely, that intelligence is related to obedience. It is only by obedience that we grow in wisdom. A scientist who would know the laws of nature must sit passively before nature. He may not dictate to nature its laws, nor may he impose his own intelligence upon nature; rather, the more passive he is before nature, the more nature will reveal its secrets. He who would play golf well must know how to hold the clubs aright, for here too wisdom is related to obedience. The more we obey the inherent laws of anything, the more that thing reveals itself to us. To obey God's laws because they are the ordinance of an All-wise and an All-loving God is the best means to discover the wisdom and the beauty of life. One whole Psalm of the Scriptures, Psalm 118, is devoted to the idea that in obedience to the ordinance of God, we grow in intelligence. Our Blessed Lord, developing this idea later on in His Life, said, "If any man will do the will of My Father, he shall know of the doctrine, whether it be of God or whether I speak of Myself." Because obedience is the secret of perfection and wisdom, which fact was revealed to us by Our Lord when He was subject to His parents, He insisted in His great upheaval of values that "unless you become as little children, you shall not enter the Kingdom of Heaven."

The great gates of the Kingdom, which are resistant to the poundings and thumpings of the mighty, will swing back at the simple touch of a child. No old people will ever enter the Kingdom of Heaven if they have grown old in their own conceit. Childlikeness, with its accompanying obedience, is an indispensable qualification for membership in His community. Childlikeness is not childishness. To be childish is to retain in maturity what should have been discarded at the threshold of manhood. Childlikeness, on the contrary, implies that with the mental breadth and practical strength and wisdom of maturity, there is associated the humility, trustfulness, spontaneity, and obedience of the child. It is the proud, and the bullies and prigs, who make social life difficult—the people who love the first places, who insist always on their own right, who refuse to serve unless they can be chairmen, who throw their weight around whether by fair means or by foul. Against all of these, Our Blessed Lord sets Himself: first of all, by being obedient to His parents, and then, at the end of His life, by taking a towel and washing the feet of His disciples.

If He Who is the Son of God makes Himself subject to His Mother and foster father in reparation for the sins of pride, then how shall children escape the sweet necessity of obedience to those who are their lawfully constituted superiors? The Fourth Commandment, "Thou shalt honor thy father and thy mother," has been broken by every generation since the dawn of man. At Nazareth, children were taught obedience by Him Who really is the Commandment. In this particular instance, where the Child is Divine, one might think that He at least would have reserved for Himself the right of "self-expression." Mary and Joseph, it seems, with great propriety could have opened the first "progressive school" in the history of Christianity—in which the child could do whatever He pleased; for the Child could never have displeased. And yet Our Lord says, "And He Who sent Me is with Me; He has not left Me all alone since what I do is always what pleases Him."

By making Himself subject to Mary and Joseph, the Divine Child proclaims authority in the home and in public life to be a power granted by God Himself. From this follows the duty of obedience, for the sake of God and of one's conscience. As later on He would tell Pilate that the civil authorities exercised no power except that given them from above, so now by His obedience He bears witness to the solemn truth that parents exercise their authority in the name of God. Thus parents have the most sacred claim on their children, because their first responsibility is to God. Obedience in the home is the foundation of obedience in the commonwealth, for in each instance conscience submits to a trustee of God's authority. If it be true that the world has lost its respect for authority, it is only because it lost it first in the home.

XI

Courtesy
and Honor

A Thousand Tiny Delicacies

POLITENESS IS A way of showing externally the internal regard we have for others. Good manners are the shadows cast by virtues. As the spoken word is the audible sign of an idea we have in our mind, so politeness is a telltale and token of reverence for others in our own spirit. Politeness differs from etiquette in two ways: etiquette can be a pose, a posture, or an air that is put on like a garment; politeness is a habit of the soul. Secondly, etiquette has certain rules for special occasions, such as what to do when you drop a fork under the table. On the contrary, politeness is a spirit which suffuses all situations and meets the requirements of a given situation without any specific rule to cover the case.

One wonders if politeness and courtesy have declined in our civilization. Schools do not teach courtesy and there are some homes that do not. But politeness never loses its hold on society because of the goodness and greatness of some souls. It is said of George Washington that many would slap him on the shoulder and call him "George." Yet he took off his hat and bowed his head to an old slave who first took off his hat, saying, "Good morning, General Washington." General Lafayette, who was in the company of Washington at the time, asked him why he bowed to the slave. The answer was, "I would not permit him to be a better gentleman than I!"

One of the elements of courtesy would certainly be attention to details in kindliness to others. The human heart is more satisfied with a thousand tiny delicacies scattered through the days and years than one sudden outburst and costly token of esteem, thereafter lapsing into forgetfulness and indifference. Our Divine Lord promised that those who would be put over the great things were those who were faithful in the little things. Boaz of Old Testament history was a man who not only greeted with courtesy, but also gave a blessing to the workers in his fields. Then he instructed the gleaners purposely to leave some of the sheaves after them that Ruth might have what she desired. His thoughtfulness extended not just to heroic sacrifice, but to trivial donations.

The courteous man will always give more than the law requires. Therefore, courtesy can manifest itself not only in trivialities but also in excesses. Judged by external standards, the widow's mite was too little a contribution to the temple, just as the penitent's costly ointment was too much in the eyes of a moneygrubber. But both had in them that inner generosity which is the essence of love's excess of the law. Courtesy, it would seem, must also be what St. Paul described as "love without hypocrisy." Love is to courtesy what the soul is to the body. Without it, we have formalism and stiffness but no real politeness. Courtesy is affection and not affectation. It reaches a point where, in a true lowliness of mind, one esteems others better than self. We know the worst that is in us and of that we can be certain, but we can never know the worst that is in others; we can at best only suspect it. Conscious of this, our feelings toward others become delicate and sensitive; they may even become deeply religious when they reach a point where we forgive others their discourtesies. This is done because we know that God Himself has forgiven our greater transgressions.

Politeness is not a sign of weakness when it is love without hypocrisy; it is a sign of strength because it involves considerable self-control on our part. Its root is sympathy, and sympathy is based on a consciousness of the natural order of our membership in the human race and our fellowship in the spiritual order with the redeemed sons of God the Father, through Christ Our Lord. The unsympathetic man is never courteous. St. Francis of Assisi explained it well: "Courtesy is one of the properties of God Who gives His sun and rain to the just and the unjust by courtesy; and courtesy is the sister of charity by which hatred is extinguished and love is cherished." When all is said and done, the truly courteous man is the truly religious man. As Hilaire Belloc wrote:

> *Of courtesy, it is much less*
> *Than courage of heart, or holiness,*
> *Yet in my walks it seems to me*
> *That the Grace of God is courtesy.*

[63]

Politeness

WHAT HAS HAPPENED to politeness? One cynic said that it is "an acceptable hypocrisy." Another said that he would be so polite to his wife that she would think he was a perfect stranger. Drivers of automobiles, hidden behind the anonymity of a windshield, regard other motorists as trespassers; they also often hold as a fundamental creed that every year ought to be "leap" year for the pedestrians. Boys call girls by their last names; Northerners criticize Southerners for saying "you-all," claiming that if they had manners they would say "youse guys." At parties during conversation, eyes roam around the room as if searching for a less boring conversationalist.

The passing of courtesy is one with the modern forgetfulness of the value of the individual person. The three totalitarian movements of the twentieth century absorbed the person into either the class, the race, or the nation. Furthermore, with the denial of the soul no one has value within himself, only in relation to something else. Courtesy is paid to those who sell it at wholesale or to those who permit a sharing of their limelight. But courtesy is not of these things; it is the giving to everyone his human due as interpreted by love. It is not something that is learned at a charm school, but rather is the sister of charity which banishes hatred and cherishes love.

Courtesy is based upon the Scriptural idea that everybody is better than we are. Cooks, housemaids, delivery boys, truck drivers are all men and women with joys and sorrows, hopes and aspirations, like our own. We cannot know them on the inside; but we can know ourselves on the inside. Since there is so little commendable in the garden of our heart, which we know is so full of weeds, then in the unknown garden of their hearts we must believe that there may grow flowers which demand our reverence and respect. This is what is meant by "in honor preferring one another."

A false idea is abroad that the way to make oneself popular is to flatter everyone you meet: "I hear all the great things you are doing, Joe; keep up the good work." Though there are some men who like to be told what they think of themselves, the fact is that the really lovable people are those who love others. In colleges, factories, in shops, and in business houses, it is invariably true that he who thinks the least of himself and the most about others is most popular. The whole world is like the miller "who cared for nobody—no, not he—because nobody cared for him."

Courtesy is kindness without parade of favors; it is tender and affectionate in looks and acts, always giving preference to others in every little enjoyment. Alexander the Great used to call his soldiers his "fellow foot-men"; Aristotle never taught from a podium, but walked among his disciples to be one with them. And Christ the Son of the Living God washed the feet of His disciples, saying, "You hail Me as the Master and the Lord and you are right; it is what I am. Why then, if I have washed your feet, I Who am the Master and Lord, you in your turn ought to wash each other's feet. I have been setting you an example which will teach you, in your turn, to do what I have done for you."

There was no sense of loss of dignity in this humble action, for twice He told them that He was their Lord. Making ourselves little for others does not destroy true greatness. Nor is it to be forgotten that at the moment when He girded Himself with the towel of a servant, the apostles were quarreling among themselves as to who should be the greatest among them. True courtesy descended from heaven and dwelt amongst us, and is extended to those who are undeserving of it. As St. Francis of Assisi said, "Know, dearest brother, that courtesy is one of God's own properties, Who sendeth His rain and His sunshine upon the just and the unjust out of His great courtesy."

Washington Irving once warned against the sham courtesy in which the eye is taught to brighten, the lip to smile, and the countenance to irradiate a semblance of friendly welcome, while the bosom is unwarmed by a single spark of genuine goodness. Just as an oily smoothness is the opposite of true charity in the soul, so is roughness and uncouthness in the soul that claims to be religious. Christianity, when practiced, is the etiquette of heaven.

[64]

Honor

ONE DAY THE wind said to the keyhole, "See how well I whistle?" "No," the keyhole said to the wind, "you mean how well I whistle." The old woman put a paper in the keyhole and then the keyhole and the wind no longer whistled. To the people of Corinth, Paul wrote such a message concerning those who boasted of having a certain preeminence or honor: "After all, friend, who is it that gives thee this preeminence? What powers hast thou that did not come to thee by gift? And if they came to thee by gift, why does thou boast of them, as if there were no gift in question?" As the earth is receptive to the rain and the sunflower to the light of the sun, so man is the vessel into which is poured both gifts and honors.

Honors, when the truth of receptivity is forgotten, tend to swell and inflat the ego. It is one thing for a man to wear the purple and another thing for the purple to wear a man. Every human being is like a sponge: some sponges reach a point of saturation very quickly —some humans reach a point where they can absorb no more honors; they get filled very quickly. From that point on, they drip the honor as the sponge drips water. If Daniel, after he was released from the lion's den, had gone about snapping his suspenders to attract attention, he would have proven himself unworthy of the honor of release. It will always be found that the man who has no Ph.D. or who has never worked very hard for a Ph.D. will put more store in an honorary degree than a man who went through blood and sweat and tears to get it. The ass that carried the Egyptian goddess, according to the legend, swelled with the opinion that all those crouches, cringes, bows were made for him. The peacock is beautiful while you look at its feathers, but ugly when you look at its feet.

Honors generally have a bad effect on character, unless they are tempered by humility in their possession and adversity as their precursor. First let us deal with humility, or a recognition that the honor has nothing whatever to do with character. One does not wear gold medals in the shower. On the contrary, the lark that soars so high is the bird that builds its nest so low; the branches that bear the richest fruit are those which hang closest to the ground; the nightingale sings sweetly, but in the shade and when things are at rest. Paul, after his conversion, wrote that he was not worthy to be called an apostle; thirty years later he wrote to the Ephesians that he was the least of the saints; and then, as he approached martyrdom, he told his good friend Timothy that he was the chief of sinners. That man wears honor best who knows in his own heart that he does not deserve it, and who, in the face of becoming more and more, makes himself less and less. The wise man never vaunts his learning; the real saints are the hardest to recognize, the spurious saints wear placards. Humility is the condition of greatness.

But the greatest preventative of honors going to one's head is to have them preceded by adversity and sorrow and tribulation. When James and John asked to be on either side of Our Lord in His Kingdom, He asked them if they could drink of the cup of His Passion. Many a man is called an enemy who is really a friend. Those who falsely accuse, wound, and harass may in the end be the greatest friends of the soul. They who lay crosses on another can be the creative helpers of character. Out of the humiliation and the trial and the crucifixion can come meekness, resignation, and closeness to God which could never come from kindness. The violin may not like the musician that pulls and tugs at its strings, but in the end it sees that it all made for the sweetest melody. No one can ever be sure if he is consecrated to God unless he has passed through the crucible of suffering. But to gain value from such crosses, one must see that they come not from the hand of man, but from the Father Himself. When Peter wielded his sword in the garden, Our Lord opposed to that sword His cup, saying, "Shall I not drink the cup which the Father gave Me?" All trials, when seen as ingredients of a cup which the Father has poured, become sweet. When dishonor as well as honor are seen as coming from the hand of God, then the human element becomes secondary. God can be thanked for His trials as well as His blessings.

XII

Three Ages
of Man

Teenagers

WHEN DOES ONE cease to be a child and begin to be a teenager? It happens at that point when affections of free choice are preferred to the natural affections in a family. A child wants to be loved and cared for; a teenager wants to love and care for others. A teenager is, therefore, more outgoing for the simple reason that he has discovered his personality, his ego, his separateness from others. Up until that point, he is like a chick in a shell. Now he pecks away at the shell of the family until he begins to emerge in his own right.

The first characteristic, therefore, of a teenager is the affirmation of self when he begins to discover himself. The boy begins to scratch his name on back fences, or on pews when he goes to church on Sunday; he frequents machines that will stamp out his name on aluminum strips. He protests against going in a group to visit Uncle Bill. Identification charms begin to make their appearance as if to declare, "I am I."

Not only the mind is discovered, but also the body. The boy begins to carry a comb; the girl a lipstick. As if in protest against being submerged in the family group, they go to the opposite extreme of finding companionship with those of their own age who alone can understand them, because they too have budding personalities. They develop a form of language which is peculiar to themselves in order to set themselves apart from the rest of society. They feel that a certain kind of talk or slang, a queer affectation in dress, all contribute to stamping them as "originals." Overalls, dungarees, loud socks, queer hairdos are all so many external signs of a youth which is seeking to set itself apart from the rest of the world. The very desire to attract attention, even at times by antisocial acts, is another superficial manifestation of the greatest consciousness that comes to any living thing in this world—namely, the emergence of individuality and personality.

But on the other hand, while there is this stress on individuality, there is also associated with teenagers a contrary tendency, which is that of imitativeness. While they want to be apart from others, they still want to be the same with their own group. The contradiction is not as real as it is apparent. Their ego is affirmed against adults, but their want of identity, or teenage monotony, is due to conformity with their own age group. What makes the teenager difficult to understand is this terrific tension which is set up in him between personal responsibility on the one hand and social conformity on the other hand. He becomes very fearful of doing anything which is not accepted by the group, or which is not "the thing." While he wants to be himself, he condemns himself to being like others. Hence the sameness of dress or costume found among teenagers and even among youths in college. There is not only mimicry in dress, but the same idols must be worshipped, whether they be bandleaders, movie actors, or singers. Failure to conform to the idols erected by the teenage masses is to court an ostracism which few youths can bear.

Because of this tension between wanting to be like others and wanting to be unlike others, there is considerable restlessness in youth. Though they pride themselves on the fact that there are no friendships closer than teenage friendships, wiser heads know that there is nothing quite as volatile. But this restlessness is, for the moment, essential for their development. A time will come when they will reconcile personality with social conformity, when they will see that they have certain rights that are personal and certain duties that are social. Above all, they will learn how wrong George Bernard Shaw was when he said that it is a pity that youth has been wasted on the young. Later on they will see that the Good Lord knew it was better to put the illusions of life at the beginning in order that we might better discover the purpose of living as we grow closer to eternity.

[66]

The Teenagers

ADOLESCENCE, or teenage, is the short hour between the springtime and the summer of life. Before the teenage is reached, there is very little individuality or personality, but as soon as the teens begin, the emotional life takes on the character of its environment, as water takes its shape from the vessel into which it is poured. The adolescent begins to be conscious of himself and others, and for that reason begins to live in solitude. The youth is more lonely than many parents and teachers know; perhaps the teenager agonizes in a greater solitariness of spirit than at any other time in life until maturity when the sense of unrequited guilt begins to weigh down the human soul.

As the teenager projects his personality to the world round about him, he seems to get farther away from it. Between his soul and the world there seems to be a wall. There is never a complete self-analysis. As it takes an infant a long time to coordinate his eyes and his hands, so it takes the teenager a long time to adjust himself completely to this great broad world to which he feels so strangely related. He cannot yet take it in stride; novelty, new emotional experiences, great dreams and hopes flood his soul, each demanding attention and satisfaction. He does not confide his emotional states to others; he just lives. It is hard for the adult to penetrate the shell into which the teenager crawls. Like Adam after his fall, he hides from discovery.

Along with this loneliness, there goes a great desire to be noticed, for egotism is a vice that has to be mastered early in youth. This craving for attention accounts for the loudness in manner of some teenagers. Not only does it attract the gaze of others, but it also experiences a latent sense of rebellion against others, and affirms that he is living for himself in his own way and as he pleases.

Along with this quality of impenetrability, the teenager becomes an imitator. Being in rebellion against the fixed and being governed largely by fleeting impressions, he becomes like a chameleon, which takes on the colors of the objects upon which it is placed. He becomes a hero or a bandit, a saint or a thief, depending on the environment or his reading or his companions. This spirit of imitation reveals itself in the dress. Overalls, shirts sticking out of trousers, haircuts fashioned after the savages of Oceania—all these become universal among youths who are afraid to march "against the grain."

There are few natural leaders among teenagers, most of them being content to follow others. In this unconscious mimicry of others is a moral danger, for character is dependent on the ability to say "No." Unless education can give to teenagers a training of the will, many of them will slip into adulthood and become slaves of propaganda and public opinion the rest of their lives. Instead of creating, they imitate. To create is to recognize the spirit in things; to imitate is to submerge personality at the lowest level of the mass.

Elders must not be too critical of the teenagers, particularly when they rebel against them. From one point of view they are not in rebellion against restraint, but against their elders for not giving them a goal and purpose in life. The teenager's protest is not conscious. He does not know why he hates his parents, why he is rebellious against authority, why his fellow teenagers are becoming more and more delinquent. But the real reason is under the surface; it is an unconscious protest against a society which has not given him a pattern of life. The schools he attends have never stressed restraint, discipline, or self-control. Many of the teachers have defined freedom and even democracy as the right to do whatever you please. When this temporary phase of rebellion is past, the teenagers will look for some great cause to which they can make a total dedication. They must have an ideal. In many instances today, they have no greater object of worship than to wrap their emotional lives around a sports hero, a movie star, a rock band leader or a pop singer. This sign of decaying civilizations will pass when the catastrophe comes. Then youth will look for a different type to imitate—namely, either heroes or saints. A sad commentary it is on our civilization that the teen-agers have never rallied around our war heroes. This is because they are not yet ready for the more solid ideal. But it will come. And when it does, education must be careful lest in reacting against "progressive" education devoid of discipline, they follow the false sacrificial gods, like the youths of Europe in prostrating before Nazism, Fascism, and Communism. The latent capacity for doing the brave and heroic which is in every youth will soon come to the surface, and when it does, please God, it will be both for heroes and saints that they center their affection. The ascetic ideal has passed away from the elders, but God sends fresh generations into the world to give the world a fresh start. Our teenagers will one day find their right ideals, in love of country and love of God and particularly the latter, for it is the function of religion to make possible to men sacrifices which in the face of reason or egotism would never come to the surface.

[67]

The Danger of Middle Age

THE EMPHASIS of the modern mind is on youth; almost all advertising is directed to youth. Music is, for the most part, directed to juveniles; forums specialize in youth telling the world what it ought to do, before youth has learned how to obey.

The stress on youth manifests itself also in early retirement age enforced by industry and government. It is practically a negation that experience is a teacher, and forgets that though the body grows old, the mind does not necessarily grow old with it. Moses, for example, was eighty when God called him to lead the Israelites out of the bondage of Egypt; Cato at eighty began the study of Greek; Verdi wrote his Ave Maria at eighty-five; Goethe wrote *Faust* when he was beyond eighty.

But what of middle age? What is apt to be its greatest weakness? In middle age a man begins to know himself, and to find out one's limitations is always an occasion for sorrow. Youth looks forward in hope, expectation, and promise; middle age sees that not all dreams and hopes come true. Youth presses forward because of what will be; middle age becomes lost in the drabness of what is. Reality confronts middle age without the mask which it wore in youth. One is no longer sitting in the theater watching a romance; in middle age, one is taken behind the scenes and allowed to see the shabbiness of the costumes, the tinsel instead of the gold, and the painted forests.

Success there may have been. The middle-aged man holds in his hands most of the things he coveted. The danger is that he may settle for just that, refusing to see anything beyond success and the monotony of repeating it.

Money becomes important not because it has value to purchase, but because it is "more"; it gives a sense of power; it salves the conscience by making the possessor believe that he must *be* worth something since he *has* something of worth. Bigger and bigger barns must be built. Expansion becomes the rule, not only around the middle but also around his factories or his stores. There is no slackening of his ability to do things; there is, however, a complete inability to decide what is worth doing. The hardening of the will not to make other choices than those that have been made in the past is one of the greatest tragedies of middle age. Men can be long at sea and yet make such a short voyage.

The desire for possession, which is God-given, often tends in middle age to become a passion. It could very well be the sublimation of the carnal excesses of youth. When the flesh becomes jaded, a substitute is often sought in the unlimited desire for *things*. Every power of the mind and body is pressed into service to augment the store of what can never be used in a lifetime. Finally, money becomes the scale and the measure of everything; it determines the worth of a man rather than his virtue. The neighbor with the most sublime dedication to truth is regarded as an impractical visionary, unless he reads the market quotations. The purseless saint is nothing. The heart of the modern man points not to eternal hills, but to golden mountains.

There is a limit to natural or real wealth—for example, the amount of ice cream a boy can eat; the number of beds in which one can sleep a night; the amount of food that can be eaten in a day. But there is another kind of wealth that is infinite—namely, the measure, or the token, or the symbol of real wealth, such as money, credit, stocks and bonds. Because these are without horizon or limit, it is possible for them to become a kind of god, and therefore an object of worship. It was this danger of allowing the soul to become materialistic in middle age which prompted Him Who was rich with heaven to become poor as a carpenter to say, "Woe to the rich." But only because they have their reward. The using of wealth as an exchange for spiritual and heavenly reward makes the rich man the wise man.

[68]

The Tide Comes In

A LITTLE OVER one percent of our biological efficiency is surrendered on an average every year. At this rate, at about the age of eighty it is completely exhausted. What then? That question is evaded. In the meantime many act like a child on the beach who builds a castle of sand, extends ramparts, mounts towers, constructs moats, and fortifies outer walls. All the while, the tide comes in. At first the child is unconcerned; then as it lays siege to the outer fortifications, he begins to bail out the water. Suddenly he gets caught in the tide. Oh, if he had only learned to *swim!* But the child happened to live in a generation that never gave thought to the sea, and was never taught to think of the tides—until he was caught in it.

The moral is evident: Pile is added to pile, stock to stock, and bond to bond; vitamins are swallowed, but with medicated survival there still comes the moment of non-survival, as far as time is concerned.

All this is better told in the parable showing that a man's life does not consist in the abundance of things he possesses.

> There was a rich man whose lands yielded a heavy
> crop: and he debated in his mind, What am I to do,
> with no room to store my crops in? Then he said,
> This is what I will do; I will pull down my barns, and
> build greater ones, and there I shall be able to store
> all my harvest and all the goods that are mine; and
> then I will say to my soul, Come, soul, thou hast
> goods in plenty laid up for many years to come; take
> thy rest now, eat, drink, and make merry. And God
> said, Thou fool, this night thou must render up thy
> soul; and who will be master now of all thou hast laid
> by? Thus it is with the man who lays up treasure for
> himself, and has no credit with God.
>
> (LUKE 12:16–20)

But the castle in the sand and the filling of the barns both prefigure the end of this life, but not of life itself. The Greeks had two words for life: one the natural or biological life, which is common to worms and to highly developed bipeds. That word is *bios*. But the Greeks had another word which also meant life—*zoe*—but which is used throughout the New Testament and refers to eternal life. The end of the spiral of the *bios* does not mean the decline of the *zoe*. On the contrary, it often happens that the spiritual life increases as the biological life declines. So true is this that in the liturgy through the centuries, the day on which saints die or are martyred is called their *natalitia*, or birthday. The reason is this: age is measured by nearness to the source of life. A child of six is older than a child of four because he is two years more distant from the source of his physical life, his parents. But there is a source of life other than our parents, and that is the Divine Life. It follows that the closer we get to it, the younger we become. That is why the day on which saints die and are born to God eternally is called their birthday.

The mind often grows stronger with age; hence the ridiculousness of enforced retirement at sixty-five. If the mind were only material, it would suffer the lot of the body and decline with it. But the higher a spiritual life is, the more independent it is of the physical frame. In Goethe's *Faust,* when the aged hero feels that night is about to close upon his eyes, at that instant his world becomes flooded with inner illumination. John had the great vision of the Apocalypse in his old days.

The castle in the sands and the bigger barns represent the two sides of contemporary civilization that blind man to the inner life. The first is technology, the second is administration. It has almost reached a point where it is difficult for an American to believe that anyone should want any other aim in life than to make more money and to be more comfortable. And all the while, the tide keeps coming in, and the Divine Judge comes. What then?

XIII

The Family

Love Dreams

EVERY PERSON carries within his heart a blueprint of the one he loves. What seems to be "love at first sight" is actually the fulfillment of desire, the realization of a dream. Plato, sensing this, said that all knowledge is recollection from a previous existence. This is not true as he states it, but it *is* true if one understands it to mean that we already have an ideal in us—one which is made by our thinking, our habits, our experiences, and our desire. Otherwise how would we know immediately, on seeing persons or things, that we loved them? Before meeting certain people we already have a pattern and mold of what we like and what we do not like; certain persons fit into that pattern, others do not.

When we hear music for the first time, we either like or dislike it. We judge it by the music we already have heard in our own hearts. Jittery minds which cannot long repose in one object of thought or in continuity of an idea love music which is distracting, excited, and jittery. Calm minds like calm music: the heart has its own secret melody, and one day when the score is played the heart answers, "This is it."

So it is with love. A tiny architect works inside the human heart drawing sketches of the ideal love from the people it sees, from the books it reads, from its hopes and daydreams, in the fond hope that the eye may one day see the ideal and the hand touch it. Life becomes satisfying the moment the dream is seen walking, and the person appears as the incarnation of all that one loves. The liking is instantaneous—because, actually, it has been there waiting for a long time.

God, too, has within Himself blueprints of everything in the universe. As the architect has in his mind a plan of the house before the house is built, so God has in His Mind an archetypal idea of every flower, bird, tree, springtime, and melody. There never was a brush touched to canvas nor a chisel to marble without some great preexisting idea. So, too, every atom and every rose is realization and concretion of an idea existing in the Mind of God from all eternity. All creatures below man correspond to the pattern God has in His Mind. A tree is truly a tree because it corresponds to God's idea of a tree.

In marriage too, love begins with a dream. As a French author put it, "To know a woman at the hour of desire, one must first respect her at the exquisite hour of dream." Love then is an act of faith, a declaration of the unseen as the real.

If ideals are not high, if the blueprints of love are not beautiful, then the marriage itself will not be beautiful. As some minds can listen to the barbaric tom-toms of anti-music, so there are hearts that can be satisfied with a body without a soul. Hence the need of a moral preparation for marriage. St. Francis de Sales once said that "in marriage, one takes a vow. But it is the only instance where a vow is taken without a novitiate. If it had a year of novitiate, how few would enter into it." The novitiate of marriage must necessarily embrace two elements: the spiritualization of personal lives in order that the sublime architectural blueprint of life's partner be formed within, and a constant prayer that God Himself will dispose historical conditions to make the dreams come true.

With marriage and its ripening with the fruit of love, there will dawn a new understanding that everyone carries with him a blueprint of the one he loves, and that One is God. The other partner then is seen as the Lord's John the Baptist, preparing the way and making straight His paths. God was just half seen through the flesh, but thanks to life's companionship, one becomes more and more attuned to the Divine Fork that gave the original melody on the wedding day.

Love which began as Passion, then became an Act, and now in the autumn of life becomes once again a Desire born of Memory; the new "passionless passion" strains at the leash of life to be one with Life, Truth and Love. The words of Our Lord now repeatedly come to their minds: "Those who are found worthy to attain that other world, and resurrection from the dead, take neither wife nor husband." That means that sex, which reflected the animal kingdom, will not exist in eternity, but love, which is a reflection of God's unbodied essence, will remain their eternal ecstasy. There will be no faith in Heaven, for we will already see; there will be no hope in Heaven, for we will already possess; but there will always be love. God is Love!

[70]

Motherhood

HUMAN MOTHERHOOD is twofold in its essence, and is a more complex thing than motherhood among the animals. There is, first, the physical act of giving birth, which women share with all of nature. As the tree bears fruit and the hen hatches her eggs, so every mother, by the act of birth, is bound up with the life of all living things, and of her it may be rightly said, "Blessed is the fruit of thy womb."

But human motherhood has a second and far lordlier aspect—that of the spirit. The soul of a child does not emanate from the mother's soul or body, but is freshly created by God Himself, Who infuses it into the body of the unborn child. Physiological motherhood is glorified by this cooperation with God Himself, Who fathered the baby's soul and then permitted a woman to clothe it in her flesh. The human mother does not bear a mere animal but a human being, made to the image and likeness of the God Who created him.

Every child born of woman has, then, two fathers: his earthly father, without whom he could not have life, and his Heavenly Father, without Whom he could not possess a personality, a soul, an irreplaceable "I." The mother is the essential partner through whom both fathers work. Her own relationship to the child has two resulting aspects: there is the mother–baby aspect, wherein the child is physically and almost absolutely dependent on the mother. But there is also the mother–person relationship (expressed at baptism, when the child is given its own name). This confirms the dignity and separate selfhood of even the smallest infant, and foreshadows his right eventually to lead his own life and to depart from his parents to cling to a wife of his own.

Every birth requires a submission and a disciplining. The earth itself must undergo harrowing before it passively accepts the seed. In woman, the submission is not passive: it is sacrificial, consciously creative, and for this selflessness her whole nature has been formed. It is well known that women are capable of far more sustained sacrifice than men; a man may be a hero in a crisis, and then slip back to mediocrity. He lacks the moral endurance which enables a woman to be heroic through the years, months, days, and even seconds of her life, when the very repetitive monotony of her tasks wears down the spirit. Not only a woman's days, but her nights—not only her mind, but her body must share in the Calvary of motherhood. That is why women have a surer understanding of the doctrine of redemption than men have: they have come to associate the risk of death with life in childbirth, and to understand the sacrifice of self to another through the many months preceding it.

In a mother, two of the great spiritual laws are united into one: love of neighbor and cooperation with God's grace—and both of them are applied in a unique way. For love of neighbor, to anyone except a mother, is love of a non-self; a mother's neighbor during pregnancy is one with herself, yet to be loved differently from the self. The sacrifice sometimes involved in neighborly love now takes place within her flesh; the agent and the object of her sacrifice are both contained within her.

And the cooperation with grace in a mother, although it may be unconscious on her part, yet makes her a partner of Divinity: every human mother is, in a sense, "overshadowed by the Holy Ghost." Not a priest, and yet endowed with a kind of priestly power, she, too, brings God to man, and man to God. She brings God to man by accepting her mother's role, and thus permitting God to infuse a new soul into her body for it to bear. She brings man to God in childbirth itself, when she allows herself to be used as an instrument by which another child of God is born into the world.

If motherhood is seen as a matter involving only a woman and a man, it is seen too astigmatically and without the honor that is its due. For to comprehend the real significance of motherhood, we must include the spiritual element that goes to make a child—we must see the human woman cooperating with her husband, the father of the human baby, and with God, the Father of a soul that is eternal, indestructible, and unlike any other ever formed throughout the history of the world. Thus every human motherhood involves a partnership with the Divine.

[71]

Freedom and the Child

HE WHO GIVES freedom takes a risk, but it must be taken. God foresaw the risk of making man free, and planned redemption from the slavery of sin. Parents, too, run a risk when they give their children liberty.

In the course of history there are two extreme errors: one, of too little freedom; the other, of too much. One would dam up the river; the other would destroy its banks and make a swamp.

There are also the two extremes of: "Don't you do it" and "I don't care." Life for some children is one perpetual "don't." A child of five was kept in during a storm; his mother was sewing as she chatted with a friend. "Don't do that, Freddy," she said as the child beat a tattoo on a carpet with his feet. He stopped his feet, then he began thumping his fingers. "Don't make a noise, Freddy." The boy turned to the window and then began drawing pictures on the windowpane. "Don't mark that window" was followed by "Don't go into the hall," as Freddy was looking for some way to escape from the "don't." The little boy with a resigned air remained perfectly still for a moment and then, with a long drawn-out sigh, he said, "Mom, is there anything that I can do?"

The other extreme is the "Do whatever you please" attitude. A child who always played games that had no rules and "out of bounds" began to hate life that was so capricious. He finally complained to his mother, "Must I always do what I want to?"

A father who was listening to the mother read a psychology book that allowed unrestrained freedom said to her, "Where does it say we are to apply that free hand we are supposed to have?"

Too often freedom is regarded as a source of all indiscipline. Repressive measures then are resorted to, which create fuel for rebellion. St. Augustine recalled the bitterness of his first days of school. He wrote, "I would prefer death rather than to be a child again."

Liberty often permits indiscipline, but it does not cause it. Liberty is merely a condition, and out of it may come slavery or self-government. Liberty is the condition of both obedience and disobedience.

Liberty manifests itself sometimes in sheer negation on the part of the child, and sometimes by bare affirmation. To will to destroy this liberty under pretext of order is to destroy the child. Nothing inferiorizes the child more than brutal imposition or constraint which prevents the unfolding of personality.

The education of liberty in a child must possess two qualities:

1. It must be gradual.
2. It must be associated with the moral order.

It must appeal to the conscience of the educator and also to the one who is educated.

There is to be a gradual unfolding of liberty according to the age of the child. In infancy, this liberty is developed sometimes by sheer imitation or by suggestion which prompts the child to act spontaneously, or as if he did not feel that any order was being given.

The peak of moral authority is in the attitude of the parent who says, "I ask for obedience, because I am responsible before God for you." The child in his turn, if morally educated, will have in his heart the sentiment, "I will obey my parents because they take the place of God in my home." Where there is love, there is obedience; where there is obedience, there is the discovery of the secrets of happiness, as the scientist, by obeying the laws of nature, learns more of their secrets.

[72]

Spanking

IF THE WORD "spanking" may be used as a symbol of any kind of discipline, it is safe to say that there is a direct ratio between juvenile delinquency and want of discipline in the home. Putting it more lightly: two of the causes contributing most to juvenile delinquency have been, first, safety razors which have dispensed with the razor strap, and, second, garages which have done away with the woodshed. If one may take the verbiage of a ship, spanking is known as "stern" punishment. It is a form of depressing one end to impress the other end. It takes much less time than reasoning and penetrates more quickly to the seat of wisdom. There almost seems to be a very providential ordering between a parent and a child. God gave parents a hand, and he also gave the child an extremely well-padded part of his anatomy; one was made for the other in extreme cases.

The former headmaster of Phillips Andover Academy said, "I was whipped as a child, thank goodness. But time and time again I had to throw boys out of the school, and all they needed was a good spanking."

The Divine word of God in Scripture is certainly not opposed to discipline on the part of the parent, but rather recommends it. The Book of Proverbs states, "A rod for the back of him who is devoid of understanding." And again, "He that spareth the rod, hateth his son; but he that loves him chasteneth him betimes." Scripture does not seem to anticipate any evil effects from spanking: "Withhold not correction from the child, for if thou beatest him with a rod, he shall not die." Later on we read, "Chasten the son while there is hope, and let not thy soul spare for his crying."

Not very long ago, a child psychologist who had written much against spanking saying that it was "cruel" was arrested for locking his crying children in the car for eight hours while he and his wife went to the theater and to dinner. One is not to fear evil results because the child is overpowered. Every child is intellectually overpowered by his teacher, inasmuch as there is the superiority of truth; he is musically overpowered when he starts trumpet lessons, and he is physically overpowered when he takes boxing lessons.

If parents say they feel ashamed afterward, this is because their discipline may have been excessive and out of all proportion to the offense. But these same people are not the least bit ashamed when they reprimand a cook.

If it be said that spanking is the expression of an authoritarian system, let it be admitted that it is not an expression of authoritarianism, but authority. It is to be noted that in the commandments of God, the first three express our duties to God. The last six commandments are duties to neighbor. In between is the fourth commandment, which is the duty that is owed to parents by children. The very order of the commandments indicates that God intended the parents to take His place in the home, and the obedience which is due them is the reflection of the obedience which is due to God Himself.

There is nothing that develops character so much as a pat on the back, provided it is given often enough, hard enough, and low enough. Spanking is one of the most easily understood lessons in the world. It requires no explanation and no fine points are involved. It is quick, clean-cut, clears the air, allows no long periods of disfavor, and helps the parent by preventing an accumulation of emotional worries.

[73]

Duties of Children to Parents

SOME LEARN what is right only by having their fingers burned. Psychologists who suggested that children never be restrained and be permitted to do whatever they wanted to do have learned the folly of their theories by the heavy harvest of juvenile delinquents. From the beginning they misunderstood the mentality of children who are not happy when they are left undisciplined and undirected, for children love to be under guidance and direction. They may often test the limits of their liberty and sometimes chafe under the necessity of having their license restrained, but as dogs want a master, so children want parents who guide them.

Obedience is the law of the universe and without it the stars and the planets would fall in chaos and anarchy. The scientist learns the laws of nature only by obedience; he must sit patiently at the lap of Mother Nature and watch attentively all her actions. Once he begins to dictate how nature should operate, he shuts the door of wisdom in his face. The more passive the scientist is before the heavens, the more quickly the heavens tell the story of their fiery encampment in the skies.

St. Paul in a few sentences once gave the true relationship between parents and children. To children he wrote: "You who are children must show obedience in the Lord to your parents; it is your duty—Honor thy father and thy mother—that is the first commandment which has a promise attached to it. So it shall go well with thee, and thou shalt live long to enjoy the land." It is to be carefully noted that all arbitrary commands on the part of the parents fall outside the scope of this advice; the children are not bound to obey every whim and fancy. There is a limitation imposed for their sake, namely, "in the Lord." The parents can claim obedience because they themselves are under obedience to the Lord: authority does not start with them; it channels through them. They are not the source of law any more than Pilate, who was told that he would have no authority if it did come to him from above.

The parents, in giving commands, have this thought in the background: "I ask obedience of you because I am obedient to the Lord and responsible to Him." Then the children will understand that in obeying their parents, they are obeying the Lord. Though it is never analyzed, it is certainly true the reason parents complain, "I cannot do a thing with them" is because they never do a thing with themselves. One cannot expect the second floor of a building to stand if one pulls out the first floor; neither can we expect the children to respect their parents when their parents do not respect the God Who gave them their children.

A young boy who would climb into a boat and say, "I am starting off for New Zealand" would be restrained by his elders—it is to be hoped. But there would be less fear if he were placed on a ship with a good and wise captain to guide him. Parents, to some extent, are like captains of ocean liners; they know all storms and winds and currents, know where to anchor and what pitfalls to avoid. But it is not their experience which gives them authority over their children; it is rather that, as windows transmit the light of the sun, so they communicate to their children their own obedience to the Lord.

Juvenile delinquency may be corrected in this or that individual, but the root of it is beyond the children themselves. Every child is given to the parents by God as so much wax or clay to be molded into the image and resemblance of Life and Truth and Love. If the parents take their eyes off the Model, the image will become imperfect. Only those who have learned how to obey know how to command. As the dispensing of money should never be given to anyone who has not worked hard to earn it, so neither should the dispensing of authority be given to him who has not served in the ranks. If the parents themselves are like pendulums separated from the clock, because they have uprooted themselves from obedience to the Divine, how shall they, with justice, tell the children that they must honor their elders? When the big wheel breaks off the axle, all the little gears cease to work. The disobedience of children increases in direct ratio and proportion as the parents decline honor to the God above them.

[74]

Duties of Parents to Children

IN THE LAST ARTICLE the problem of juvenile delinquency was discussed in terms of children being disobedient to parents. It was pointed out that because parents are not obedient to the Lord from Whom they derive their authority, children refuse to be obedient to them. A young man sentenced to be electrocuted was visited by his parents in his cell. He said to them, "If it had not been for you, I should never be here." The father, speaking for the mother also, answered, "But we never told you to do any harm." "No," he rejoined, "but you never told me to do any good." The child who is allowed to do anything he pleases will eventually identify good with whatever he wants to do—whether it be stealing or raping. It was no wonder that Plato, seeing a child do some serious mischief, went and reprimanded the father for it.

But the other side of the problem is, what is to be the attitude of parents to their children? St. Paul tells them, "You who are fathers, do not rouse your children to resentment; the training, the disciplines in which you bring them up must come from the Lord." Parents can irritate children, provoke them to wrath, which is the opposite of being too soft and indifferent to their wrongdoings. The Chinese have a proverb that when a son is born into a family, a bow and arrow are hung before the gate. The Psalmist used the same analogy: "Children are like arrows in a warrior's hand. Happy whose quiver is well filled with these; their cause will not be set aside when they plead against their enemies at the gate." Kahlil Gibran in his beautiful poem on children says that when God gives parents children, He sets up the target which is Himself:

> You are the bows from which your children
> as living arrows are sent forth
>   The Archer sees the mark upon the path of the
> infinite, and He bends you with His might that His
> arrows may go swift and far.
>   Let your bending in the Archer's hand be for
> gladness;
>   For even as He loves the arrow that flies, so
> He loves also the bow that is stable.

The parent, who holds the bow, must be careful not to abuse and rankle the arrow. Discipline and authority are not the same as exasperating and tantalizing severity. To provoke children may gain a sullen submission, but the child himself is smart enough to know of the injustice. Parents can incite resentment in children in several ways: one is by giving too many commands, with the result that the child hears none. There recently appeared in a magazine a list of some of the directions that children never hear; one of them was, "Kiss your Aunt Lucy." When the requirement is more than can be reasonably rendered, it becomes an annoyance and a vexation. Another way to make children think less of their parents is continually to blame them for the wrong they have done, or else give all commandments in terms of "Don't." To condemn when there is no sure ground for complaint is to sting the child with injustice. The child who is never encouraged or praised when he does well, but always criticized when he does wrong, is apt to feel there is no reason for doing the things that are good except to avoid a scolding.

Correction and submission are to be given in the spirit of the Lord. The parents who know themselves to be disciples of the Lord know best how to make disciples of their own children. Children are much more sensitive than is generally believed; their growing sense of self-respect does not like to be wounded; parents who roar and shout at children and reiterate their faults and foibles keep opening wounds which the children themselves are trying to close and forget. A balance must, therefore, be struck between the kindness of the parents and the obedience of children. If no discipline or obedience is expected of children, they will grow up suffering a moral loss which life can never remedy. Parents who selfishly grant every whim of their children later on will feel the barbed agony of their children's selfishness. Parents are like shepherds who lead their sheep as the Lord walked before His disciples, showing them the way. Then there will never be an abuse of power. If the Lord does not teach, guide, and nourish the child, the devil will. Youth is for learning, manhood is for acting, and old age is for enjoying the fruits of both. The parent is the best teacher who has God as his teacher.

[75]

Teenage Respect

SOME PARENTS complain that their teenage children never obey them; other parents deny they have any difficulty on the subject of obedience with their children. Why the difference?

The difference is not always in the children, as is too often assumed; it may lie in the parents. The rebellion against the authority of the elders is not always because teenagers are opposed to authority, but rather because of those who administer authority. One of the greatest philosophers who ever lived gave this rule in Latin which is worth quoting:

> *Ex reverentia praecipientis procedere debet*
> *reverentia praecepti.*

> The respect that one has for a rule flows from the
> respect that one has for the one who gives it.

On the subject of music, for example, teenagers are very willing to accept the authority of a bandleader, because they feel he knows his subject and is qualified to speak on it. The teenage boy will accept the authority of a well-known baseball player on the subject of sports, because he is worthy of respect in that field due to his accomplishments. It was said of the soldiers of Napoleon that if anyone had cut out their hearts, they would have seen his image engraved thereon—so much did they respect his ability as a soldier.

Little boys never have any difficulty in accepting the authority of their parents. "My daddy told me" is their final word on any subject. There is a real inner adhesion to him because of the trust reposed in him. Later on, when the little boy becomes a teenager, there is not that same spontaneous acceptance of parental authority; there must be added another reason for parental respect, and that is the moral worth of the one who gives it. Where there is love, because of the nobility of the character of the parents, there is always obedience. Our Blessed Lord based obedience to His Commandments upon love: "If you love Me, you will keep My Commandments." Before He gave Peter the authority to rule over His lambs and sheep, He asked him three times, "Do you love Me?" Once there was a love admitted for Christ on the basis of His conquest over evil, then there would be no question whatever of obedience to His commands.

When a teacher lacks that moral and intellectual value which commands respect, disobedience increases. Juvenile delinquency is in direct ratio and proportion to the decline of moral value among the parents. Every defect in character is a defect in obedience. If, therefore, the parents of teenagers are of the type who are intemperate, given to alcoholism, infidelity, quarreling, and fighting, what can be expected of the children? If parents are living in a second marriage, with first spouses still living, it is impossible for these parents to say to their children, "You must keep your word and never break it"; the children know they have already broken a word concerning loving unto death. It will not do for alcoholic parents to say, "You must not drink," if the children have seen either of the parents drunk.

On the contrary, where the parents give example to their children, obedience is not rendered by the children because of a fear of punishment, but rather because they would not hurt whom they love. This is behind the meaning of the words of St. Augustine: "*Ama et fac quod vis*" (Love and do whatever you please). The commandment of God: "Thou shalt honor thy father and thy mother" implies honor in the parents. The definition of honor is a recognition of the excellence of someone.

In conclusion, it would be quite wrong always to blame the children for failure to honor their parents. Honor and dishonor, love and aversion, respect and disgust are born in them according to what they see in the parents. Sometimes it may be the duty of teenagers to educate their parents. To parents who have not given good example, the teenagers must be given this counsel: The last generation has failed you; but you must not fail the next generation.

XIV

Holydays

Easter

As THE DEAD flowers of winter burst into blossoming life in token of the Resurrection of Our Lord and Savior, they remind us of the great lesson of Easter: that it was not Christ who died on the Cross. It was *death* that died.

The Resurrection proves He did not die. And the Resurrection was a fact—but a fact which nobody around Him was prepared to believe. Christ had said He would rise again, and He did: *"Resurrexit sicut dixit"*—but His words had never been taken literally, even by the close companions of His teaching years. The apostles believed the Crucifixion would be the end of the whole story; only one of them was present on Golgotha for what they thought would be the final chapter of His life. On Easter morning, the women followers went to the sepulcher with no thought of meeting the Risen Christ; they had gone only to embalm His body, and their great concern was how to roll away the stone before the tomb. Even when they found the stone rolled back and the grave empty, they saw these things as evidence of a shameful theft. The very message of the angel frightened them; they still did not dare believe the story had a happy ending.

The apostles were the next skeptics to reject the fact of the Resurrection: when the women told them the Good News they regarded their words "as idle tales, and believed them not." Peter and John went and looked into the empty tomb, but even then they did not understand the meaning of what they saw. Later, when they actually saw the Risen Lord, they still were so unprepared for belief in the Resurrection that they imagined they had seen a ghost.

Everyone doubted the Conqueror of Death; this was, therefore, no "hallucination," no self-induced fancy. The very onlookers of Our Lord's Easter doubted their senses and refused to believe their eyes. Mary Magdalene mistook Him for the gardener; the disciples on the road to Emmaus did not recognize Him until He broke bread with them. And when they told the story of the Resurrection to the other disciples, who had not seen Him, they met with utter incredulity. Thomas said he would not believe this fantastic story until he had put his finger into His hand, and his hand into His side. But Thomas was finally cured of his doubts by evidence even he could not refuse—the presence of Our Lord, Who spoke to him and repeated his skeptical words to him. Thomas thus became the precursor and patron of all agnostics: their healer, and their hope.

If Christ's followers had been eagerly anticipating His Resurrection, they would have accepted it at once. Instead, we have their strong resistance to belief, which was overcome only by sheer weight of unanswerable evidence. The apostles had to be convinced . . . and they were convinced, and by facts alone. They had to readjust their whole conception of death to make room for this astounding truth that Christ, Who had died on the Cross, was not dead. Life, then, could not mean what men had always thought life meant. The apostles began to see that what men mistake for life is a kind of partial death, that bodily life is not the truest life. They caught glimmerings of the Christian truth that he who surrenders his soul to go on "living," or to "live" more enjoyably, destroys even the flesh that houses that soul; that we cannot save our lives unless we lose them; that whoever lays down his life for Christ's sake, finds it. It was not Our Lord Who had died; it was death-in-life that had died.

Everyone wants life—abundant life, life that is joyous and intense and lived to the hilt. And now there is no need to look for this in any of the places which earlier generations of men have searched and found empty. We need not set up new laboratories to test new methods of fulfilling man by tinkering with his body; these give us only the old errors with new labels. We need not repeat the experiments of the ancients who believed in the supremacy of man and who found that without a God to worship, mankind becomes subhuman. We need not try indifference to the religious solutions—this has been tried and it has ended by identifying the spirit of truth with the specter of evil. We have also tried science torn from a context of religious belief; it has fed our minds and starved our hearts. We have weighed the earth and measured Betelgeuse; we have taken a census of the stars and set our thermometers in the heart

of the sun—and still we had with us our ignorance of all that matters, our heartaches, and the "dismal, universal hiss of sin."

We have tried to square the circle of human problems by man-
made laws; but instead of obeying them, we changed the laws to suit
our way of living. We have tried to raise beauty to a sacrament, and
found that it broke under the weight of those who asked of its frail
strength a substitute for the Divine. We have tried to live in a world
of unsolved riddles, and have discovered that our doubts left us in
"confusion worse confounded," for the mind cannot rest with its ultimate destiny a mere question mark. We chose wealth as a goal,
and ended up poor; we took power as our ambition, and found ourselves weak; we tried pride as our motive, and we were brought to
our knees.

Only one experiment in living has not been attempted by modern
man: the experiment of love, directed not toward Jesus the Teacher
nor toward Jesus the Social Reformer nor Jesus the Humanitarian,
but toward Him Who is True God and True Man, Our Resurrected
Lord Who alone can show us how to live by conquering death upon
our Cross. As G. K. Chesterton said, "It is not correct to say that
Christianity has been tried and has failed. Christianity has been
found difficult, and not tried."

[77]

Easter

EASTER CAN NO more be separated from Good Friday than college
graduation day from discipline and examinations, or the tightening
of the strings of a violin from the melody produced, or drossless and
purified gold from the cleansing fire. Christ the Victor over Death
and Error and Sin is the same Christ Who was the Victim of the
Death, Error and Evil.

Christianity differs from all other religions because it begins with defeat, catastrophe, and crisis. Sunshine religions make God your "partner" in a successful business or a happy marriage, but they cannot stand up in darkness, storm, and defeat. There is some mysterious and intrinsic relationship between the cross and the empty tomb. On Good Friday, evil did its worst; it unshielded its sharpest sword; it seemingly gained victory over love and righteousness. But in this world evil has its hour (and the crucifixion Our Lord always called "My Hour"), but goodness has its day. Evil was defeated when it came with its strongest arms and was accompanied in its mightiest army. Having gone down to defeat, evil can never be wholly victorious again, though it will have its hours of seeming victory, as it does now in the persecution in totalitarian countries.

The second point about Easter is that what happened to Christ as the Head of humanity must in a diminished way happen to every individual if he or she is ever to attain that glory. He is the Pattern and we are the images; He is the original Die, and we are the coins stamped from the Divine. No one can ever expect to be without trials and crosses, for these are the very condition of victory and incorporation with Him. *"For if we have been planted together in the likeness of His Death, we shall be also in the likeness of His Resurrection."* It is not merely by verbally confessing His death that we purchase that identification with the Prototype which is the condition of happiness and glory; there must be veritable crucifixion or a putting to death not of our human nature, which is good, but of our evil tendencies such as lust, avarice, and the pride which blockades the progress of the spirit.

All the psychological and biological helps in the world cannot make us rise to a new nature and power, any more than a corpse can give life to itself. What is born of the flesh is still flesh. In a world where self-expression becomes identified with license, there is but a petty hearing given to a discipline of the lower passions and instincts; but the law is inexorable. The real inner peace of soul can be attained only by being planted in the likeness of His death and crucifixion. Then we become like soldiers sharing in the victory of the general and a family enjoying the prestige and the success of the father. What has happened to the Head is assured to the members of the body.

Easter Sunday, therefore, is not just a miracle of the past, but a promise also of the future. In its light, not decay but advance, not a pulling down but a reaching forward becomes the main characteristic of both man and history. Even these hours of trial and decision through which the world is presently passing are seen in the light of the Resurrection as a kind of judgment for the evil of our ways; but they are also seen as a sharing in the dark hours of Good Friday in order that we may be given merit to see a resurgence and resurrection of those historical forces which make for the peace of the world. The remedial process is certain, though, for those who have faith in Easter. History is not an ascending hill of progress, as the false thinkers of the nineteenth century assured us; neither is it a certain catastrophe and winter and decay as Wells in his decline and Spengler warned us; it is rather a mixture of the two. There must first be the trial, the dark side, the purging out of the leaven of selfishness; then comes the peace. Easter peace is not something that comes automatically. Peace is made; "Blessed are the peace-makers." Peace is made through a Good Friday as the prelude to an Easter Sunday. The crown of thorns is the condition of the crown of glory. The creativeness of man and history are cleansed and illumined, not quenched and destroyed, by Calvary and the empty tomb. The tragedy of the world is that there are so many escapists who run from the condition of happiness; the joy of the world is that there are so many who see the glory through discipline.

[78]

Easter

No GREATER DARKNESS will ever descend upon the earth than that which fell upon Christ on Calvary. In all other wars there was a gray, or a mixture of good and evil, on both sides, but in the

Crucifixion there was black on one side and white on the other. Evil would never be stronger than it was on that particular day, for the worst thing that evil can do is not to bomb cities and kill children and wage wars; the worst thing that evil can do is to kill Goodness. Having been defeated in that, it could never be victorious again.

Goodness in the face of evil must suffer, for when love meets sin it will be crucified. A God Who wears His Sacred Heart upon His sleeve, as Our Lord did when He became man, must be prepared to have human daws peck at it. But at the same time, Goodness can use that suffering as a condition of overcoming evil. It can take all of the anger, wrath, and hate and say forgive; it can take life and offer it for another. Hence to Him it was expedient that He suffer in order to enter glory. He thus proved that evil could never be called truly victorious again. Conquered in its full armor and in the moment of its monumental momentum, evil might in the future win some battles, but it would always lose the war.

No hope can be given to a wounded world by a Confucius, a Buddha, or even a Christ who teaches goodness and then rots in the grave. No healing can be brought to broken wings by a humanism, which is brotherhood without tears, or by a gentle Christ who has no source of knowledge distinct from any other teacher, and who in the end like them could not burst the fetters of death nor prove that truth crushed to earth may rise again.

This summary that Our Lord gave of His life throws down the challenge to men: take Him out of history and what assurance have we that evil shall not triumph over good? Suppose that He was only a good man or an ethical teacher or the greatest moralist the world would ever have, then what assurance is there for the victory of virtue? What inspiration is there for sacrifice? If He Who came to this earth to teach the dignity of the human soul, who could challenge a sinful world to convict Him of sin, Who could, at the moment of death, forgive His enemies, had no other issue and destiny than to hang on a common tree with common criminals and thieves to make a Roman holiday, then each man may despairingly inquire, "If this is what happens to a good man, then why should I lead a good life?" Then the greatest of all injustices can go unredressed and the noblest of all lives can go unvindicated. Pay whatever compliments

one may to His teaching, His patience under blows, His meekness
before mobs—these eulogies do not make Him the Lord of death
and life; they rather make these virtues vain, for they have no reward.

There is no greater inspiration in the world to lead a selfish life, to
use every other person as a means to one's own pleasure, to snatch at
every person as a glass to break it if need be to get the wine, than
the spectacle of a good man going to death and having no other immortality than for His followers to dress up vainly on Easter. Those
who would make Christ a mere ethical teacher destroy ethical teaching; those who make Him a moral preceptor destroy all hope from
morality. Admire holiness as much as one pleases, but what is one to
think of a God Who would look down on this spectacle of Innocence going to the gallows and not pull out the nails and put a
scepter there? Or Who would not send an angel to snatch a crown
of thorns and place a garland there? Shall God be a party to saying
that the noblest life that ever walked this earth is impotent before
the evil deeds of men? What are we to think of human nature if the
white flower of a blameless Life is trampled under the hobnail boots
of Roman executioners and then destined to decay like crushed
flowers? Would it not send forth a greater stench because of its primal sweetness and make us hate not only the God Who had no care
for truth and love, but forever our fellowmen for being a party to
His Death? If this is the end of goodness, then why be good at all?
If this is what happens to justice, then anarchy reigns.

But on the other hand, if He can take the worst the world has to
offer and then, by the power of God, rise above it; if He the un-
armed can make war with no other weapon than goodness and pardon, so that the slain has the gain, and they who kill lose the day,
then who shall be without hope? Who shall ever despair in any
momentary defeat by evil? Who shall fail to trust when he sees
walking in the darkness the Risen One with glorious scars on Hands
and Feet and Side?

[79]

Easter

MANY MINDS REGARD our modern world as hopeless. It is indeed like a vast and horrible Good Friday where everything divine seems gone down to defeat. The future never seemed so completely unpredictable as it does today. Mankind seems to be in a kind of widowhood, in which a harrowing sense of desolation sweeps over it, as one who sets out on life's journey in intimate comradeship with another, and then is suddenly bereft of that companion forever. There are wars and rumors of wars. Economics is a tangled mess. Communism is robbing men of their souls and a false education is stealing away their faith. Lives have been made flabby with worldliness, and ill-prepared for the rigors of an enforced discipline. Platitudes abound on lips and unrealized desires embitter hearts. Everywhere there is confusion, hopelessness, and despair.

And yet there need not be such hopelessness and despair. The world seemed just as hopeless before, when it crucified its Savior; and yet with all its paganism and nationalism it arose to newness and freshness of Christian life and civilization. The miracle of the Resurrection can happen again. The world may rise once more as it has risen before, at least a dozen times since the advent of Christianity. But let us suffer no illusions. It will not rise to peace and happiness through economic and political remedies alone; it will rise only through a spiritual regeneration of the hearts and souls of men. The Resurrection of Our Lord was not the resumption of an old life; it was the beginning of a new life. It was the lesson of Christmas all over again—namely, the world will not be saved by social recovery but by rebirth: rebirth from the dead by the Power of Divinity in Christ.

We must not reconstruct our old life; we must rise to new life. There must be a new energy introduced from without, in the absence of which we must rot in our graves. Christ rose from the dead by the Power of God. It is vain for us to try to rise by any other Power. This Life and Power the Risen Savior has given to His Mystical Body the Church. His Truth comes to us through His Vicar; His Life comes to us through the Sacraments; His Authority comes to us through the Episcopacy. But here is the stumbling block of the world. It may admit that by the Power of God Christ rose from the tomb, but it will not admit that the Power of the Risen Christ continues beyond that tomb. It sees the Church on its human side, made up of weak, frail creatures, and therefore thinks it something to be ignored. It makes the same mistake Mary Magdalene made the first Easter morning. She mistook the Risen Savior for the gardener—that is, for but a human thing. The world, too, sees the Risen Christ in His Mystical Body the Church and takes it to be the gardener—something human and not divine. But Divinity is there as it was in the Garden the First Easter, and only that same Divinity can give hope to a hopeless world. We may yet attain our peace if we but seek—not the political and the economic, but the new Life of the Kingdom of God. For such is the message of Easter Day: the Resurrection of the Dead, the Triumph of the Defeated, the Finding of the Lost; the springtime of the earth, the waking of life, the Trumpet of Resurrection blowing over the land of the living.

But to all souls the Easter message rings out that there is no reason for despair. The Resurrection was announced to a Magdalene —a soul once like our own. Peace awaits you in the service of the God Who made you. No matter how hopeless things seem to be, there is still hope, for Christ is the Resurrection and the Life. He who can make snowflakes out of dirty drops of water, diamonds out of charcoal, and saints out of Magdalenes can also make us victorious if we but confess Him in His earthly and Mystical Life as Christ the Son of the Living God.

[80]

Christmas

WHY IS EVERYONE so interested in Superman and Batman? Never before has our culture been so absorbed in those who are above the human, or who come from another planet and are endowed with a supranatural strength. These giants come to the rescue of the afflicted, help damsels in distress, liberate the imprisoned, and defend the cause of goodness. Some believe that little men come out of flying saucers which transported them from other worlds to ours, saying, "Take me to your chief."

The popularity of such programs reveals our subconscious sense of human inadequacy, and also our need for a power beyond the human.

Given this credulousness, why should we find it hard to believe that Christmas is the visitation of the Super-Man Who comes from a higher source of life, and Who does things that man cannot do by himself?

While there are great similarities between Superman and the coming of God to this earth by taking a human nature, there is a great difference: Christ. The Superman comes in power; God comes in weakness—the weakness of a Babe in a cradle, Whose tiny hands cannot reach the huge heads of the cattle. Modern mind is much more ready to accept a Superman who emits electrical power from his fingertips than it is to accept a Super-Man, or God Who appears in the feebleness of an Infant. A second reason is that Superman makes no demands on us morally, requires no change of life, no reformation of morals, no self-discipline; he leaves our ego as he finds it.

They were looking for a king
To slay their foes and lift them high;
Thou cameth, a little Baby thing,
That made a woman cry.

The Superman works on the outside; the God-Man works on the inside. The Superman leaves hearts and souls as they are; the God-Man demands a revolution of spirit.

The God-Man renovates man in his heart from the inside, in the following way: just suppose a plague infected the human race; tens of millions perish just as one third of Europe was wiped out by the Black Death in the Middle Ages. Suppose also that a scientist who had already recovered from the plague developed a serum which would counteract that disease and offered it as immunity to everyone in the world, but few ever availed themselves of it because they did not like the pain of the injection.

That is precisely the meaning of Christmas. Our Blessed Lord enters into the plague of misery, sin, bitterness, war, hate. He passes through it in Calvary, recovers in the Resurrection, and then offers His Divine power to all men. They shrink from it because it demands a kind of death to that which is low and base in us. To change the figure, we know that our spiritual and moral anemia can be cured by a blood transfusion, but we dread the momentary pain.

Christmas, then, is not something that has happened; it is something that is happening. Christmas is the day when the God-Man says to every person in the world, "My Mother Mary gave Me a human nature like unto your own in all things save sin. I have shown you how one can overcome the worst of the human situation and live in joy. But what I want to do is to take your human nature, as I took the human nature from Mary. I want to give you an infusion of light for your mind, a power for your will, and a joy for your heart. What does it profit Me if I am born in Bethlehem and am not reborn in your hearts? You will find that all who have given themselves to Me are at peace. They are full of joy, they are merry." That is why we who belong to Him greet one another on this day with a "Merry Christmas."

[81]

The Christmas Star

CHRISTMAS IS the most popular season of the Western world. But it is also one in which almost everyone celebrates the feast without knowing the meaning of the festival. A time has not yet come, and may it never come, when the Fourth of July will be celebrated with fireworks but without a memory of our independence. If Christmas were just the birthday of a great teacher, like Socrates or Buddha, it would never have split time into two, so that all history before the advent of Christ is called B.C. and all history after, A.D. which means "the year of the Lord."

What happened at Christmas is the opposite of what happened to many emperors and dictators. Nero and Caligula of Rome, though men, called themselves God; the Japanese Emperor was regarded as a man who became a god. Hence for years he was made untouchable and almost unseeable, for the discovery of his human limitations would have fractured a belief in his divinity. Stalin called himself God, and Khrushchev, by denying dependence on anything beyond himself, made himself an absolute. But Christmas is not a man making himself a god, but God becoming a man, without ever ceasing to be God. In the first instance, there is exaltation or self-inflation by which man makes himself what he is not. In the second instance, there is humiliation, for God takes on the form and the habit of man.

This meant that for the first time there was a real and intimate bond established between God and man. As a man by his own power cannot touch the ceiling without the aid of some intermediary such as a stepladder, so man left to his own weak and frail nature could not reach God. On the other hand, God's love for man is something that man could not grasp in its fullness unless that love obeyed the law of love: we tend to become like that which we love.

A man who loves a woman who is a musician will cultivate a love for music; if she is a poet, he will tend to become poetic in his tastes like his beloved. So if God loves man, then God should become one with man, and that is precisely what happened in the stable of Bethlehem. There God, Who exists from all eternity, took upon Himself in time a human nature like ours in all things save sin.

He therefore became the perfect Mediator between God and man. Now there was a bridge between heaven and earth, a link between Divinity and humanity, a bond between eternity and time. More than a Jacob's ladder reaching to heaven, which he saw in his vision, was this union of God and man in the person of Christ.

If we imagine the star over the crib as five-pointed, this Light from heaven issued forth five rays which were the reasons for His coming to earth. The first ray was that now God was tabernacled among men. Proud man, who distorted his nature by deifying himself, was given the lesson of Divinity appearing as the servant of man, saying that He came not to be ministered unto, but to minister. The second ray was His sacrifice. He did not come to live; He came to die. The sin of mankind merited death, for the wages of sin is death. He would take on the sins of man as if they were His own: their blasphemies, as if His lips had spoken them; their thefts, as if His own hands had committed them. He became the Good Shepherd Who lays down His life for His sheep. The third ray was His mercy and compassion and sympathy. He knew human hearts because He made them. Hence His deep love for sinners whom society condemned and His condemnation of those who sinned and denied they were sinners, or else who sinned but had not yet been found out. Humanity was wounded, but not all men admitted their wounds. But to all who saw their guilt and came to Him, He was the Physician Who restored their souls to union with Himself.

The fourth ray was the establishment of a kingdom which would be a prolongation of His own body. As He taught, as He governed, as He sanctified through the human nature He took from Mary, so too, through other human natures who would be His apostles and their successors, He would continue to teach, to govern, and to sanctify. The fifth ray was His promise to live within us. Had He remained on earth, He would have been only an example to be copied; we could have gotten no closer to Him than an embrace or a word. But if He went back to heaven and sent His Spirit, then He would be an example to be lived. Those who possess that Spirit of Christ today, manifesting His humility, compassion, sacrifice, and love as He did, are the ones who are really celebrating the Christmas.

[82]

New Year

A NEW YEAR makes us conscious of the passing of time, and when time passes, history is made. Our fondness for the immediate and the latest news, our emphasis on science, have made us oblivious to the importance of history. Science is a record of what is happening, whereas history is a record of what *matters*. Science deals with what is determined and necessary; history, with the doings and decisions of free men.

History is a story of crisis, and "crisis" in the original Greek means judgment or verdict. The oak is a judgment on the acorn; the headache is a judgment on our refusal to eat; the double chin is a judgment on our eating too much; ignorance is a judgment on our refusal to study. Nature acts in a certain way simply because God has implanted certain laws in the universe. Some of these laws are physical, others biological, and others moral. The transcendent God, therefore, is present in the universe immanently through these laws. It is His Will that these laws be obeyed for the perfection of the creatures themselves. It is with history and human freedom that we are presently concerned.

History is the testing ground for human freedom and passes judgments on the way we use it. The seed of certain ideas is planted; it bears fruit either good or evil, and this fruit is a judgment on the kind of seed we planted. History is always passing verdicts on the ideas of an age. The religious revolution of the sixteenth century was a judgment on the way those who had the faith lived. The French Revolution was a judgment on the privileges of the monarchy and the denial of political equality to all citizens. World war is a judgment on the way we think and live, marry and unmarry, buy and sell; it is a judgment on our banks, our schools, our books, our economic system, our factories, our homes, our legislatures, our hearts and souls and, above all, on our humanist delusion that man is naturally and progressively good, either individually or collectively.

What has God to do with these judgments? God does not will these judgments directly. He does not send a war into the world as a punishment from outside history in a purely arbitrary and extrinsic fashion because He is angry with us. From the moral viewpoint of history, wars do not follow disobedience to God's Will as a spanking follows a disobedient boy's eating his mother's jam. God does not send the thunder as an applause because He is thrilled with the momentary pyrotechnics of the heavens. Rather He made the universe in such a way that, when there is lightning, there is thunder. The thunder is the judgment on the lightning, the effect resulting from the cause. In the physical sphere, certain diseases are judgment on squalid living, not because God plays favorites with the nice clean hygienic people, but simply because of an essential element in the universe. God made the world in such a way that when we freely set ourselves in opposition to His Will certain consequences follow, and the calamity attendant upon the defiance of His Will is what we call a judgment of God. Sin brings adversity in its train, and adversity is the expression of God's condemnation of evil. A wrong attitude toward nature and a wrong attitude toward fellowman or society imply a wrong attitude toward God and here, too, the consequence is inevitable.

There is a difference between the Will of God and the judgment of God. The Will of God is our peace and happiness. The judgment of God is made up of our opposition to that Will. A vertical bar stands for God's Will; a horizontal bar, which crosses it in sin, stands for man's will; the result is a Cross or a crisis. The Will of God is never defeated, because in doing evil we produce an effect which we do not intend. The frustration of the modern world, therefore, is a result of the collision of our wills with the Divine Will. History then becomes the sphere where fallen man works out the consequences of his severance from God. When war comes, then, it is not, in the strict sense of the term, a visitation from God or even an extrinsic punishment from God; it is our apostate civilization registering sentence on our thinking, on our living. Love was meant to be our consolation. When we reject it freely, love becomes our judge. We are as free to run counter to God's Will as we are free to run counter to "the law of gravitation" by throwing ourselves from a building. But in doing the latter, we kill ourselves. When society, in like manner, sets itself up in antagonism to the gospel of love, the sovereignty of God is revealed in the judgment that follows the disobedience. Without judgment, there would be no sovereignty even in our earthly courts. But God's judgment is never separable from His mercy. When we acknowledge Him to be our Judge, He becomes our Savior. The alternative before men, therefore, is either to live under the love of God or else to live under His justice and His judgment. It is under the latter that the world is in the present evil hour.

[83]

New Year

A WORLD OF difference exists between the old and the young in their attitude toward time. As St. Peter said in one of his first Pentecostal sermons: "Young men see visions; old men dream dreams." By this he meant that the old look backward; the young look forward. Horace, the great Latin poet, spoke of the young as *"laudator tem-*

poris acti"—praising the days of old. With the passing of each new year, time goes more quickly; but with youth, time proceeds slowly. A young girl of sixteen is anxious to be a girl of twenty-one. Hence, the young live in the future and in hope and promise. Lacking experience, they are apt to think that the emotions and pleasures and thrills of youth continue all through life. Though it can never be stated as a general rule, it often happens that the man a girl would marry at eighteen is not the man she would marry at twenty; the man she marries at twenty is not the man she would marry at twenty-two. Time has made her wiser and less apt to judge the moment as a token of what will always be.

Hence when a new year rolls around, the aged are amazed that time has passed so quickly. The young would like to give time more wings in order that it might speed both their pleasure and their hope.

But both are apt to forget that time is a part of eternity; that just as our present moment has a memory behind it and a hope in front of it so, too, time is like one circle that is locked in another circle or, better still, time and eternity are like two hearts carved by lovers on an oak tree as if to give perpetuity to their love. Each new year is actually a testing and proving ground for eternity, a kind of novitiate in which we say "aye" or "nay" to our eternal destiny, a season of plenty from which we shall later on reap either wheat or weeds. A beautiful example of this consciousness of how time is bound up to eternity was revealed when we gave First Communion to a little princess. After the ceremony, when she had received the greetings of friends she said to her mother, "I am ready." Her mother said, "Ready for what?" She said, "Ready for Heaven. I have received Divine Love this morning and why should I go on living? For living is nothing but waiting for Perfect Love."

The beginning of a new year is an opportunity for improvement. It makes little difference what the past has been, for we are not to look back to see if the furrow be crooked. What matters most is the sanctification of the now moment. Time is so precious that God doles it out second by second. If life in the past has been evil, the new year is an opportunity for penance. In such a way is time redeemed. If life, however, has been virtuous, the new year is an opportunity for greater self-perfection.

It is not to the point to say that our life is merely like the light of a match when it is struck, for we perish like the squirrels and the foxes to rot in the earth. Even the very analogy of the match which is used suggests immortality, for once that light is struck, the light goes out into space at the rate of about 186,000 miles an hour and exists forever in the universe. So, too, when the human light of the soul is struck in the entrails of a mother, the light continues through eternity. Though there be such things as deathbed conversions, nevertheless as the tree falls, there it lies. One man who led an evil life always boasted of the fact that he needed never worry about his soul when time would end, for he could save it with three words which he quoted in Latin: *"Miserere mei Deus."* He was right about saying three words at the moment of his death, but they were not the words he expected to say, for his life had not been so lived as to pronounce them from his heart. As his horse threw him over the cliff he said: *"Capiat omnia biabolus,"* which means, "I'll be damned."

Time is equivalent to what can be done or gained by it. At the beginning of the new year, therefore, we wish everyone that it be happy because we know that there is no greater melancholy or sadness than to use time for any purpose but the supreme one, which is the salvation of the soul.

XV
Knowledge and Reason

Self-knowledge

SELF-KNOWLEDGE demands the discovery of our predominant fault, of the particular defect which tends to prevail in us, affecting our sympathies, our decisions, desires, and passions. The predominant fault is not always clearly seen, because it acts as a fifth column in our souls. A man who by nature is gentle and kind may easily have his spiritual life ruined by the hidden fault of weakness toward ethical and moral issues. Another person who by nature is courageous may have as his predominant fault a bad temper, or fits of violence which he calls "courage." The existence of a predominant fault does not indicate that there is no good quality in us; yet our good qualities may possibly be rendered ineffective by this hidden defect. The quickest way to discover the predominant fault is to ask ourselves, "What do I think about most when alone? What fault irritates me most when I am accused of it, and which sin do I most vigorously deny possessing? Where do my thoughts go when I let them go spontaneously?"

The predominant fault varies from person to person. It can be any one of the seven capital sins, and their correlated failings. The seven capital sins are actually the seven pallbearers of the soul. We hate to acknowledge any one of them as being our own, for we see their ugliness; self-knowledge is not easy, because self-love cannot endure humiliation. It hurts us to tear off a layer of our conceit. If a thought suddenly crosses the mind of "how rotten I am," the ego is alert to drive it away. When the real self—the I—sees itself in God's Light as it really is, the ego vanishes. But the ego does not want to vanish. That is why some people try to avoid the painful process of self-knowledge on the ground that it develops an "inferiority complex."

Of all the towering nonsense in the modern world, nothing is greater than this dread of an inferiority complex; the roots of such a fear are always pride. Pride tells us, "I am not as proud or bold or self-assertive as I might be if my conscience were quieted by self-deception. I know that I am not so learned or so beautiful as my neighbor, and this fact hurts me, makes me miserable. I had better forget it." But the acceptance of our natural imperfections is desirable; we cannot all be giants. To accept both our talents and our lack of talents as God's will is true humility. It is realism to say, as John the Baptist did, "I must decrease." He saw his true inferiority when he was confronted by Divinity, yet Our Lord said that he was the "greatest man born of woman." The real self must be accepted for what it is. Perhaps it is not learned, nor beautiful, nor charming. But what of that? The real self can have its own wisdom and its own beauty if it yields to God, for "the beauty of the King's daughter is from within."

It is further objected that self-knowledge brings despair, as it reveals our true defects. There is no doubt that such despair is likely if we view ourselves apart from God revealed in Christ. A materialistic psychoanalysis necessarily makes one pessimistic about human nature; the soul naturally shrinks from the discovery of a disease which cannot be cured. Atheists shudder at the prospect of going down into the pit of their real selves, for there is no exit for them toward happiness. Not having the humility to face the fact that their real selves are guilty, they deny the very existence of guilt, although seeing their sins would be the essential condition of their cure. Self-knowledge is never despairing to those who acknowledge the power of God. Who fears to reveal sickness to a physician who can cure him? Who fears to reveal his guilt to a Savior Who redeems? Self-examination to the Christian is the digging of a foundation. The deeper the foundation, the higher the building will finally soar. The more humble the soul, the greater will be his exaltation when God touches him.

[85]

Knowledge and Wisdom

OF ALL THE erroneous zones of thinking, none is worse than the one which identifies freedom with the absence of responsibility. The most unhappy people are those who say, "I gotta be me," "I gotta do my thing," "nobody is going to tell me." Their heart is like a clogged sewer because there is no outflow: hands are always out to receive, never to give. Their hell does not begin in the next life; it begins here, for what is hell but isolation, alienation, and separation?

Let the sober mind examine how much happier the heart is when there are some limitations to license. Do not all games have handi-caps and hazards? Why sand traps on a golf course? Why boundary foul lines on a football field? Why speed limits on highways? Ulti-mately, why did the Lord give ten commandments? To limit our freedom or to tell what sand traps to avoid? With the purchase of every new car there is given a set of rules and instructions: the cor-rect pressure for the tires, the reminder to put water in the battery and when to change the oil, and so forth. The manufacturer has no intention to restrict our freedom to drive; he merely gives hints on how to make driving more effective and attractive.

So it is with the commandments. God gave them to us to prevent us from choosing the *second-best*. Killing is one way of avenging a wrong, but it is second-best. Stealing is another way of increasing our possessions, but it is second-best. The pendulum of the clock, if it were conscious, might deny it was dependent on the mechanism, but that is not the best way to achieve the right to swing. So, too, boasting that we are our own creator makes our own Savior a second-best way to live, which is not best at all.

Every Declaration of Independence is a Declaration of Dependence. Our own national Constitution, while affirming our sovereign right to be free and independent of the political power, also states that we are dependent on God for our rights and liberties. The more we affirm the autonomy of the imperial self, the less help we have from the outside. For too many, life is like a locked box with the key on the inside. It is puzzling and confused because there is not outside help. The electric bulb supplies its own energy. Likewise, the wisdom one needs to guide our lives has to come from outside our intellect. "If any of you lack wisdom he should pray to God to give it to him; for God gives generously and graciously to all."

A world of difference exists between knowledge and wisdom. T. S. Eliot asks, "What has happened to our wisdom in our conquest of knowledge?" Knowledge is acquired; wisdom is infused. Knowledge comes from the outside; it is learned and absorbed. Wisdom is infused, and comes to us as an illumination. Think, for example, of the many decisions youth have to make. What college should one attend? Whom should one marry? What career or profession should one embrace? Should a wife be chosen on the basis of sex appeal? We need wisdom to make big decisions, and the right answer comes from God Who has a destiny for us. He is longing to fulfill it in us for the benefit of ourselves and others.

Too often we ask God to rubber-stamp our own wishes—for example, to win the hand of a girl friend or to pass a certain examination. This does not mean our prayer is unanswered. God has two answers: one is yes; the other is no. When Michelangelo was working on the great Cathedral of Saint Peter's he had much criticism from ecclesiastical superiors and workmen on the building. To these critics the great architect said, "Even if I were able to make my ideas and plans clear to you—which I am not—I am not obliged to do so. I must ask you to do your best to help me, and when the work is completed, the completion will be better understood." In like manner, we must recognize the following facts: we often lack necessary wisdom, but we must believe that God wants to guide us and make us wise.

[86]

"How Noble in Reason!"

EVERY MAN coming into the world has one great light sealed upon him, which is reason, or the faculty of knowing the true and the right. Some have an additional light, which is that of faith. The latter are fortunate, inasmuch as they have the extra illumination for the problems of life. As the eye has not its own light, but needs the sun, so too the reason for its perfection needs the gift of faith. We have the same eyes at night as we have in the day, but we cannot see in darkness because we lack the additional light of the sun. The reason those with faith have a keener insight into values and a deeper moral sense is because they are blessed with a light others lack.

But here we are concerned solely with first light, or reason. In these days of propaganda, superstition, denial of intellect, the exaltation of sentiment, and the domination of instinct, it is well to remind man of his dignity, as Shakespeare did in saying, "How noble in reason!"

Every person in the world is illumined with the light of reason, which is a reflection of the Divine wisdom. We are like so many volumes issuing from the Divine press. To each is given the freedom to write on those pages and thus do the autobiography of our character. Even though we write badly or well, indisputably stamped on the cover is the name of the Divine Author. Despite inkblots of moral value which are due to our moral carelessness, the Divine watermark is stamped on each page, untouched by our poor scribbling.

Reason manifests itself in different ways at different times. In the ancient world it was art that made civilization and culture; in our world it is science. Art is the expression of beautiful ideals through the real. Michelangelo said that inside every block of marble is an admirable form; one need only hack away the nonessentials in order to reveal it. Science, however, is more concerned with law and order.

Every new invention, every newly discovered law, whether in biology, or astronomy, or physics, is in the truest sense of the word a "discovery." Columbus could not have discovered America if America had not been "there." A scientist actually unwraps a secret, a rhythm, a melody, a law that God has already placed in the universe. As Michelangelo "unwrapped" marble, so the scientist unwraps what has been hidden in the cosmos since the beginning.

Every scientist is a kind of proofreader. He is not the author of the law he enunciates. Few indeed are the great scientists who ever think so, even by confusing the carbon copy with the original. They know the difference between discovery and invention. Many have the vision of Wordsworth, who said that "the meanest flower that blows can give thoughts that do often lie too deep for tears." But such thoughts are not given to those who do not think, and search for reason. The window lets in the light, but not to the blind.

The scientist of our modern civilization has a blessed advantage over most men, for to him is given a deeper vision of creation. One great scientist, Eddington, became so enamored of his findings in mathematical physics that he ended up his scientific treatise with a chapter on mysticism. This was going too far. But at any rate he did acknowledge, with Jeans, that all our scientific discoveries take us only to the edge of the picture. Then the philosopher must take over.

Blessed is the man to whom the universe is not opaque like a curtain, but transparent as is a window, and to whom reason's Author is seen behind every true act of reasoning.

As George Herbert expressed it:

> A man that looks on the glass,
>   On it may stay his eye;
> Or if he pleaseth, through it pass,
>   And then the heavens espy.

[87]

Reason or Emotion?

THOUGH THE WORD "think" is placarded on many a desk; though a filter had been provided for the "thinking man," the sad fact is that reason today is held in but little repute. The symbol of justice for centuries was the blindfolded woman with scales in her hand, the implication being that she is blindfolded in order not to be influenced by favoritism, the dignity of persons or the size of bribes or anything that might possibly strike her emotions. The weight of rational arguments, not emotional appeal, decide which way the scales will fall or rise.

All this has changed. Dietrich Bonhoeffer, who was hanged by the Nazis some weeks before the atomic bomb was exploded, pointed out that reason today fails to guide men; conscience, duty, justice, sin no longer appeal to the modern man. George Bernard Shaw said, "the modern man is too busy to think about his sins."

Whether we like it or not, the world is comparing the use of reason and Christianity with its Logos or Reason Incarnate and its message and its method to the figure of Don Quixote, the knight of doleful countenance who took a barber's dish for a helmet and a miserable hack of a charger and rode into endless battles against windmills for the love of a lady who did not exist. This is the picture that is so often given of the attempts of reason and the Church to meet the evil of our day. The assumption is that we are using rusty swords with which our fathers performed great feats, but which we cannot use today. Today, if a man puts his head between his hands to think out some question, he is often asked if he has a headache. As Newman said, "the syllogism makes but sorry rhetoric with the multitude."

What has taken the place of reason? Emotion, feeling, sentiment, repetition, subliminal suggestion, the irrational and glandular reaction. The blindfolded lady of reason has given way to the Aeolian harp, which was a musical instrument made of fine strings of wire attached to wood, through which the wind blew. Aeolius, the god of the winds, was presumed to have let loose the wind from his cave, producing sounds which entranced and captivated.

One notices this particularly in the Aeolian harps of the twentieth century: radio and television. Practically no advertisement appeals to reason. In fact, the more products such as autos, cigarettes, and detergents resemble one another, the greater is the appeal to emotion, such as cigarettes bringing you to the land of cowboys or to running brooks or to he-men on top of oil rigs. News, too, is made emotional through concentration in tragedies, accidents, floods, disasters, and excesses against the moral order. "A plane just fell, killing 102 persons in the worst accident in aviation history. Details after this important announcement about how Dora the adorable deodorant will open the door to the adorable world of femininity." The singing commercial is the one thing least calculated to convince a thinking person. Just go up to a friend from whom you want to borrow a hundred dollars and sing it to the tune of "Yankee Doodle" and you will not be taken seriously. But to the emotional, the insistent drip, drip, drip of repetition, like drops of water on the skull, finally makes the animal jump through the hoop of the animal trainer.

The nonrational is further evident in the young, who are so receptive to the sensual, rhythmic, dynamic stimuli of the Aeolian harp. There is not much emphasis on the words of a song or on meaning. Sometimes the words are even unintelligible. What matters is that winds keep blowing through Aeolian harps until life becomes a "beat" rather than a program and a drama.

What effect does the antirational or Aeolian harp have on religion? Religion which appeals to reason, justice, sin, and Word Incarnate has little appeal to the emotional masses of people. Religion is aboveground with reason and theology; the masses are underground with doubts, fears, frustrations, anxieties, dreads. The conscience of which the Church speaks does not touch the unconscious; the ethical order does not contact the frustrated man. Modern man is locked in the closet with a lot of his skeletons. As T. S. Eliot said: "I have very seldom heard people mention their consciences except to observe that their consciences were clear." Are the masses irreligious? Definitely no! But where has their interest in religion moved? To their subconscious minds.

XVI

Education

Education for Life

MAN HAS AN infinite capacity for life, truth, love and beauty; he alone, of all creatures on this earth, has the possibilities of attuning himself to the Infinite. Since he craves the perfect, and desires to be attuned to the highest, it follows that only an infinite God can satisfy him. Man above all other creatures has been made to conquer new worlds. Man alone has a soul to be converted—converted to God and His holy purposes.

Education cannot be understood apart from the plastic nature of man. Taking due cognizance of it, one might say that the purpose of all education is to establish contact with the totality of our environment with a view to understanding the full meaning and purpose of life. But the purpose of life cannot be understood without God, nor can anyone enter into contact with the whole of environment unless he enters into relationship with God, in Whom we live and move and have our being. Imagine a man in a boat in the center of a lake. He sees approaching him a series of little ripples becoming increasingly wider and not leaving off their play until they have reached the distant shore. The man in the boat knows that the ripples did not cause themselves. If he is to account for their existence, he must look out beyond to the distant shore where perhaps stood a man who threw a stone into the lake that caused it to awake with its watery vibrations. So, too, it would be necessary for any mind that sees the concentric orbs of knowledge round about him to go out beyond the worlds to Someone who stood on the seashore of eternity and threw the planets into being from the tips of His Almighty fingers. And that Someone who explains the totality is God. No mind has entered into communion with the whole of all that is, and hence no man can call himself truly educated unless his mind has carried him out beyond the uttermost rim of space, out to that beauty which leaves all other beauty pain, and to that love we fall short of in all love, out to the Life of all living, out to God, the Creator and Lord of the world.

Are the schools and universities throughout the country that ignore God really educating the young men and women entrusted to their care? Would we say that a man was a learned mathematician if he did not know the first principles of Euclid? Would we say that a man was a profound physicist if he did not know the first principles of light, sound, and heat? Can we say that a man is truly educated who is ignorant of the first principles of life and truth and love—which is God?

To leave God out of a university curriculum is to leave out the First Cause and the intelligibility of all that is.

There is not a difference in degree between modern education and traditional education, but rather a difference in kind. The difference between the two is the difference between education and instruction. Education means drawing something out, as the Latin root itself signifies. Instruction seems to mean putting something in. There can be no education in any system of training which asserts that man is just a glorified animal, or that he has no supernatural destiny or a soul that has potentialities for communing with the Infinite. Such a system by its very nature can never draw anything out. On the contrary, education should assert that we are not risen beasts, but fallen angels; that we have had a Golden Age in the past when our ancestors walked with God; that we have a nature which has a capacity for being lighted with the faith of God, and becoming veritable children of God.

With the passing of time, students will forget the refinements of Latin syntax, they will no longer remember a delicate point of law or the year of the battle of Bull Run. The one thing that will endure in true education, however, will be the assurance and the joy that they have reached out not only to those concentric orbs of knowledge which make the ripples of the universe, but have gone out even to the Hand that created those ripples in the immensity of space.

[89]

Youth and Education

THE SUGGESTIONS concerning youth and education contained herein are brief, but they represent the matured reflections of one who was a university professor for twenty-five years and has never ceased to be interested in those who are future citizens of both time and eternity.

1. Reduce the elementary school training to six years and the high school to three, through harder work and more intensive teaching.

2. College education should be an intellectual privilege, not a social necessity. Presently "it is smart to go to college" when we should say "one must be smart to go to college."

3. Introduce two kinds of high schools and colleges: one Standard, the other Honor. The Standard schools would be partly vocational and adapted to the average students. The Honor school would have high intellectual standards with rigorous examinations. It will be objected that such an arrangement would create an "elite." Certainly; those who drive Cadillacs are the economically "elite"; football players are more the "elite" to high school students than brilliant students are. Why not have an intellectual elite? The purpose of the division would be to prevent the leveling down of education to a point where the dumb and the mediocre have the same classes and take the same amount of time as the learned and the industrious. We do more in America for the delinquent than for the intellectual.

4. Meet the rising cost of education in colleges not by raising tuition, but by decreasing the number of courses available. Students would be better educated if certain so-called "life adjustment"

courses were eliminated. Many students take "snap" courses, provided they do not come at nine in the morning. The President of Yale recently received a transcript from a high school student who had courses in chorus, physical education, personality, marriage, English, and speech. If thirty percent of the elective courses were eliminated and the professors given not only sabbatical leave, but Monday to Friday leave, education would improve and the expenses of education would be reduced. Many college courses a good student could absorb without going to class, provided he did ten hours of serious reading.

5. Certain courses should be required in college, such as History, English, Science, Philosophy, and a foreign language. In Switzerland, the students of elementary schools learn three languages. The California State Board of Education has a regulation: "No Foreign language shall be required by a State college as a condition of graduation." The purpose of studying a foreign language is not necessarily to speak it, but to open a door to culture and knowledge not otherwise available. If more Americans spoke French during their visits to Paris, they would not have to shout at the waiter in English, as if he were deaf, instead of them being dumb.

6. When juvenile delinquents destroy any property, their parents should be made to make reparation by paying the damages. It may be hard on the parents, but it is harder on other parents whose property is destroyed.

7. Juvenile delinquents who have been guilty of repeated serious offenses should be sent to a camp for a period of one or two years or more. In this camp there would be a combination of education and hard outdoor work, both under army discipline.

8. In teacher-colleges, the stress should not be on the *methods* of education as it has been up to the present, but on the knowledge of subjects. Too much "how" and too little "know" has depreciated the content of courses and made "know-how" a substitute for "knowledge."

9. Make examinations bear more on the ability of the student to think and to utilize his knowledge, rather than be a guessing game in which he chooses between what is true and what is false by merely marking a paper with a check.

10. Stress quality rather than quantity. A contestant may not go

on "The $64,000 Question" without having passed a test proving familiarity with a subject, before he ever appears before a television camera. Would it not be a good idea for colleges and high schools to give tests to their professors before they go into the classroom? This is necessary because today a teacher who has a Ph.D. is not necessarily educated. He may have written a thesis on "Four Ways of Cooking Ham," which is the subject of one Ph.D. in an American university.

[90]

Differences:
The Training of Man and Woman

EDUCATION TODAY makes no difference between the training of man and woman. This is right from the point of view of opportunities that are open to both, but it is shortsighted when one considers the psychological differences between the two. One of the most obvious and most pointed-out differences is that man is rational and woman intuitive. The man often stands bewildered and confused at what are called a "woman's reasons." They completely escape his understanding because they cannot be analyzed, taken apart and arranged in an orderly sequence. Her conclusions seem to come as a "whole piece." There are no vestibules to the house of her arguments; you walk right into the parlor of a conclusion, and, it seems, often by a trapdoor. The very immediacy of her conclusions startles a man because they obtrude without any apparent foundation. But they are just as unshakable as the reasoned deduction of the male.

A second difference is how they react on one hand to trifles such as the souring of cream and, on the other hand, the great crises such as the loss of a job. Man is much less disturbed by trifles, with the exception of the morning paper's being taken by the neighbor's dog. The daily shocks of life disturb man less; the little things are like drops of water he can absorb in the sponge of his masculinity. The woman, however, is more readily upset by inconsequential things, possessed as she is by a rare talent of turning molehills into mountains.

But when it comes to the great crises of life, it is the woman, in virtue of her gentle power of reigning, who can give great consolation to man in his troubles. She can recover reason and good sense at the very moment the man seems to lose his. When the husband is remorseful, sad, and disquieted, she brings comfort and assurance. As the ocean is ruffled on the surface but calm in the depths, so in a home the man is the rippled surface, the woman the deep and quiet stability.

Another difference is that a man governs the home, but the woman reigns in it. Government is related to justice and law; reigning, to love and feeling. The orders of the father in a home are like written mandates from a king; the influence of the woman, however, is more subtle, more felt and less aggressive. The commands of the father are more intermittent; the quiet pervading radiation of the mother is constant, like the growth of a plant. And yet both are essential for the home, for justice without love could become tyranny, and love without justice could become toleration of evil.

A fourth difference is that woman is less satisfied with mediocrity than man. This may be because man is more attached to the material and the mechanical, and woman more to the biological and the living. The closer one gets to the material, the more one becomes materialized. Nothing so dulls the soul for the finer values of life as counting. But the woman, being the bearer of life, is less indifferent to great values, more quickly disillusioned with the material and the human. This may account for the judgment often made that religion is more natural for women than for men. This is not because woman is more timid and is more likely to seek flight and refuge in the spiritual; it is rather because being less trapped by the material, she is more likely to pursue ideals that transcend the earthly.

These differences, instead of being opposites are actually in a marriage correlated. Man is like the roots of a plant; woman more like the blossom that bears the fruit. One is in communion with the earth and business; the other with the sky and life. One is related to time; the other to eternity. The fusion of both is the prolongation into the home of the Incarnation where Eternity became time and the Word became flesh and the Divine became the human in the person of Christ. Differences are not irreconcilable; rather, they are complementary qualities. The functional differences correspond with certain psychic differences which make one in relation to the others like the violin and the bow, producing the music of a home and the joys of a marriage. They symbolize the mystical marriage of Christ and His bride, the Church.

XVII
The Common Weal

Capital and Labor

THREE THOUGHTS about capital and labor are here offered to those who wish to look beyond petty interests to the graver side of justice and peace of the world.

1. Neither capital nor labor alone is always right in a dispute, because no class is always right simply because it is a class. It used to be the injustice was more often on the side of capital—for example, when it refused to allow collective bargaining, and when it held that the opportunity for a worker to become president of the industry proved there were no limits to individual enterprise. But there is little consolation for the thousandth donkey to receive a carrot if 999 others died of starvation.

But now nothing is more absurd than to claim that one side rather than the other is always right. Take certain criticisms embodied in such words as "monopoly," "controlling Congress," "anonymous power," "violence." Which of these is exclusively the characteristic of capital or the characteristic of labor? The fact is that there is a little of the Old Nick on both sides. Divine Justice implied as much when He was asked to decide a question of inheritance as two sons quarreled over money. His counsel was "Beware of covetousness." In other words, there can be egotism, selfishness, avarice, and oppression, sometimes on one side, sometimes on another.

2. There is something bigger than capital and labor—namely, the public good, the common weal or the citizenry. It used to be that capital and labor were like a husband and wife throwing dishes at each other in the privacy of their home. But now the conflicts of capital and labor are like a husband and wife shooting at each other on the street; they are injuring property, endangering life, and disturbing the peace. In like manner, when there is a strike or lockout everybody suffers: the stockholders, the families of capital and labor, business, the nation, and even we who beg for the poor of the world.

The lepers of the world suffer, for there are fewer deeds of kindness to that work which seeks to heal the afflicted.

Capital and labor, therefore, are not the objects of our national economy; they are the subjects to the economy. The national good does not exist for them; they exist for the national good. Hence there should be found some way of settling these disputes somewhat as other disputes are settled. If two persons quarrel on a street, the magistrate settles the case; domestic courts settle family quarrels; civil courts settle disputes between social and business bodies; international courts adjudicate between nations; the only collectivity which is allowed to throw a nation into confusion is capital and labor. What is bigger than either is humanity, and they must bow down in their particular egotisms to the common good. They must not be like the vested interests of the Gerasenes who expelled Our Lord because He favored the good health of man to two thousand swine. Humanity comes first.

3. The spirit which should animate both capital and labor should be one of retrenchment of desires and the stifling of egotism. In the Christian philosophy of life production exists for consumption, consumption exists for a measure of earthly happiness to acquire virtue and eventually to save one's soul. Today, production exists for consumption and profit, profit exists for more production, more production is increased through advertising which makes us want what we do not need, and want it because it gives us a superiority over others, and also through credit which makes us believe that a credit is not a debt.

The spirit which should animate both capital and labor is that we live in a world wherein the other half is about ready to jump at our throats because of our luxuries. The crushing of our desires for the sake of the poor of the world will do much to bring world peace. We have a rich banquet. Our Lord said to invite not the rich to our banquet, but the poor, the halt, and the lame. Thus will the gap between the rich and poor nations of the world narrow, through the generosity of those who have and the thankfulness of those who have not.

[92]

A Primer on Politics

WHEN A NATION is more concerned with politicians than with states-men, and when politics become identified with expediency, it is well to recall some basic principles of government.

A democracy survives only by rethinking its beginning, as a wheel makes progress by going backward. Four such important principles are:

1. The family is a community prior to the state, because every in-dividual in the state owes his existence to the unity of man and woman. Every citizen is a member of a community of the family be-fore he is a member of the community of the state. That is why the family has rights prior in nature and in time to the state. Demo-cratic states always respect this priority of the family and the right of the family to educate children. The breakup of the family is the beginning of the breakup of the community, and therefore of the nation itself. A democratic state is built up from below—that is, from families and persons, each with inalienable rights; the totalitarian state is built from above by the edict of law or the decree of a dictator. Since totalitarianism admits of no community outside the state, it begins with the destruction of the family through the anarchy of free love or the ethics of the stud farm. The preservation of the family and other natural associations is democracy's first fighting front against the absolute state. A planned society is a slave society.

2. The less individuals and families do for themselves, the more the state must do for them. As citizens cease to feel themselves re-sponsible for the way they live, they increasingly shift responsibility

to the state. The political health of any nation can be measured by how much the people expect the state to give them and how little they expect to do for themselves, or how much they believe the world owes them a living. There are no Community Chests, no Charity Appeals in Russia. The basic principle of totalitarianism is that the state assumes all responsibility for the welfare of its citizens. Slavery cannot only be imposed from the outside but can also be self-imposed, namely by the surrender of a duty to do all one can for himself before he asks the state to do it for him. The larger the state becomes, the less personal are its relations with its citizens. The family, being small, admits of personal affection; the town hall and the village green, in which everyone knew everyone else, made for a community spirit and feeling. But the larger the political institution, the more impersonal it becomes.

3. The more evil people become, the more powerful the state must become to suppress the evil. The less the power of evil in citizens, the less they need the state to suppress evil. The sheep who stay in the green pastures have no need of a dog to bark at their heels. Suppose everyone in a village of one hundred homes was honest. Everyone had the custom of leaving the door unlocked at night. A thief robs one house; it now becomes necessary to buy a hundred locks. If thieves broke into a dozen houses, or the citizens began to steal from one another, a police force would have to be organized to meet the evil. So it is with the state. As a moral sense declines in a democracy, as freedom becomes equated with license, anarchy appears. Then it becomes necessary to suppress that anarchy with power. On a big scale this is the origin of totalitarianism and socialism. Totalitarianism is the forcible reorganization of a chaos created by a false freedom in which everything is allowable. The only way known to history in which people can prevent the state from controlling their lives is for them to control their own.

4. Democracy prospers by avoiding two extremes when confronted by social problems on a vast scale. One false extreme would be to accept them while blaming them on the lack of individual initiative—this is the pessimism of the right. The other way is to forget the individual in need and be conscious only of people in the mass—this is the pessimism of the left. Both dispense themselves from personal efforts toward a social reformation. Those on the right

separate themselves from their fellowman in distress by blaming his failure to cooperate with their will; those on the left separate themselves from their fellowman in distress by being concerned only with the social problem in the abstract.

Democracy makes progress only by realizing that while there is a social problem, its solution must proceed from the individual, first through sacrifice and then through political institutions. In a democracy we will all be bound together, either by the interior bond of affection and love which springs from morality and religion, or by the exterior bond of invasion, war, or atomic destruction. The leaves that are not nourished by the same sap are carried away together by the wind.

XVIII

Communism

Communism and Equality

LIBERATION BEGAN with the idea of liberty, but liberty understood as freedom *from* something rather than freedom for something. Communism began with the idea of equality, in which it was hoped to make everyone happy by establishing a classless society. Communism was not so much concerned with political equality won, by which all men were made equal before the law, but rather with economic equality which was not yet won.

The argument of the Communists was as follows: The reason there are inequalities in the economic order is because of private property. By its very nature, private property is the basis of exploitation, Communism argues. It has built up a system in which one man works for another for wages, and as a result has divided society into two classes: the exploiting class and the exploited class. The way, therefore, to do away with all inequalities is to do away with private property by putting all productive private property into the hands of the state; then all become equal because all are the servants of the state.

Such a solution attributes all the wrongs in the social order to something outside of man instead of something inside—namely, to private property instead of avarice and injustice. But apart from this general observation, there are two great defects in the Communistic scheme of equality. These defects are:

Communism purchases equality at the cost of freedom. Equality is indeed desirable, but not when it is purchased at the cost of freedom, and man being what he is, there is no other way to achieve it. There is no freedom to assert personality, for man is absorbed into the state very much in the fashion that a drop of water is absorbed into a glass of wine. There is no freedom to own property, for the state is the sole employer and reserves for itself the right of exploitation. There is no freedom of religion, for that is equivalent to admitting that God is above the Party. There is no freedom to dissent politically, for no rival parties are tolerated, each one being poured into the mold of the state. There is no freedom to think, for propaganda backed up by terror determines what one shall think, what one shall do. Freedom thus becomes identified with the will of the Party, which in Russia represents only one and one-half percent of the population. The result is that the state, instead of being a policeman as it was under liberalism, becomes a nurse which takes care of men from the cradle to the grave. Planning becomes a mania; personality is mechanized down to the very core of being, and the noble creature who once was regarded as a child of God, and who came to be regarded under capitalism only as a hand, was now under Communism regarded only as a stomach that had to be fed to pile up wealth for the state.

Despite the fact that Communism condemns capitalism, it ignores the best features of capitalism and preserves only its worst. The worst feature of capitalism is that it makes the economic the principal end of man; Communism says that the economic is the unique end of man. One of the worst features of capitalism was its individual selfishness; Communism transforms individual selfishness into collective selfishness. It claims that it hates capitalism and yet it imports specialists in capitalism to build up a capitalistic system in Russia. It hates capitalism only because it wants to be capitalistic itself. The Communist is scandalized by the injustices of the economic order not because he is poor in spirit, but only because he is tempted by the wealth of others' possessions. Capitalism in its worst form could exercise only economic rights over the employee, but under Communism not only economic rights but even juridical rights are exercised over the worker, for Communism decides where he shall work and when he shall work, at what salary he will work, that he shall not strike, that he shall not have a minimum wage, and that if he does not work where he is told to work, the words "disorganizer of labor" will be written across his passport. The result is that man under Communism simply becomes a chattel.

Wealth is held in common under Communism, but administration is not common. It is only natural, therefore, for everyone to wish to become an administrator in order that he might divide for himself the choice spoils. It is one thing to ask a thousand boys to put all of their marbles into a barrel and it is quite another thing to be sure that the ten boys who were picked out to divide the marbles will distribute them equally among the 990. Where find the economic eunuchs who will be so free from the passion of both wealth and power that all will receive equally? Communism is not the answer.

[94]

Imperialism

TODAY MEN AND nations fight not with ideas, but with words. A slogan endlessly repeated or an epithet repeatedly hurled is presumed to brainwash the need of further thinking. The most common charge thrown by the Communists against the "unbelievers" of the Western world is that of "imperialism." The Soviets had a quarrel with Tito and they blamed it on the imperialism of the United States; the missionaries of China were arrested and tortured by Communists on the ground that they were "agents of the imperialistic governments of the West."

In order to understand what the Communists mean by imperialism, it must be recalled that the Soviets have as a basic principle that they should always accuse others of the crime of which *they* are most guilty, and to do it first, thus making it difficult to hurl the charge back at them. They deprive millions of the right of suffrage and free press, then accuse the other nations of being "destroyers of freedom"; they initiate a one-man rule with absolute autocratic authority, and then blame the other nations of being "enemies of democracy." So it is with the charge of imperialism.

The Soviets today possess over one third of the earth's surface and over one third of the earth's population, and frankly state that they are bent on bringing the whole world under the servitude of Communism. Obviously, this would be imperialism. What better way is there to distract the world from their imperialism than to accuse the nonimperialistic nations of the world of being guilty of that crime?

What is happening in the world today is actually what happened to the Roman Empire after the spread of Christianity. The Roman Empire was imperialistic. There was one ruler, Caesar; one capital, Rome; one official language, Latin. Most of the emperors called themselves a god, a pontiff, or a lord. Both body and soul belonged to Caesar; there was no worship but state worship, no God but the state god who was Caesar.

When Christianity appeared, the very word which was used in Greek for emperor was "Lord"; it was also applied to Christ, Who was called *Kurios,* or Lord. It was a falsely divine title with the emperor; it was a truly Divine title with Christ the Son of God. At the birth of Christ, the angels announced that "the Lord was born." That was why Herod was troubled, because there was now another Lord besides Caesar. Later on, Our Blessed Lord distinguished between the political power of emperor and the religious authority of God, saying that to Caesar should be given the things that are Caesar's, but to God the things that are God's.

A persecution followed. There was no lord but Caesar. Christianity challenged the belief that the worship men owed to Caesar was total and complete; it affirmed that man had a soul and hence was not obligated to the political in the totality of his being. But the emperors, in claiming divinity, sentenced hundreds of thousands of Christians to death, for there was only one lord to them, which was Caesar.

The Communists today are somewhat like the Caesars: man belongs to the state; there is no thought of his which escapes state control; there is only one lord, one god, one master, and his name is the dictator. But there is this difference: the Romans admitted that they were imperialists; the Communists do not, because the word has changed its meaning in the course of the centuries. Imperialism to the Soviets means all those who are opposed to the Communist rule or, really, to Communist imperialism.

In that sense, the charge which the Communists hurl against the Western world, instead of being one of opprobrium, is one of glory.

If "imperialism" today means opposition to the identification of Caesar and God; if "imperialism" is a protest against the seizure of Eastern Europe, North Korea, and Vietnam; if "imperialism" means a diplomatic protest against the murders of those in Hungary who sought liberation from the Soviet yoke; if "imperialism" means that man has another imperium than that of the Communist state, then let imperialism prosper, and trust in the one *Kurios* who can overthrow the regime bent on the servitude of the human race.

[95]

Is Leprosy a Point of View?

THE ATTITUDE OF politicians and nations to the Soviet Union is the best public index to the character of either a person or a state. He who would contend that it makes no difference whether one has leprosy or not is already judged, for he has failed to make the most radical and fundamental distinction of physical life—that between disease and health. Communism is to the social body what leprosy is to the physical body; in fact it is more serious, for Communism affects personality directly, while disease affects the mind and soul only indirectly. In moral language, Communism is intrinsically evil. It is evil because it submerges and destroys personality to the status of an ant in an anthill; free government is made impossible through its basic principle enunciated by Engels, that freedom is necessity or obedience to a dictator.

There is no need to draw up other reasons why Communism is wicked or why the world has been more unhappy since 1917 than it has in any other equal period of time. The point is that if our world blurred the distinction between health and disease as it has blurred the distinction between right and wrong, we would have little reason for hospitals, nurses, or doctors. If those who say that cancer is bad are expressing only "a point of view," then health is no longer a standard. What is curious is that as the distinctions between true and false, right and wrong, good and evil have become confused, there has been an almost scrupulous dedication to the importance of health. Everyone is germ-conscious, but few are conscious of evil.

So too, when Soviet leaders talk "peace," there are not wanting statesmen who will say, "Communism is no longer evil"; which being translated means tuberculosis is no longer a disease, leprosy is no longer an affliction. But can the leopard change his spots or the Ethiopian his skin? Has there been a single repudiation of the slavery principle on the part of the Soviets? Would it not be better for the Free World to take an entirely new attitude toward the new tactics of Communism, such as the following:

Instead of the Free World always being in the position of answering the notes of the Communists, would it not be well to have them answering our notes for a while? Why should the robber who wants to keep the jewels he has stolen be the one to open negotiations with the rightful owners for keeping them? Should peace notes always begin with the supposition that the jewels of Poland and Hungary are to remain within the iron setting of the Soviets? The Free World is on the defensive, instead of being on the offensive. Liberty, truth, right to self-government, which were the bulwarks of Western civilization, are now no longer invoked against a regime which tramples on them. Day has become night and night has become day. What Nietzsche once said as an individual has become true of a world power: "Evil, be thou my good." By becoming indifferent to the hard, fast line which divides justice from injustice, right from wrong, the Western world has ceased to be militant about those political virtues on which its great civilization has been built.

There come moments when buyers and sellers must be driven out of the temple. Why should not the Free World, instead of being obliged to acknowledge a note, begin mailing notes out first, like bills long overdue, and let them be mailed often. Why should not the first note rehearse the injustice to Poland, the second to Hungary, and so on through the countries behind the Iron Curtain; then let there be notes about North Korea and Vietnam and Afghanistan. What courage it would give to the enslaved peoples to know that we were pleading for their liberation! It would certainly stir their souls more to hope, than the knowledge that we had given more dollars than Russia had given rubles. Right is right when nobody is right, and wrong is wrong if everybody is wrong. Besides, if we defend right, we shall have God on our side, and if He is with us, who can be against us?

[96]

Betrayal with a Kiss

No ONE HAS ever written a philosophy of betrayal, unless it was Machiavelli who told kings and princes how to deceive their fellow-men. But his counsel was not actual betrayal, but just sheer worldly, pragmatic advice in which the useful became identified with the true. Actually, the pattern and the model of betrayal has been written—and forgotten. Take, for example, the principle upon which the Soviets conduct their international policy. It can be reduced to three principles: 1. Materialism; 2. Coexistence; 3. Betrayal at the moment of greatest friendship and coexistence.

First, materialism. Its basic principle is denial of God and the soul. God must be denied, because if there is a power other than the Party or the dictator, then men have other rights and liberties than those given them by the Party. The foundation of our rights and liberties as given in the Declaration of Independence is that they are given by God. The soul must be denied too by the Communists, because the soul contemplates and thinks for itself. But any personal thought which cannot be socially controlled must be denied by the Communists in order that there be only one thought—namely, the Party thought.

The second principle is coexistence. This is a Soviet word, not the word of free peoples. The latter never ask themselves if they should coexist. Such talk would be nonsense between Canada and the United States. Coexistence is a Soviet suggestion that relations which exist between the free peoples of the world who believe in decency, morality, honesty, and truth should be extended to the Soviet Union which Lenin said must use every lie, stratagem, ruse, and deceit in order to foster world revolution.

The basis of coexistence talk is given in an article published in the Soviet Union in 1954 by a certain Leontyev. His argument was that the atomic bomb makes war mutually destructive of the powers which engage in it. The Soviets can no longer rely upon their mighty armies and those of the satellites to conquer the world. Hence, there must be "long periods of coexistence" with democratic and free peoples, until the historical moment arrives for the world conquest of Communism.

The third principle is that the betrayal of those who fall for coexistence must be at the moment of greatest intimacy and friendship. For example on August 31, 1939, the Soviets signed a pact recognizing the independence of Estonia, Lithuania, and Latvia. On this occasion the Soviet Government published the following: "These pacts of mutual assistance strictly stipulate the inviolability of the sovereignty of the signatory powers, and the principle of non-interference in each other's affairs. We stand for the scrupulous and punctilious observance of the pacts on the basis of complete reciprocity, and we declare that all the spreading of nonsense about Sovietizing the Baltic countries is only to the advantage of our common enemies, and of all Soviet provocateurs."

The following year, the Soviets annexed the three countries. Is this pattern of betrayal new? Or does it follow a line which brought upon the world its greatest blackness? The model of deceit and betrayal was actually set by Judas. First of all, avarice was not his basic sin; it was materialism, or a denial of spiritual values. The first mention of avarice as regards Judas comes at the very end of his life, though he is described as a traitor much earlier when Our Lord spoke of Himself as God, and foretold that He would suffer and die, rise and ascend again into heaven. When He refused to be King of the masses, when He refused to establish a kingdom based on earthly bread, Judas broke, for he had nothing but contempt for the spiritual.

Then came coexistence. Never once during the public life did anyone know that Judas was the guilty man; when he spoke of the poor, some of the disciples joined in with him; and at the Last Supper when he left the table, it was thought that he had gone out to give money to the poor or buy food for the feast. His coexistence was so clever that only John knew who he was—and, of course, the all-knowing Lord. Even the best were deceived.

The third stage came at the moment of greatest affection, when Judas kissed Our Lord and then delivered Him over to the soldiers. Sacred things can be betrayed only by some mark of affection and esteem. Let America beware! To pleas for coexistence, America must ask, "Wilt thou betray with a kiss?"

[97]

Why Don't They Say It?

IF A NEIGHBOR across the street from where you live had knowingly and certainly robbed every other house on your side of the street save your own; if he had murdered some of the homeowners or else sent a few of them into exile; if he had stripped many rooms of furniture and brought the contents into his own house and then begun accusing you of being a robber and a thief and a murderer, even writing articles to the paper to that effect, what would you do? Would you merely say that you were not a robber, or would you write to the newspapers and merely state that you are not a thief? Or if he made these charges in court, would you be silent about the plundering of the houses and the enslavement of some of the children? Then why is it that when the United States and the Western world are accused of being oppressors of people, wanting to start a nuclear war and enslave people, of being imperialistic and an enemy of peace, do we merely make denials at the United Nations instead of giving a list of the countries that they have robbed, pillaged, raped and confiscated? Why do we not name names, and remind the Soviet Union of some of the countries they have confiscated, such as the Ukraine, Rumania, Hungary, East Germany, Estonia, Latvia, the Karelian Isthmus of Finland, Poland, Lithuania, Bulgaria, Armenia, Albania, Outer Mongolia, Azerbaijan, Kirghiztan, Uzbekistan, and others? Why do we not bring up before the United Nations, day after day, the problem of the liberation of each of these countries? When they were taken over Molotov said, "The carrying into effect of the present pact must in no way affect the sovereign rights of the contracting parties." Within a short time, the contracting parties were deprived of all rights.

Instead of being on the defensive, would not our strength lie less in constantly dealing with the Soviets than in pleading for the liberty and independence of the submerged populations of Eastern Europe? There is nothing that so much disturbs a thief as to be caught with the stolen goods in his own hands, and not all the waters of the seven seas are enough to wash the blood from the Soviet hands that suppressed the freedom fighters of Hungary.

As Molotov lied when he said that he would allow the nations of Eastern Europe to preserve their integrity and sovereignty, so too Soviets today continue the dictum of Lenin to lie, deceive, and distort in order to further the Soviet revolution. In one of the very best books that has been written on the Soviets, Lin Yutang in *The Secret Name* wrote about the conferences at Yalta: "Churchill believed Stalin; Roosevelt and Truman believed him. Roosevelt smoked a puny cigarette, Churchill smoked a long cigar, and Stalin smoked a pipe and he won. Stalin lived up to the words he had spoken before Yalta: Words have no relation to actions—otherwise what kind of diplomacy is it? Words are one thing; actions another. Good words are a mask for a concealment of bad deeds. Sincere diplomacy is no more possible than dry water or wooden air." So long as the Soviets can make the United States discuss nuclear warfare, space, summit meetings, and the free city of Berlin, it distracts the

Western world from the basic problem of taking the stolen goods from their hands. The last World War started because of Poland. Its modern history has been that of a crucifixion between two thieves—Nazism and Communism. Nothing will happen to the world until something happens to Poland.

[98]

The Great Jailer

ONCE UPON a time, there was a Great Jailer who was invited to visit a people who boasted they were not captive or imprisoned. What made his visit so unique was that this Great Jailer had millions and millions of people in his prison; some of them he put to death before they even got to jail, and others who tried to break out of their jail were driven back with tanks. The problem that faced the free people when the Great Jailer came to their free country was: "What should I think?" "How should I act?"

1. Do not think you will make the Great Jailer anxious to throw away the keys of his prison simply because he sees that you have longer automobiles, better hair-dos, more electric gadgets, more rooms in your apartment, richer food at your table, and the greatest per capita income in the world. Remember that the Great Jailer is already a rich man—richer than anyone in America; he owns all the lumber, all the steel, all the railroads, all the autos, all the housing in his own land. The Great Jailer who became rich through "confiscation" does not envy your national wealth; he envies your *personal* wealth. Personal wealth is the economic guarantee of your freedom. He knows that your right to call property your own is yours because you already have a soul which you can call your own.

This is a great challenge to the Great Jailer. If the Great Jailer believed in the Spirit, he would rejoice in your well-being, because the spiritual man rejoices in the property of others. But being a materialist, the Great Jailer envies your freedom; it embarrasses him before other nations of the world. As Chesterton said, "There is a spirit which drives men incessantly on to destroy what they cannot understand, and to capture what they cannot enjoy." Think not, therefore, that seeing your comforts will make him work hard to catch up to you in a peaceful world. Rather, he may think it wise to destroy what you already possess. Do all men in the face of saintliness seek to be good? Are there not some men in the face of goodness who seek to crucify? Your freedom is not an object of pious emulation; it is an object to be destroyed.

2. As your economic prosperity and freedom will never change him, so neither will a visit to you change his philosophy of life. *Remember that the Great Jailer is himself a prisoner.* He is the prisoner of a collectivity from which he cannot escape. The leopard cannot change his spots, nor the Ethiopian his skin. In brainwashing others, the Great Jailer has become brainwashed. The touch of Christ's Lips did not make Judas less the traitor. The Great Jailer's life is not his own; it belongs to the anthill; the moment he changes his mind or heart, he will suffer the liquidation he has ministered unto others for changing their hearts. There are some who will not believe, though one rise daily from the dead. His basic philosophy is that freedom is not in the person, but in the Party; it is the Party who decides who shall live and not live. It is, therefore, not a person who is visiting you; it is a *Philosophy*; it is a *Party*; it is the *Great Jaildom*.

3. Think not that because the Great Jailer comes, not with the prison keys rattling from his hammer and sickle, that he has nothing to do with bars and cells. In all human relations with the Great Jailer, remember the prisoners! Prisoners who are so thin they stand like poles in their imprisonment; who are so hungry they even make the name of their country sound like their starvation; remember that in some jails the prisoners wear not stripes but checks. Look then at the Great Jailer as if he were transparent; see through him to the millions who weep tears at the sight of a free man from a free country; see through the Jailer to the hands lifted saying, "Betray us not. The world is upside down! Those who should be in prison are the

jailers. Now is verified the words of Innocence behind bars: 'I was in prison and you visited Me.'"

Finally, do not insult or injure or be unkind in word or deed to the Great Jailer. Freemen must not lower themselves to the level of those who would destroy freedom. There must be moments of silence before the Great Jailer as Christ was silent before the Jailer Herod because he sent John to his death; but there should be moments of speech, warm and sincere, as the Great Jailer is shown not just our reactors, but our churches and our synagogues. Take him to a synagogue, to a Protestant Church and to a Catholic Church during services, that he may see that we are great, not because we challenge God and seek to destroy Him as is done in his Jaildom, but because we love and worship Him Who has endowed us with, as our Declaration of Independence says, "unalienable rights" and among which are "life, liberty and the pursuit of happiness."

XIX
The World

The Atomic Bomb: A Symbol

It is so easy to justify ourselves in the face of that which is evil, like the story of Mark Twain's young lad of Tahiti, who, on hearing the story of how Cain killed Abel, asked the missionary: "What was Abel fooling around there for, anyway?" The modern version of this was the American comedian, who, on hearing of Japan's sneak attack, asked: "What was Pearl Harbor doing in the Pacific anyway?"

It is often the custom of those who have done what is wrong to picture themselves as the victims of unjust attacks and reprisals. In some such way, the use of the atomic bomb is justified. But the point to be kept in mind is that even if there were no atomic bomb, people would still face the future with misgiving. What makes the modern man uneasy, apprehensive about the future, and fearful of what is before him is not so much something *outside* himself as something *inside* himself. The atomic bomb is only a highly concentrated symbol of the two subjects which most engage modern dramatists and philosophers: fear and death.

Men feared fear before, and they feared death before, but there is a new element in the fear and in the death. Previously their fear was directed to something *outside* themselves, like a wild beast, or a pestilence, or loss of fortune; now it is directed to something inside themselves, which makes psychiatry so necessary. Death before was regarded as individual; now it is regarded as social. It is not only that the ego must die, but that we are in danger of collective death. Kirkegaard and Sartre, Heidigger and Jaspers, Marcel and Lavelle— so runs the litany of modern writers who have been tearing their brains out, trying to find an answer to these two problems.

Atomic energy is a great God-given gift, but in the bomb that energy is unloosed without a principle of internal or moral control. As such, it is a symbol of the modern mind that has lost the inner control of mind and soul, and thus becomes panicky about fear and death. Mockers of religion used to say that man made God to his own image and likeness. But now it is certainly true that men have made the atomic bomb to their own image and likeness; the split self in fear of living, and dread of dying.

Is it possible that the split man, who feels civil war inside himself, will use the split atom to destroy himself? In the last century, when scientists were boasting that they were just beginning to lisp the alphabet of destruction, some prophetic words were uttered by Goncourt. He had been visited by the two great scientists Berthelot and Bernard. In the course of the conversation, they unfolded to him the tremendous forces of destruction which the science of physics would unleash in the next century. To which Goncourt observed, "And when that day comes, I think that God shall come down from the heaven, rattling His keys, like a night watchman, saying, 'Gentlemen, it's closing time, and we'll have to start all over again.' If such a time comes, then will be fulfilled one of the beatitudes. When the great cities like Babylon are burned like papers, there will still be left the coolie in his rice patch, the cowboy on his plains, and the farmer with his plow. Then shall be verified: 'The meek shall inherit the earth.' "

Other ages went to God by reason, still others by faith; our age will go to Him through trial and error. Having burned itself on atomic fires, it will learn to have Hope in the Divine Physician. In the bright cloud which Constantine saw over the battlefield, he espied a cross, and under it the words: "In this sign thou shalt conquer." Modern man has already seen over Hiroshima and Nagasaki, and maybe over a future city yet unnamed, another cloud, the sign of the split atom, and under it the words: "In this sign thou shalt not conquer." It will be trial through error, but man can come back again to God even by writing with crooked lines.

[100]

Revolution

SUPPOSE ONE took a thousand feet of movie film, cut it up into a thousand pieces, scrambled them, and then showed them in succession on a screen. That would be a sample of how some people look on world events—namely, as a meaningless succession of happenings tied together by no common thread other than the fact that they constitute "late news." Social and political upheavals round about us are seen as happening in a vacuum, without any relation to what has gone before, without any relevance to the future. Nothing is so holding up the modern man's understanding of world events as his neglect of history. Actually, there is nothing really very new happening in the world today; there are the same old things happening to different people.

How pitiable is a loss of memory or a mind with amnesia which cannot make any adjustment of a present experience to past life. What memory is to man, history is to civilization. As no one can think unless he goes back into the storehouse of his memory to draw out thoughts and experiences as the basis for new thoughts, so neither can one rightly interpret news and events when one recoils from history. If there is anything that distinguishes man from the monkey, it is his consciousness of duration. But today the emphasis on youth, the catering preponderantly to juvenile tastes, the decline of parental authority, and the identification of progress with contempt for the past have all conspired to an amnesia which tokens a betrayal of the heritage of civilization.

We live in a revolutionary age, but the revolutionary spirit did not start with the Russian Revolution. Actually there have been three great revolutions in the last four hundred years. Within the last two centuries, one that gave impetus to the present was the French Revolution, which was political in nature. This was a revolution on the part of the middle classes against the Royalists, as the Communist revolution later on was a revolution of the masses against the bourgeois or the middle classes who had become capitalists. There has actually been a continuous revolution for several hundred years, one growing out of the other.

Now turn to the East and to Africa, where the vast majority of people are like giants being roused from a long slumber, but endowed with new power after long repose. Are the revolutions, even the nationalistic ones, unrelated to the West? It would seem so at first, because most of them have a contempt for the West. The answer is in the negative. First of all, the leaders of the revolutions in Asia and Africa for the most part received their education in the West; second, the Communism which inspired some revolutions such as China is Western in origin, inasmuch as the entire ideology of Marxism was the result of the decadent European thought of seventeenth- and eighteenth-century Europe. Third, the constitutions which the new states adopt are somewhat in the line of the French Revolution; fourth, hidden in the hearts of a small proportion of the people, as a leaven in the mass, are those who live by the superior insights given to them by Christian missionaries who came from the West. Thus the revolutionary movement which began in Europe and was spread first to the bourgeois, then to Eastern Europe, then to the proletariat, is now fomenting in Asia and Africa. Thus there is a paradox: the debt of the new nationalisms of the world is to the West, but on the other hand they are anti-Western, due principally to Communist propaganda and to the bad taste left from the era of colonialism.

History still has a deeper meaning than this revolutionary background, but only those with faith in God can see it: namely, the rise and fall of civilizations are a kind of a way of the Cross or a roadway on which is worked out the advancement of the Kingdom of God. Judgments come to nations which are their fall, as a headache, which is a judgment, comes to those who do not eat. Each nation has its moment of grace, its decline, and then its disaster. The real problem of the world is to find unity—materialism cannot do it, for materialism divides and separates; men can quarrel over the division of a dollar. Only the spiritual unites—the more men know poetry and the more they say prayers together, the more they are united. The unifying spirit comes from religion, and it is to the Divine that men must look for unity. Nations cannot unite any more than one hundred twenty pencils can tie themselves into a bundle; there must be something outside of the UN to make the Nations United, and that is the Spirit.

[101]

Poland or World War III*

THE PRINCIPAL READING of the vast majority of people is the daily newspaper. This means that their thinking is to a great degree standardized, that their knowledge of the world is derived principally from one source, and that what *has* happened is of little importance, for nothing is as old as yesterday's newspaper. But the past is not a dead past, but a living past. As our memory influences our present actions and our future decisions, so what has transpired in our political world determines to a great extent what will happen in the future. Among the past events, perhaps no one of recent years so much summarizes our problems as the forgotten tragedy of Poland.

We remember some years ago writing these lines for a radio broadcast: "Poland has been crucified between two thieves." By the two thieves were meant the Nazis and the Soviets. The American people in those days believed that the Soviets were sincere, despite Lenin's dictum that "we must use every lie, deceit, and cunning in order to establish world revolution." We received a telegram from

* In view of the dramatic events that took place in Poland in 1980–82, it is of interest to note that this article was written in 1953. —Editor.

one of our censors saying that we could not make that statement over the air because it would be offensive to the Soviets. We sent back a wire saying: "How would it be if we call Russia the good thief?" But the censor did not think it a bit funny.

The fact was and still is that Poland has been crucified between two thieves. Eighty-five percent of its homes were destroyed first by the Nazis, and one million were made homeless. Then came the Soviets to give permanence to ruin and add new links to the chains of slavery. It was because of Poland that the Second World War began, and so it was understood as men spoke of "Danzig or the Second World War." Though journalists today speak of Russia and the Third World War, a more just appraisal would be "Poland or the Third World War." Poland is the cameo of the world situation; the knot of political Europe; the key to whether we will have justice or force in the world for the next hundred years.

The uniqueness of Poland is derived not from the fact that the Soviets have raped Poland and taken it into their imperialistic harem, but because at the end of World War II Europe concurred in the crime. What disappeared was the Poland for which England and France took up arms, the Poland which was at the heart of the Atlantic Charter to which Stalin subscribed. The Atlantic Charter promised that every people and every nation would be allowed to choose the government it saw fit; Poland was denied this, first by the invasion of the Soviets and then by the concurrence of Europe in the murder of Poland.

The United Nations never seems to see the inconsistency of the Soviets stirring up trouble through Africa and Asia and South America by inciting nationalism, while at the same time denying it to Poland and the other countries behind the Iron Curtain. Russia had no right over Poland—that is elementary international ethics. For Europe to give juridical sanction to what was taken by force was to agree in the robbery.

Just suppose that the whole emphasis of the Free World in the United Nations were changed. Suppose that, instead of organizing political forces against the "enemy" Russia, it changed the emphasis and reopened the question of Poland? The stress would then be not on resisting an evil, but on defending a right. No nation is strong when it opposes another nation because it steals; but every nation is strong when it affirms that honesty shall be the policy in all international relations. There is more vigor in uniting for the rights of Poland than in uniting against the imperialism of Russia.

If free nations take not the position of loving the good, then the hope of Poland must be beyond all hopes of politics. Then there must be combined in our hearts a faithfulness to the duty of restoring Poland, along with a recognition of the enormous inequality of the task. Our hopes then must be likened to the flowers and trees that shed their verdure in the long winters, only to be reborn in another spring. One hundred years ago one of the heroes of Poland, Mickiewicz, wrote: "Poland, you will be taken out of the tomb, because you are believing, loving and full of hope." If the nations fail, then Poland must trust in the Christ Who wept over the tomb of Lazarus, and Who weeps now over Poland. Poland will then find its glory assured in Him Who says, "I am the Resurrection and the Life."

[102]

Collectivity or Community?

HE WHO CONCENTRATES too much on the succession of letters in a word is apt to miss its meaning. He who knows the world through the hourly commentator or the daily headline is apt to miss the deep current that underlies these events. The closer the hand is to the eye, the less the eye sees; mountains are seen best from the valleys and the world is best understood when we stand apart from it. Otherwise our understanding of it is likely to become like an impressionist painting in which fascination lies in segments instead of the whole.

What is actually going on in the world today is what might be called fragmentation or a splitting of wholes, unities, and organisms. One sees it in politics in the wave of nationalism that is sweeping through Asia and Africa, in which small ethnic groups dissociate themselves from the commonwealth of nations and the peace of the world. It is seen in family life in which husband and wife are fragmented when both work in different occupations, or when the only unity in the home is a common financial return or else its status as a dormitory. Fragmentation appears in literature when stories do not end, they just stop. Having no one basic idea to present, writers piece together meaningless chatter between spineless characters, hoping that "free association" will supply the plot. Fragmentation appears in medicine when doctors are made specialists instead of physicians, and when organs are treated instead of sick people. The splitting or fission process continues in psychology when the total personality is no longer studied, but only one very small and unimportant part of it, such as subconsciousness or instinct. Advertising, too, breaks up the personality when it assumes that people have no God-given reason, but are rather like animals who can be trained to do certain things if a suggestion is repeated often enough, for example, "*Allium sativum* tastes good like garlic should."

But the fragmentation is more serious when the world, a nation, and a people become split up into tiny little loyalties that are permitted to hold precedence over the common good. It used to be that people lived in what might be called "community." On a large scale, this might have been the Roman Empire, or the great Medieval unity called Christendom. Community could also be applied to small groups such as farmers who at harvest time help one another so the good of all is served. But today the splitting and fragmentation has produced what might be called a "collectivity," or group which serves only the purpose of the group and ignores larger interests outside the group. Politicians in Congress who vote with the party when their consciences tell them that the best interests of the public are not served are typical of "collective" activity. Members of economic groups, such as labor unions or management councils, have the "collective" spirit when they blindly follow the group self-interest to the detriment of the public.

In the community, the movement is toward unity, togetherness, and its motive force is within persons. But in the collectivity, the semblance of unity comes from without, from a dictator, from a leader, from a directive which must be followed whether one believes it or not. In the community, there is communion of one person with another; in the collective there is proximity and spatial contiguity of members, like bricks in a house.

Communism is the supreme example of collectivism. Its unity is achieved through common ownership of property. The assumption is that if the State divides an apple between the citizens, all will be equal and united. The supreme example of community is that of the Spirit. Before the Spirit of God descended on the apostles at Pentecost, each had his own separate interest; they quarreled for first place and disputed as to who would have authority. But their unity came through sharing of the same spirit. Only the spirit unites men. Fifty men can learn a poem, and yet no one person who learns it deprives another of knowing it, because learning is a spiritual process. But divide a melon between twenty men and quarreling begins, because materiality is division, and division is dispute, and dispute is selfish interest, and selfish interest is "collectivity." Christianity teaches that no man can save himself alone; he must save himself with others or be lost. This is "community," fraternal charity, union of capital and labor, and international unity.

[103]

The Dark Side of Good

BECAUSE OF cold wars, high taxes, threats of Communism, and general insecurity, we have become accustomed to take a dark view of the world. There is some justification for this, for never before in the history of Christian civilization has there ever been such a mass attack on decency, honor, personal rights and freedom as there is at the present hour. While there is justification for looking on the dark side because of evil, there is, however, no justification for the present tendency to look upon the dark side of good. It is one thing to be gloomy about starvation, but it is quite another matter to be gloomy about good health; disease has its shadows, but why see shadows in health? In a word, why is it that so many see the dark side of virtue, goodness, honesty, purity, and honor?

In other ages, though men lost virtue, they still admired it; though they ran from the battlefield at the first need of courage, they still admired the hero who fought and suffered; though they threw away the map of the roadway of life, they never denied the need of a map. But, in our generation, men look for shadow in the radiance of every virtue. Love of truth is called harshness and intolerance; purity is called abnormality or fear of totems or myths; humility is termed weakness; the meek are made to appear as lacking in force and strength; those who pray and believe in God are labeled "escapists"; the generous are accused of seeking acclaim; the contemplative are sneered at as "useless"; the husband of one wife and a devoted father of a family is "in a rut."

A civilization can be forgiven for seeing the dark side of evil, but should it not examine its conscience when it begins to fear the dark side of the good? The right and normal reaction when one sees a shadow is to think of the light; in fact the darker the shadow, the brighter the light. Goodness needs but little explanation, for good is self-propagating and self-explanatory; it is evil, darkness, and suffering which need explanation. One does not only conclude to the existence of God because there are good things in the world; but one argues that because there is evil in the world, therefore there must be a God, for evil is a parasite on goodness. It has no capital of its own. Darkness is not a positive entity; darkness is the absence of light and is intelligible only in terms of light. Most of the suffering of the world is intelligible in terms of the abuse of something that is so profoundly good that not even God will take it away for all eternity, and that is our freedom.

Whence, then, comes the tendency to see the bad in things, if it be not that our consciences are already so burdened with guilt and hidden distortions that to ease them we have to minimize the good in others and drag them down to the level of the worst or else reduce heroism to mediocrity? Public officials are thought to be best described when not the good that they do is recounted, but when some suspicion or slur is cast upon their characters. The kettles are unhappy unless they call the pots black.

How our outlook on the world would change if the makers of public opinion, instead of seeing the dark side of the evil alone would see the bright side of the good; if they would single out politicians, businessmen, labor leaders, parents and others who mirror forth great virtues and moral integrity, then the evil of the world would be more quickly overcome. When pestilence is abroad, it is encouraging to know that there are recoveries and there are many who are not stricken. But if our doctors are accused of being diseased and our teachers are accused of ignorance; if our public officials are all crooks, then who shall hope?

We do not make children give up writing because they spill the ink. The world is discouraged enough; it needs encouragement, inspiration, good example; above all, it will be happier when it sees a standard and a Redeemer Who invites us away from the dark side: "I am the Light of the world; he that followeth Me walketh not in darkness."

XX

Renewing
the World

A Recall to the Inner Life

A FATHER GAVE his little son a cut-up puzzle of the world and asked him to put it together. The boy finished the picture in an amazingly short time. When the astonished father asked him how he did it, the boy answered, "There was a picture of a man on the other side; when I put the man together, the world came out all right." Such is the key to the understanding of all the political and economic problems of our day. Nothing ever happens to the world which does not first happen inside man. Wars are not made by politics, but by politicians with a certain philosophy of life. No explanation of war has ever been as clear as the Biblical one which declares that wars are punishments on man for his sin. Not a punishment in the sense that God sends a war as a father spanks a child for an act of disobedience, but rather that a war follows a breakdown of morality, as thunder follows lightning, and as blindness follows the plucking out of the eye.

The people of this century have lived through an era where war is more "normal" than peace. There has been literally fulfilled what Nietzsche prophesied—namely, that the twentieth century would be a century of wars. War is a symptom of the breakdown of civilization. There are only different degrees of guilt among the combatants. All is not black on one side, and all is not white on another. When a body becomes diseased, the germ does not localize in one organ to the exclusion of all others; it infects the whole bloodstream. So the evil of our day is the evil not of the East or the West, but of the world. It is of the world because men generally have become estranged from the true center of their spiritual life. Having ceased to fear God, in the sense of filial fear such as a child has for a father, they have begun to fear man with a servile fear, such as a slave has for a tyrant.

Modern man has become passive in the face of evil. He has so long preached a doctrine of false tolerance, has so long believed that right and wrong were only differences in a point of view, that now when evil works itself out in practice he is paralyzed to do anything against it. Political injustice, chicanery in high office, and organized crime leave him cold. While keeping very busy and active on the outside, he is passive and inert on the inside, because he rarely enters into his own heart. Remedying the evil therefore falls to agencies and mechanical realities external to man. No government or state can put the screws on personal freedom, unless the citizens have already abdicated in themselves the basis of that freedom—namely, their responsibility to God.

Having lost his inward unity, man is more and more compelled to seek the unity outside himself in the unity of organization. Disclaiming all responsibility, he surrenders it more and more to the state. The sheep that will not obey the shepherd must be retrieved by a dog barking at their heels. The citizens who will not obey the moral laws of God must be organized by a dictator snapping at their souls. The weakening of the inner spiritual life is the basic cause of the disharmony and discord which prevail throughout the world. The forcible organization of the chaos created by the enfeeblement of the moral sense always calls forth some dictator who makes law personal rather than a reflection of the Eternal harmony that rules in the heavens.

A great burden is thrust upon men who call themselves religious. In this fatal hour, all of their energies should be spent recalling man to his spiritual destiny and summoning him to invoke the God Who made him. Instead of that there are some who would accuse their neighbors, who also believe in God, of being disloyal to their country, or else of trying to impose their faith by force on their fellow citizens. Such lies do a disservice both to God and to country. And their supposed faith in God is to be questioned, because no one who loves God hates his neighbor, nor does he try to incite citizen against citizen through slander. Let those who call themselves Catholics, or Protestants, or Jews recall that the function of their religion is to intensify the spiritual life of man and not to empty the vials of bitterness into hearts, stirring up one against another. It is not to the politicians and the economists and the social reformers that we must look for the first steps in this spiritual recovery; it is to the professed religious. The nonreligious can help by repudiating those who come to them in the name of God or America and say that their neighbor does not love either. Religion must not be a cloak covering the dagger of hate!

[105]

Three Suggestions

THREE RADICAL solutions for the preservation of the peace of the world are here submitted.

1. *Our prayer life must shift from petition to reparation and intercession.* This does not mean that petitions in prayer are wrong; they are right and good. It does mean, however, that in a crisis it is not so much for ourselves that we must ask favors, but that we should make intercession for the entire world. As a loving father would take on himself the debts of a wayward son, as Divine Innocence took upon Himself the guilt of the world, so must we begin to feel the guilt of the world and realize that it is what it is because we are the way we are. Ten just men would have saved Sodom and Gomorrah, and a sufficient number of good souls praying and making reparation for the world would balance the scales in favor of Divine Mercy. We must suddenly begin to realize that it makes a tremendous difference to us because Our Lord died on a Cross, rather than in a bed. Therefore, repentance, reparation, and metanoia, or a complete change of our outlook on life.

Our Lord's first sermon, St. Peter's first Pentecostal sermon, the first words of John the Baptist, and the first sermon of Paul at Athens all stress the same idea: "Do penance. . . . Repent." If our eye had a speck in it, the hand would come to remove it. If a friend were suffering from anemia, we would give our blood to cure the person of that condition. As it is possible to graft skin, so it is possible to graft prayer; as it is possible to transfuse blood, so it is possible to transfuse sacrifice. But to do this we have to revive ourselves to a consciousness of sin and then seek to make amends for its injustices.

2. *Before attempting to alter the world, we must begin to alter ourselves.* To alter the world, we must be unworldly. The world can be helped only by those who are not directly involved in the crisis. A sick man is cured by medicine outside himself; the eagle flies only because of the non-eagle, which is the air; we cannot lift ourselves by our own bootstraps.

Our Lord came to renovate the world, and He did it. But He did not begin with the world; He first altered hearts. He left Herod in his court, Pilate on his judgment seat, Caiaphas with his council, Roman coins in the pockets, Caesar's emblems flying on the streets, Roman eagles screaming on banners of invading armies, and He took twelve men apart from the world, purged their hearts, then sent into them His Spirit, and after they were changed they revolutionized the world.

In other words, it is a few saints rather than social crusaders that we need. It does not take many. Stalin once said, "It takes ten thousand men to build a bridge; it takes only two to destroy it." So, too, a few souls that are full of energy and the spirit of Christ can do more than thousands who are just busybodies washing the outside of the cups. There are already too many who, like Peter, would substitute action for prayer. When the soldiers came to arrest Our Lord, Peter swung his sword and cut off the ear of the servant of the High Priest. If the world is to rebuild from its foundations, then the way to make clean politics is to make good politicians; the way to have a sound economics is to have moral economists! There is nothing that ever happens to the world that does not first happen inside the heart. Until hearts are renovated, nothing is saved.

3. *There must be a shift of emphasis from social justice to conversion of souls.* This does not mean that social justice must not be pursued with unrelenting energy, because it must. But it means that we have moved too much from the center to the periphery, and the direction must be reversed. We have to realize that social amelioration is conditional upon spiritual regeneration, that social justice is

an *effect* of moral living, and not its cause. A man is not made moral because he possesses all he wants. So long as envy is in the heart, it will do little good to talk social justice. Greed, envy, and lust must first be uprooted, and it was this approach that Our Savior suggested when He said, "Seek ye first the Kingdom of God and His Justice and all these things shall be added unto you." Nothing is saved until souls are saved.

The Communists, it would almost seem, have almost stolen the Pentecostal fires, for they show an energy for their doctrine of hate which puts to shame those of us who claim to live by a gospel of love. They have zeal and no truth; we, who have the truth, have no zeal. Our fires are going out; our salt is losing its savor.

How can eyes that never wept for the sins of the world expect one day to see the King of Kings? How shall hands that never busied themselves in handing out sacrifices for the spread of the faith in the mission lands expect to be clasped in friendship by the Hand that has the scar marks of a nail? How can hearts which never throbbed in love for the unfortunate of the world ever beat with that love we fall short of in all love? How shall lips that never speak of God expect to answer these searching questions on the last day? It behooves the good to be better; the better to be saintly; and all to start the serious business of saving a remnant that may be the spearhead for future morality, decency, and freedom in a better world.

[106]

The World Around Us

MOST OF THE psychologies we read about our human nature center on emotions and feelings. This is because we live in what might be called the "sensate age." In earlier centuries men lived by faith, then

by reason, now on quivers and throbs. When ruled by faith, there
was another source of light than the mind. Just as the eye has no
light within it but depends on the light of the sun, so above the confused rationalizations of the human psyche was the light of revelation. For example, the commandments enabled man to have a more
certain moral guide than Aristotle could give us in his Ethics. When
civilization lost the light of faith, it fell to total dependence on
reason. The mind was thought to be the one certain rule of life. Our
Declaration of Independence, for example, states it to be a self-
evident principle that the Creator has endowed man with certain
unalienable rights. But as the world lost its faith, it then lost its
reason, and now it has tumbled into a reliance on sensation. How
often we hear it said, "I feel it in here." Never before was truth so
dependent on gas in the stomach.

Among the feelings, the one that was given primacy was sex. Since
there is no standard outside of a sensation by which to judge it, everything becomes allowable. The feeling of relief at sneezing is not
more moral than the easement of blowing one's nose. It then becomes normative to smoke pot, to denude, to adulterate. Hitler did
"his thing," Stalin did "his thing," and a rapist does "his thing."
Any referee who calls a foul on a basketball court for jumping on
the back of another player is restraining "freedom," and if certain
lawyers are paid enough to do "their thing" they could prove that
the referee violated the First Amendment.

This degeneration of culture has been so progressive through the
centuries that we have hardly noticed it. As Vergil said over two
thousand years ago, "The descent to hell is easy." The temperature
of water suited to a frog's organism may be raised the smallest degree day by day. Eventually the water will reach a point where it
boils. But nowhere during the increase of the heating of the water
could anyone tell when the frog died. At no point does it struggle
against death. So it is with culture and civilization. They perish so
gradually . . . they do not realize that all the lights have gone out.

For those who realize that falling off a cliff does not mean increased healthy mobility, it is worthwhile to recall the true nature of
man and how he can perfect himself. Man is composed of a triple
bond to reality: he has a spirit, a mind, psyche, or soul, and he has a
body. The spirit is his capacity for communicating with God. It is

only a potentiality or a dynamic recovery for the Spirit spelled with a capital S. His soul or mind, which expresses itself through the body, constitutes his "personality" and enables him to establish communion with persons. Thanks to the soul or psyche, man can know sciences, arts, philosophy, law, and the thousand and one disciplines which help perfect his humanity. Below this is the body, which through sight, sound, touch, smell, and taste makes it possible to absorb the material universe into itself.

In other words, we have a capacity for three kinds of consciousness: God-consciousness, self-consciousness in relation to other persons and knowable things, and finally sense-consciousness, which establishes our contact with the physical universe. In each instance there is a power to assimilate either the Divine, the human, or the cosmic. No two persons actualize this triple power in the same way, but for each there is something "given" or "outside" us which can be absorbed, thus making us more perfect and more happy. When Paul wrote a letter to the Greek-speaking people in Thessalonia, he prayed that each of them might be kept holy and sound in "spirit, soul, and body." Every person in the world lives on one of these three levels, and his happiness varies with each level.

XXI
Plain Talk

Equity and Woman

Is WOMAN attaining her full dignity by insisting on equality, or should she be insisting on equity?

Equity is the perfection of equality, not its substitute. It has the advantage, which equality does not have, of recognizing the specific difference between a man and a woman. As a matter of fact, they are not equal in sex; they are unequal, and it is because of this that they complement each other.

Law takes care of exactness or equality, but equity goes beyond it and considers the particular circumstances which might extenuate an extreme application of law. In the Christian ages there were courts of equity, as well as courts of law; the former have almost all passed out of our contemporary civilization. In the Cathedral of Chartres there are two sets of priceless stained-glass windows on either side of that magnificent edifice. One was given by Blanche of Castile; the other by her rival family, Pierre de Dreux. As these families face one another vicariously through their windows, they seem to carry on a kind of war in the very heart of the cathedral. But over the main altar sits the Virgin Mary as the Lady of Equity, presiding over the courts, listening serenely to pleas for mercy in behalf of sinners. She signifies the humane and merciful power, as against the stern mandates of law.

Law has broken down today. Obligations are no longer sacred. The choice, therefore, before women in this day in the collapse of justice is whether to continue equating themselves with men in rigid exactness, or to affirm equity, mercy, and love, thus giving a cruel and lawless world something that equality can never give. Where there is equality, there is justice; but there is no love. If man is the equal of woman, then she has rights—but no heart ever lived on rights.

The level of any civilization is the level of its womanhood. This is because of the basic difference between knowing and loving. When we know anything, we always bring it down to the level of our intelligence. In instructing children, we give simple examples drawn from our own experience. But in loving, then we bring the object up to our level. If we love music, we submit to its discipline, its scales, its rhythms; if we love a person, we meet the demands of a person. When a man loves a woman, then it follows that the nobler the woman, the nobler will be the love of a man. The higher the demands made by the woman, the more worthy that man must be. That is why every woman is the measure of the level of our civilization.

What is contributing to the degrading of women is the intellectualization of sex. It has been said that the United States is the most sex-obsessed country in the world. Today sex is thought about, placarded, advertised in a kind of erotic pyrotechnics. As Professor Crane Brinton says in his *History of Western Morals*, "It may be true that homo sapiens spend more time and energy fantasying, thinking, talking and writing about sex than doing anything else about it." Many people are driven to sex as a kind of refuge from or compensation for other frustrations, as they might be driven to drink or to opium. There is less a desire for another than there is a demand to escape from anxiety. One may even attempt to make the intensity of an experience make up for a want of goal or purpose in life, as youngsters speed on highways for the same reason. Sex is replaceable, but a person is not.

[108]

Birth Patrol

BIRTH PATROL is a new kind of sentry affecting life. Hitler believed in birth patrol of the Jews; Stalin in birth patrol of Christians; Khrushchev in birth patrol of the Hungarians, Poles, and Ukrainians. Now there are those who would patrol life, not after it becomes a harvest but while it is seed in the granary. The new kind of vigilance would not wait until the fruit appeared on the tree, as did Hitler and others, but would stifle the blossoms and the buds. They would take up their watch at the borderline of love and life and say, "They shall not pass."

Those who believe in birth patrol find it very hard to justify why they should worry about an increase of population on the one hand, while on the other, they live in a nation which pays farmers not to raise an excess supply of foods. "There will not be enough food," is muttered in the same breath as "There is a surplus which is hurting prices." Another inconsistency appears in the fear of a "population explosion" on the one hand, and the multiplication of atomic bombs on the other. The very phrase "population explosion" shows that human birth is equated with a chemical reaction, and that the multiplication of human beings can be as dangerous as an explosion of an atomic bomb.

If we, as a people, had the fear of God's justice in our hearts, knowing that He is the Giver and the Preserver of life, would we not shrink from fumbling with the levers of life, lest our fingers fumble with the atomic bomb? Even the phrase "population explosion" could turn against us, for has it not been estimated by military experts that on the first day of atomic warfare, fifty million people will be killed?

The attitude of birth patrol is negative, failing to see beauty, truth, love, and life as a whole. Everything is dissected, analyzed, fragmented, split. Picasso paints a man; but the man he paints has been exploded into a thousand particles. He puts the pieces together, but never as they are in a human. The painted man has only one eye and it is in the wrong place. Cynically, a violin solo has been described as the drawing of the hair of a dead horse across the entrails of a dead cat. A poem is so analyzed in its meters that it no longer carries meaning; the conscious and subconscious in man are probed to a point where they look like a watch a naughty boy has torn apart—wheels, ratchets, hands, face, jewels are scattered about as time is destroyed.

Love is distorted and its disfigurement has gone through two phases. Both have one thing in common—namely, the denial of the "other." First, through the influence of Sartre, Proust, Stendhal, and Nietzsche, love denied the partner as love was defined as the projection of the self into something else in order to intensify the pleasure of the ego. The other is not loved; the other does not exist except as an occasion of egocentric satisfaction. The ego gives the other the illusion that he or she is loved, but once the water is drunk, the glass is forgotten. Then came the second phase—the denial of the other in the sense of the offspring; birth is patrolled. Love is denied a fruit. Lover and beloved become like two ships that pass in a night of epidermic contact. Their mutual self-giving ends in exhaustion and boredom. And because the other is denied either as partner or parent, there is a breakup and a search for another partner in a wild ecstacy of being alone together.

Life is a whole; so is love. Love is like eating; there is something personal that belongs to us, and something impersonal and reflex that belongs to God. We can choose what we eat, but after we eat, digestion is automatic. Thus does God assure the preservation of individual life. Love is personal; we decide where we will live. But in the act of love there is something automatic, reflex, beyond personal control. This is where God steps in to preserve the human species as digestion preserves the individual. We can, of course, tickle our throats and vomit; we can fumble and tear at the blossoms of life too; but will God look with favor on such perversion of His laws?

These words are written for the future, and may it be distant. We do have to fear a "population explosion," but it will come from fumbling with a bomb because we have thwarted a womb.

[109]

Sneeze Morality

THERE IS A tendency among many shallow thinkers of our day to teach that every human act is a reflex over which we do not exercise human control. They would rate a generous deed as no more praise-

worthy than a wink, a crime as no more voluntary than a sneeze. Men are believed, by such false thinkers, to be "conditioned" to act this way or that—with no freedom of choice, no responsibility for their good deeds or bad. They tell us that crime and sin are caused by an insufficiency of playgrounds or by a childhood shock which turned the child into a "problem child" and prevented his ever "adjusting" to reality and its demands.

Such a philosophy undercuts all human dignity. It confuses conduct, which is human, with behavior, which is animal. It ignores the spiritual faculties of man, which enable him to act against his impulses, to refuse the course of least resistance because of his allegiance to an ideal. This false conception of human nature contradicts our own common-sense experience: you do not *have* to finish reading this book, nor do you *have* to set it aside. You are conscious, now, of your freedom to follow one course or the other in the next three minutes. All of us have the power of choice in action at every moment of our lives.

"I couldn't help doing it," is the weakest and least likely of excuses. It is particularly favored by liars; they say, "She asked my opinion of her new hat, and I couldn't tell her the truth!" Why not? The truth need never offend if it is told with charity and friendliness. "I simply *had* to" is not a valid excuse for committing any sin, and lying is a sin.

The notion that men act because of "forces" stronger than their wills leads to great dangers in the social scene. Even killing is justified by some, who say that economic necessity makes wars inevitable. No one in the age of faith ever spoke of wars as a necessity. Wars are made by men, not by economies, and men, in saner ages than our own, were known to be free agents, deciding their own destinies.

St. James told us, "What leads to war, what leads to quarreling among you? I will tell you what leads to them: the appetites that infest your mortal bodies. Your desires go unfulfilled, so you fall to murdering; you set your heart on something, and cannot have your will, so there is quarreling and fighting."

Atomic warfare is not "sure" to come; men will decide in their hearts whether such a war will come or not. The lifeless bomb does not create the problem of our times: men's cruelty creates our problem. A stockpile of bombs in the hands of St. Francis of Assisi would be as harmless as a flower. But a single bomb in the hands of a tyrant (or of a President willing to release it) can menace New York or prove a scandalous calamity to Hiroshima.

Christian tradition attributes evil to a personal choice, an act of the free will which misuses the liberty that God gave to man. Freedom is vastly prized today in the speeches of politicians, but it is only political freedom which they praise; nobody takes the microphone to remind the individual listener that he is morally free, that his sins are of his making. Such liberty is derided: we sometimes have to sneeze—therefore, according to the confused thinkers, we have to sin and nothing can prevent it. This effort to deny man's freedom would, if it could succeed, turn people into so many animals.

The "sneeze morality" recommends itself particularly to those who wish to escape the voice of conscience. They long to believe in a philosophy which will allow them to be cruel and untruthful and proud without a sense of guilt. Their own consciences, their uncorrupted reasons, tell them that what they are doing is wrong and that they will be held accountable for it. To escape this uncomfortable knowledge, some of them attempt to bribe their consciences into bringing in a more favorable report. They set up a new morality, gauged to fit their actions and to measure them as good. Since the true conscience has caused discomfort, they will devise a false conscience to reassure and flatter them.

The man who has created a new conscience in this manner has set himself up as a rival to God, able to determine right and wrong. When he does something good (such as contributing to a charity and getting his name in the papers for it), he takes full credit. When he does something bad, he says, "It is because I am built that way," or, "My childhood was unhappy, so I cannot be expected to behave."

False consciences seem to succeed—but only in the daylight hours. Even sneeze moralists, in the long nights, know remorse—and their uneasiness is the Voice of God, summoning them away from their self-made slavery to the glorious freedom of the children of God.

[110   ]

"Kicks"

A YOUNG MOTHER ran away with five different lovers in five months, abandoning her children. She appeared before a judge who belonged to the new school advocating that compassion be shown to the criminal rather than the victim. Some "sob sisters," who shared his view that nobody is guilty, made it appear that the one to be condemned was the husband who was not "humanistic" because he was a science instructor. The judge relieved the wife of the responsibility of her two children, allowed her to keep the nice home that she had obtained in an original settlement with her estranged husband; he then allotted $200 a month until she could get settled "emotionally." The judge, in concluding the case, said, "she is more to be pitied than censured."

A federal judge in Washington assailed what he considered to be "an unfortunate trend of judicial decisions which strain and stretch to give the guilty not the same, but vastly *more* protection than the law-abiding citizen." Bleeding hearts, some of whom are supposed to administer justice, are so concerned for criminals and terrorists that today the good citizens are considered off the reservation, as the new compassion exalts the guilty and condemns the innocent.

What is the cause of this reversal of judgment? The loss of a moral sense. Dostoevski wrote that in a future day men would say there is no crime, there is no sin, there is no guilt, there is only hunger; then men will come crying and fawning at our feet saying to us, "Give us bread." Nothing will matter except the economic.

A spirit of license makes a man refuse to commit himself to any standards. The right time is the way he sets his watch. The yardstick has the number of inches that he wills it to have. Liberty becomes license, and unbounded license leads to unbounded tyranny. When society reaches this stage, and there is no standard of right and wrong outside of the individual himself, then the individual is defenseless against the onslaughts of cruder and more violent men who proclaim their own subjective sense of values. Once my idea of morality is just as good as your idea of morality, then the morality that is going to prevail is the morality that is stronger. It has been put:

> Pale Ebenezer thought it wrong to fight,
> But roaring Bill, who killed him, thought it right.

Why is Communism so anxious to see the moral degeneracy of the United States? Because it produces chaos, and chaos is the door it enters to seize power. Communism is the forcible organization of chaos created by license. When the sheep disperse, the shepherd sends a dog barking at their heels. The transition from "nothing matters," which is indifference to virtue and justice, to "everything matters," in which even our thoughts are controlled, is short and slippery.

Another effect of the growth of "everything goes" is a passion for more and more excitement. One notices that many juvenile delinquents state that they became dope addicts because alcohol no longer gave them a "kick." This is true of every sensation: to produce an equal effect or "kick" over a long period of time, one must increase the stimulus. One can get used to noise in a boiler factory. Weber and Fechner tried to tie up the psychological law with mathematics, stating that to increase the "kick" in the ratio of 1, 2, 3, 4, one had to increase the stimulus 2, 4, 8, 16. Now, after the delinquents become used to dope, what new thrill will be necessary? History proves that such emotionally exhausted punks begin to be masochistic and take pleasure in inflicting cruelty on others. Could persecution of any social or religious class be in the distant future? It is my guess that our jaded and sated appetites will demand an intermediary "kick" and perhaps it will come in a new "sport"—namely, bull fighting. Will we thrill to cruelty to animals, even though done skillfully? Perhaps! But this we do know: the policy of not restricting degeneration on the ground that it destroys freedom may

lead to a love of seeing others "punished" to take the blame off ourselves. Even in television, the realistic and the possible already bore
us; we must have the impossible, the supernatural. What faith!
What credulity! Believing in the Resurrection of Divine Justice and
Love demands less credibility and gives a thousand times more
peace, and no demands for more violent "kicks."

[111]

Slobbering Over the Criminal

SOME PROBABLY remember the famous Victorian "tearjerker" *Hearts
and Flowers*. It was played in practically all melodrama, especially
when the poor family was about to be dispossessed by a vicious landlord on a snowy night. Modern literature, as Edmund Fuller has
pointed out, has now gone to the opposite extreme where pity is for
the rapist, not the raped; for the criminal, not the victim. This false
compassion started with novelists like William Saroyan and John
Steinbeck, who presented the "lovable bums," the shiftless, the
drunks, as "beautiful little people."

The next stage was to excite pity for the genial rapist, the jolly
slasher, the dope pusher, the adulteress playing musical beds, the
rich kid who sells "goofballs," knifers, sluggers, muggers, and the ho-
mosexuals.

In one novel, as a girl takes up dope and tries a little prostitution,
she says to her friend, "You think I am a tramp." The compassionate one answers her, "Shucks kid, just going around and doing
everything a tramp does doesn't make a good, sweet, clean little kid
like you a tramp."

What is true compassion? It is a sharing of sorrow, a pity and
sympathy, a desire to help, a bearing of another's burdens as if they

were one's own. Compassion can be moral, material, or physical. In the moral realm, it shares guilt as if it were one's own. A judge who might sentence a murderer to death and then take the punishment would be a faint example of Christ taking on our sins—dying for them as if they were His own. Compassion is physical when one helps another carry an extra burden. A boy with another boy on his back was asked if he could bear up under it and he answered, "He's not heavy; he's my brother." Material compassion is a sharing of one's goods with the poor. Compassion, in a word, is vulnerability. It is a sympathy so deep and keen that one feels the wounds of others as if they were his own.

Compassion also makes a distinction between a man destroyed by his own fault and one destroyed through no fault of his own. No valid compassion can exist without a separation of right and wrong. Otherwise there is no difference between a saint and a sinner, a murderer and his victim.

But today, thanks to a few social workers, a few incompetent judges and woolly-minded thinkers, and many "sob sisters," compassion is extended not to the one who was mugged, but to the mugger; not to the policeman, but to the dope pusher; not to the girl killed by a dope fiend, but to the rich boy from an interesting family. No blame may be laid at the door of the criminal or the degraded. The new saviors of a perverted society say, "Neither do I condemn thee. Go, and sin some more."

Nobody is "bad" because there is no right and wrong. Criminals are "sick." One professor in a large university had just finished his lecture on social work, advocating compassion to punks and criminals. On his way home, he was mugged and severely beaten. He insisted on going to the police station before being taken to the hospital to complain against the city for not protecting life and property. He wanted compassion. Gone was his compassion for muggers. May those judges and social workers who deny the difference between right and wrong learn the lesson that not every criminal is "sick" without being mugged themselves.

[112]

Idleness and Relief

NOTHING would probably surprise the Communists more than to be told that their Constitution contains a quotation from St. Paul's Second Epistle to the Thessalonians: "If a man will not work, neither should he eat." Since there are too many in our American life who would rather take their philosophy from the Communists than from the Scriptures, it might be well for them to ponder over the text. Social workers in democracies too could learn much from the discussion of the first problem of relief that vexed the Christian community. Who in a society will become the objects of what used to be called "charity" and now is called "relief" [and today is called "welfare"]?

The answer here stated is that all who are willfully idle shall not receive public funds. Actually there are people who choose to "go on relief" knowing they are better off receiving public bounty than if they worked and paid income tax. The law of nature here reaffirmed is rigid and inflexible: no work, no life. The hens scratching the barnyard for worms, the squirrel busily storing nuts for the winter, robins carrying worms to their young, sheep walking miles a day to gain their living—all these bear witness to the mandate that life and labor are inseparable.

A man cannot live the life of a musician without hours of routine practice, nor can he live in the order of grace while doing nothing to acquire merit. Unless there are the sharp blows of the chisel on the marble of the ego, the fine form of Christian character will never emerge. Peace of conscience, the joy of pardoning love, the knowledge of the mysteries of life, all are the results of toil. In the realm of religion the drones are not always doubters, but the doubters are always drones. The worst fifth column in any civilization are its idlers, its loungers who eat the fruit of others.

Abraham Lincoln once wrote to his stepbrother Johnston, who requested a loan of money: "The great defect in your conduct is not that you are lazy, but that you are an idler. This habit of uselessly wasting time is the whole difficulty, and it is vastly important to you and to your children that you should break this habit. Go to work for the best money wages you can get, and for every dollar that you will get for your own labor, I will give you another one. If you will do this you will soon be out of debt and what is better you will have gained a habit that will keep you from getting into debt again."

Country people have a way of catching wasps which illustrates Lincoln's principle that idleness gets people into trouble. They put something sweet into a narrow-necked bottle. The do-nothing wasp goes in for its "relief," plunges in, and is drowned. The busy bee may come by and smell for a second, but she will not go in because she has honey of her own to make. Work is a great preservative for the soul: it parries the thrusts of those who urge us to evil; it helps drain off the libido of the body, and gives man an assurance of being a cooperator with the Creator.

There will, of course, always be some in society who are not willfully idle, who cannot work, and who do not have the means of sustenance. These fall into a different category. They ought to be not just the objects of relief, but rather the recipients of charity on the part of those who "never weary of doing good." Work may be a duty, but the kindly service of the sick and the needy is a work of love. Love is always lavish; it does not stop to compare values; it breaks the alabaster vase and fills the whole neighborhood with its fragrance of kindness before legalism has even begun its calculation.

The legitimate needs of others must not be considered as a burden, but rather as an opportunity for sacrifice in God's name. But citizens must never allow the whole burden of relief to be taken over by the state, or by city government. A nation is greater when we care for our own as much as possible. Otherwise we would be idle in the face of a fellowman's need, and that would be the worst kind of idleness.

Old-fashioned Words

WHAT WOULD BE the general effect on the nation if newspapers changed their vocabulary and began using old-fashioned words to express some unvarying and eternal truths? The question is pertinent because today words are so often used out of context that it is sometimes believed there is no reality behind them: no such things as turnips and cabbages when we use the word "vegetable," and no such things as horses and cows when we use "quadrupeds." The Communists have had much to do with this, since they began using the word "democracy" to describe their tyranny, and "peace" for war through fifth columnists, and "liberation" for occupation. The word "progress," which means an approach toward an ideal, now means the changing of the ideal. A man was said to be making "progress" in driving to Washington from New York when he got as far as Philadelphia; now he is said to make "progress" when he ends up in Portland, Maine.

A boy is arrested for shooting another boy whom he has never seen, but does it on a "dare." The newspapers describe him as "delinquent" or "psychopathic" whereas a few generations ago, when Davy Crockett lived, the press would have called him "bad." A woman under forty who kills a man is described as "attractive," "social," "rich," or a "café singer," as the case may be—none of which adjectives has anything more to do with the case than if a baseball reporter stressed the color of the batter's eyes rather than the hits he made. "A redhead hits a home run" misses the point as much as "Beautiful blues singer kills her father."

There seems to be an insane dread of using moral terms, or even condemning anything on moral grounds. Psychological terms, the lingo of sociology, even medical terms such as "complexes" are invoked with an air of scientific certitude, but "bad" or "good," "right" or "wrong" seem to be scrupulously avoided. About the only time the word "good" is used is when the mother of a bad boy, a mother who completely neglected her husband and her children, is quoted in the press as saying of her son who has just committed murder, "He was a good boy."

It reminds one of G. K. Chesterton's description of what would happen if he killed his grandmother. He said everyone who heard of it would describe it in a thousand other terms except as "wrong." Some would call him insane, others would say that he had a low IQ or was vulgar or lacked manners; or it was a loathsome spectacle or a revolting scene, or pathological or the effect of an Electra complex, or that it was "an economic waste of a good grandmother." The only real point worth mentioning is that the action was wrong because the grandmother had a right to live. The conspiracy is to use any word at all except the one word which would take one into the field of ethics—on which every civilization is built.

Unless there is some sharp and fast law to resist the psychological and economic descriptions of crime, it will not be long until a wrong thing will be called a right thing if it is done in a nice manner. The moment is not far off when dramatists, authors, and even murderers will describe the taking of human life as the "perfect crime." This is like describing leprosy as the "perfect disease."

Sour notes in music do not become sweet because the musician is in white tie and black tails; juvenile delinquency will never be conquered as long as it is seen in the abstract, instead of in the concrete youths who constitute the problem. No doctor can cure a disease by changing its name; nor can a teacher cure ignorance by saying that if she did not pass every student every year, she would create in them an "inferiority complex." Right and wrong do not change, even though one seek the escape of the Fifth Amendment. Right is right if nobody is right, and wrong is wrong if everybody is wrong.

[114]

Stupid Maybe, but a Sinner Never

A GENERATION ago, George Bernard Shaw said that the modern man was too busy to think about his sins. Shaw admitted that there was such a thing as sin. What might be called contemporary thinking does not admit even the existence of sin. A man might reach a point of self-condemnation, saying, "How stupid I am," but he would never reach the horrid depths of guilt, crying out, "I am a sinner," as did Peter when he cast himself at the feet of Our Divine Lord. In fact, a consciousness of sin in these times is equated with a psychological abnormality. There is such a thing as a "guilt complex," but the term has come to include the denial of all guilt and the identification of guilt with a deviation from the normal.

From a spiritual point of view, the denial of sin makes salvation impossible. If the blind deny they are blind, there is no hope of ever seeing. But despite all denials of sin, this fact still remains: though a person may deny the reality of sin, he nevertheless feels the effects of sin. Not all, certainly not even the majority, but many who are consulting psychiatrists are suffering from the effects of repressed or denied guilt. Lady Macbeth denied sin when she murdered the king, but she could not rid herself of the psychological effect of hand-washing, which became a compulsion neurosis. The manifestation of her guilt was abnormal, but the guilt itself was real.

No civilization is healthy which denies that it ever did wrong, or affirms that it is responsible when it does good and should be praised for the good it does, but when it does evil and is irresponsible should never be blamed. It may be interesting to note how sin has been

regarded in various civilizations. The Greek word for sin in the New
Testament is *hamartia,* which originally meant missing of the mark.
The greatest of the Greek poets, Homer, who lived about a thousand years before Christ, used that word about a hundred times—for
example, when a soldier missed his mark with his arrow or spear.
Thucydides, who lived about five hundred years before Christ, used
the word to signify a missing of the right turn in a road. In the Old
Testament, the word meant a missing of the mark or goal which was
signified by the law given to Moses.

Whenever a thing is used for a purpose for which it is not intended, there is a missing of the mark or goal or purpose—for instance, to use a fountain pen to carve wood will result in double failure, ruining the instrument itself and not carving the wood. So
when a man fails to attain the purpose for which he was made—
namely, the attainment of happiness or truth and love, which is God
—he not only misses happiness, but he also hurts himself psycho-
logically and sometimes physically, and always morally or spiritually.
In this sense, sin then becomes a transgression against the law of
God.

But in the New Testament sin takes on a more refined meaning
and is to be understood in terms of love, rather than law. Here
human love again serves as an example of the meaning of sin. A
devoted husband would not make any serious distinction between
giving his wife a punch in the nose or cutting her throat, simply because he would not want to hurt someone that he loves.

When, therefore, Divine Love becomes Incarnate, as it did in the
person of Christ, Who is God in the form of man, there is a shrink-
ing from departing from His Spirit, not just because one will be
punished, but rather because one does not want to hurt someone he
loves. The crucifix then becomes a sinner's autobiography. He sees a
personal and intimate relationship between himself and Christ.
Pride crowned Him with thorns, lust tore and buried His Body, avarice nailed His Hands to a tree. Yet, at the very moment that he
feels such compunction, he hears from the crucifix the words: "Father, forgive them, for they know not what they do." The worst
thing in the world is not sin; it is denying that we are sinners.

[115]

Ingratitude

WHEN Our Divine Savior cured the ten lepers, only one returned to thank Him—and that one belonged to a despised race, the Samaritans. Aptly, the Miracle Worker asked, "Where are the other nine?"

The Gospel story is repeated in all centuries and circumstances: thankfulness is rare, ingratitude is common. It is likely that the nine did not return to express gratitude for the same reason: preoccupation with some selfish interest that outweighed the claims of gratitude. But this single excuse can be broken down into nine probable reasons for staying away:

1. *Hardness:* One man may have thought, "I would have become healthy anyway, so why thank God for what was mine by rights?"

2. *Thoughtlessness:* Many people lack the habit of ever turning back, in reflection on their own lacks: they are therefore unconscious of the benefits they have received, taking them for granted and acting like the kind of husband who never thanks his wife for the happiness that she has given him.

3. *Envy:* There is the person who cannot enjoy the favors he receives as much as others do if they are younger or wealthier or in other ways outstrip him. Such persons, on receiving any favor, immediately advert to what a neighbor has received and make themselves unhappy because the gift they won was not unique. Envy always turns sour the milk of human kindness.

4. *Cowardice:* There are some who refrain from gratitude because the One who gave to them is not popular with the mob; they avoid showing that they are beholden to Him for fear of being associated with Him in the public mind.

5. *Fear:* Some refuse to be grateful because the favor granted has strings attached to it—the obligation of discipleship, perhaps, or of moral betterment. To avoid these commitments, they refuse to offer thanks.

6. *Worldliness:* Excessive devotion to business makes some souls so insensitive that they cannot take time out to notice the favors they have received.

7. *Pride:* To acknowledge that one has been helped is, to some souls, to admit inferiority; their pride makes them prefer to withhold thanks, rather than belittle themselves.

8. *Gregariousness:* Some people are incapable of doing anything alone. Unless they have the mob supporting them when they act, they refuse to act at all. If the majority of the others had given thanks, then so would the man of the gregarious temperament; but if the others remain silent, so will he.

9. *Procrastination:* Some people fail to fulfill their human obligations by putting every gracious gesture off until "tomorrow," when "tomorrow" never comes. The road to Hell is paved with stones of *postponed* resolutions.

Underlying all these varied and distinctive reasons for ungratefulness is forgetfulness of the Benefactor and of what *He* wants. Such an attitude, in human affairs, is extremely common among children; they do not ordinarily give thanks for the blessings of life and care to their parents until they have children of their own and learn how much their own families have had to endure for them. Even then, many adults refuse to admit that *they* as children could have been as troublesome as they actually were.

Ingratitude to God is even commoner than ingratitude to the men who have deserved our thanks. A legend says that one morning His angels set out with ten thousand baskets of food for His children—but that, at evening, a single basket was enough to carry back to Heaven the thanks that He received.

Some may ask, "Why *should* we thank God?" Yet surely it is clear that the merest justice requires our gratitude to Him. *God* does not need our thanks, but *we* need to perform the act of thanksgiving in order to acknowledge, of ourselves, that under the law of truth we have been blessed beyond all our deserts. In thanking God, we are a little like the child who brings a gift of dandelions to his mother; the mother does not need the dandelions, but she is happy to receive them because the child needs the experience of love, honor, obedience, and gratitude that are involved in making such a gift. We, too, when we give thanks to God, become better merely by recognizing that all good things come from Him and are the tokens of His love. To blink at this fact would be to forfeit the strength which comes to us from an admission of the truth.

Character is tested when we receive a gift—when we get the thing we want. As soon as this has happened, the benefactor ceases to be necessary to us in our ambitions: will we forget him, as we forget the dentist when the aching tooth is cured? After we have received the gift we craved, we can see the benefactor in a quite different light than we did formerly: the delivery from our need of his assistance is also the delivery from the bias in his favor which our selfish aims dictated. The benefactor, who was once a necessity or a convenience, is no longer needed—and the very same self-sufficiency often intrudes into man's attitude toward God. Beneath the seeming reverence for the Divine Benefactor there may have lurked a querulous temper which chafed at the calamities of life, as if living under an unpleasant dispensation of Divine Providence. When God has granted such a disposition what it craved, then that temper rises to the surface, and ingratitude results.

Gratitude is characteristic only of the humble. The egotistic are so impressed by their own importance that they take everything given them as if it were their due. They have no room in their hearts for recollection of the undeserved favors they received.

Gratitude is not only an obligation, however—it is also a means of curing the sick soul. Those who suffer from despair would do well to sit down and count their blessings. They would then see that even some of the misfortunes of their lives have turned out, under God's Merciful and Guiding Hand, to be blessings; either they disciplined character in a needed way, or they acted as a preparation for greater favors still to come.

Thanksgiving redeems wealth by ridding it of that terrible complacency which chokes the spirit; it redeems work by purging from it pride and selfishness. Thanksgiving is the one act by which a man may become free. An atheist, who believes that everything is predetermined and that nothing is a free gift from the Love Divine, cannot honestly give thanks to anyone for anything—if he is logical in carrying out his barren, sad philosophy, he cannot even thank his neighbor for lending him a cigarette!

[116]

Fanaticism

IN A HEATED discussion, the man who cannot argue always wants to bet. It is his way of withdrawing from the field of logic into the area of chance and daring. This is not necessarily a sign of fanaticism, but it suggests the first element in fanaticism—namely, flight from argument, logic, and objective standards of truth. Fanaticism is never primary either in a person or in a civilization; it is always preceded by a breakdown of reason. Any age which denies that there are objective standards of right and wrong, or which says that one view of the universe is just as good as another, or that right and wrong are relative to the observer has already given up the yardstick for measuring the cloth of truth, and is in danger of becoming fanatical.

The decline of logic and sound reason brings in its wake the second condition of fanaticism. When truth, goodness, and absolutes lose their value, it is only natural for fanaticism to center itself around certain persons who have the capacity to drag the nonthinking after them. Fanaticism never centers on an idea as such; for example, no one becomes a fanatic about all the angles of a triangle being equal to two right angles, but he can become a fanatic about a mathematician who says they may equal three right angles in the stars. At first sight, it would seem that the fanatics of Communism love its dialectical philosophy as such, just as the fanatics of Nazism and Fascism loved the race philosophy and nationalist philosophy of each system. But it must be noted that when Hitler, who was the symbol of Nazism, and Mussolini, who was the symbol of Fascism, disappeared, so did the fanatics of the two systems, except for isolated islands of insanity here and there.

Communism had its appeal under Lenin; it had its appeal later under Stalin, and presently the *locum tenens* of both, whoever he may be. The leader keeps the fanatics together. Any fanaticism against Jews or Christians, however abstract its expression, is basically directed against the persons of Jews or the persons of Christians.

The third basic attribute of fanaticism is that the soil in which it grows is the masses. There is a world of difference between the masses and the people. The constitution of our country speaks of "We the people," not "We the masses." The people are persons, each with his own individuality, each guided by his own conscience and determined by some well-defined objectives. The masses are the people without consciences; they are people who become like individual nuts and bolts without reason or self-determination. All their actions are determined by equally irrational forces outside of them. The masses can never be identified; they have no faces; they just have the name "they" or "everybody." They all read the same books, see the same movies, listen to the same commentators, without ever asking themselves whether these standardized means of communication should completely determine one's own set of values. They thrive on scraps and shreds of predigested ideas in capsule form, find it difficult to read anything without pictures, and would not dare be out of step even if everybody were walking to a precipice.

Fanaticism is born when all these three are put together: the loss of reason and a sense of values, the rallying around a leader who satisfies emotions, and the enthronement of mediocrity in the masses.

On the lower levels, fanaticism wants to bet, instead of appealing to objective standards. On the higher levels, it wants to persecute instead of plead. The fanatics never think of ideas that have to be answered by logic; they only think of the persons who hold contrary ideas, as something to be overthrown and put out of the way. Every fanatic is the enemy of truth because he is the enemy of ideas, the foe of logic. The man who believes in truth will die for it, but he will never hate those who oppose Him. Rather, he will plead for those who hate Him, saying, "Father, forgive them for they know not what they do."

[117]

Does Mercy Stand Alone?

As THE WORLD grows soft, it uses more and more the word "mercy." This could be a praiseworthy characteristic if mercy were understood aright. But too often by "mercy" is meant letting off anyone who breaks the natural or the Divine law, or who betrays his country. Such mercy is an emotion, not a virtue, when it justifies the killing by a son of his father because he is "too old." To avoid any imputation of guilt, what is actually a murder is called "euthanasia."

Forgotten in all such mercy pleas is the principle that *mercy is the perfection of justice*. Mercy does not come first, and then justice; but rather justice first, then mercy. The divorce of mercy from justice is sentimentality, as the divorce of justice from mercy is severity. Mercy is not love when it is divorced from justice. He who loves anything must resist that which would destroy the object of his love. The power to become righteously indignant is not an evidence of the want of mercy and love, but rather a proof of them. There are some crimes the tolerance of which is equivalent to consent to their wrong. Those who ask for the release of murderers, traitors, and the like on the grounds that we must be "merciful, as Jesus was merciful" forget that that same Merciful Savior also said that He came not to bring peace, but the sword. As a mother proves that she loves her child by hating the physical disease which would ravage the child's body, so Our Lord proves He loved goodness by hating evil, which would ravage the souls of His creatures. For a doctor to be merciful to typhoid germs or polio in a patient, or for a judge to be tolerant of rape would be, in a lower category, the same as for Our Lord to be indifferent to sin. A mind that is never stern or indignant is either without love or else is dead to the distinction between right and wrong.

Love can be stern, forceful, and even fierce, as was the love of the Savior. It makes a scourge of ropes and drives buyers and sellers out of temples; it refuses to give the courtesy of speech to moral triflers like Herod, for it would only add to his moral guilt; it turns on a Roman procurator boasting of totalitarian law, and reminds him that he would have no power unless it were given to him by God. When a gentle hint to a woman at the well did no good, He went to the point ruthlessly and reminded her that she had had five divorces. When so-called righteous men would put Him out of the way, He tore the mask off their hypocrisy and called them a "brood of vipers." When He heard of the shedding of the blood of the Galileans, it was with formidable harshness that He said, "You will all perish as they did, if you do not repent."

Equally stern was He to those who would offend the little ones with an education that was progressive in evil: "If anyone hurts the conscience of one of these little ones that believe in me, he had better been drowned in the depths of the sea, with a mill-stone tied about his neck." He told men to pluck out eyes and cut off hands and feet, rather than to allow these members to become occasions for evil and the occasion of the loss of their immortal souls. When one of His disciples asked to be excused from his apostolic work to bury his father, Our Lord said, "Do thou follow Me, and leave the dead to bury their own dead." While Martha waited on Him at table, he pointed out that something else was needed more than service. When His apostles slept, He awakened them ruthlessly and chided them for their want of prayer; and in spite of Thomas's full confession, He rebuked him for his want of faith. One of His looks was so soul-piercing, revealing the weakness and evil within, that a disciple was moved to tears.

If mercy meant the forgiveness of all faults without retribution and without justice, it would end in the multiplication of wrongs. Mercy is for those who will not abuse it, and no man will abuse it who has already started to make the wrong right, as justice demands. What some today call mercy is not mercy at all, but a feather bed for those who fall from justice; and thus they multiply guilt and evil by supplying such mattresses. To become the object of mercy is not the same as to go scot-free, for as the word of God says: "Whom the Lord loveth, He chastiseth." The moral man is not he who is namby-pamby, or who has drained his emotions of the sterner stuff of justice; rather he is one whose gentleness and mercy are part of a larger organism, whose eyes can flash with righteous indignation, and whose muscles can become as steel in defense, like Michael, of the Justice and the Rights of God.